Perichoretic Salvation

Perichoretic Salvation

*The Believer's Union with Christ
as a Third Type of* Perichoresis

JAMES D. GIFFORD, JR.

WIPF & STOCK · Eugene, Oregon

PERICHORETIC SALVATION
The Believer's Union with Christ as a Third Type of *Perichoresis*

Copyright © 2011 James D. Gifford, Jr. All rights reserved. Except for brief quotations in critical publications or reviews, no part of this book may be reproduced in any manner without prior written permission from the publisher. Write: Permissions, Wipf and Stock Publishers, 199 W. 8th Ave., Suite 3, Eugene, OR 97401.

Wipf & Stock
An Imprint of Wipf and Stock Publishers
199 W. 8th Ave., Suite 3
Eugene, OR 97401
www.wipfandstock.com

ISBN 13: 978-1-61097-114-0
Manufactured in the U.S.A.

All scripture quotations, unless otherwise indicated, are taken from the Holy Bible, New International Version®, NIV®. Copyright ©1973, 1978, 1984 by Biblica, Inc.™ Used by permission of Zondervan. All rights reserved worldwide.

Contents

Preface vii
Abbreviations ix

1 Introduction 1
2 Biblical Evidence 33
3 Historical Development 78
4 Theological Issues 127
5 Possible Implications and Conclusion 175

Bibliography 193
Subject Index 219

Preface

ONE OF THE THINGS that makes Christian theology so exciting is the challenge to interpret the doctrines of the faith anew in each generation. Christianity has been in existence for almost two thousand years, and it has a rich history of people who labored to proclaim the message and probe its depths in their social and cultural contexts. At the first decade of the twenty-first century draws to a close, Christian theologians remain faced with the need to revisit the great doctrines and form them into language that resonates with the faithful. At this time, the doctrine of salvation has multiple controversies swirling about it, such as the perspectives on the meaning of justification, atonement theories, living a meaningful Christian life, election and preservation, the existence of a central motif in salvation, and a host of others. This book is a humble attempt to start a conversation about the nature of the believer's union with Christ and its ramifications for Christian theology and life. It is only a conversation starter. It certainly is not the last word. This book is designed to offer a paradigm that may help begin to solve, or at least soften, some of the controversies swirling about the faith. Doubtless it will raise as many, if not more, questions than it answers, requiring more theological investigation and interaction. At least, as the author, I hope that is the case.

This book is a revision of my doctoral dissertation I completed and defended at Southeastern Baptist Theological Seminary. It is more than just an academic exercise for me. It is part of a lifelong quest to better know my Savior and to more fully understand his boundless love. For me, it is more an act of devotion than a stale academic exercise. Although the study will get technical at times, I don't want to lose sight of the forest for the trees. The end result of any good theological work is to know and love God more richly than before. I humbly pray that reading this will do that for you.

Abbreviations

AffCrit	*Affirmation and Critique*
AnBib	Analecta Biblica
AB	Anchor Bible
AThR	*Anglican Theological Review*
ANF	Ante-Nicene Fathers
ATJ	*Ashland Theological Journal*
BECNT	Baker Exegetical Commentary on the New Testament
BIS	Biblical Interpretation Series
BSac	*Bibliotheca Sacra*
BBR	Bulletin for Biblical Research
CTJ	*Calvin Theological Journal*
CBQ	Catholic Biblical Quarterly
CTSJ	*Chafer Theological Seminary Journal*
CD	Church Dogmatics
Colloq	*Colloquium*
CBET	Contributions to Biblical Exegesis and Theology
CCR	*Coptic Church Review*
CCSL	Corpus Christianorum: Series Latina
CR	Corpus Reformatorum
CurTM	Currents in Theology and Mission
DiAl	*Dialog and Alliance*
DRev	*Downside Review*
EvQ	*Evangelical Quarterly*

FC	Fathers of the Church	
GTJ	*Grace Theological Journal*	
GOTR	*Greek Orthodox Theological Review*	
HNTC	Harper's New Testament Commentaries	
HSM	Harvard Semitic Monographs	
HS	*Hebrew Studies*	
Hor	*Horizons*	
ICC	International Critical Commentary	
IJST	International Journal of Systematic Theology	
Int	*Interpretation*	
IST	Issues in Systematic Theology	
JSNT	*Journal for the Study of the New Testamnet*	
JSNTSup	Journal for the Study of the New Testament: Supplement Series	
JBL	*Journal of Biblical Literature*	
JETS	*Journal of the Evangelical Theological Society*	
JGES	*Journal of the Grace Evangelical Society*	
JTS	*Journal of Theological Studies*	
LCC	Library of Christian Classics	
LQ	*Lutheran Quarterly*	
LW	*Luther's Works*	
MBPS	Mellen Biblical Press Series	
MTh	*Modern Theology*	
MNTC	Moffatt New Testament Commentary	
Neot	*Neotestamentica*	
NAC	New American Commentary	
NASB	New American Standard Bible	
NFTL	New Foundations Theological Library	
NICNT	New International Commentary on the New Testament	

NICOT	New International Commentary on the Old Testament
NIDNTT	*New International Dictionary of New Testament Theology*
NIDOTTE	*New International Dictionary of Old Testament Theology and Exegesis*
NPP	New Perspective on Paul
NSBT	New Studies in Biblical Theology
NTS	*New Testament Studies*
NTT	New Testament Theology
NPNF¹	Nicene and Post-Nicene Fathers, First Series
NPNF²	Nicene and Post-Nicene Fathers, Second Series
OLA	Orientalia lovaniensia analecta
NovT	*Novum Testamentum*
PG	*Patrologia Graeca*
PL	*Patrologia Latina*
PRSt	*Perspectives on Religious Studies*
PNTC	Pillar New Testament Commentary
PrTMS	Princeton Theological Monograph Series
ProEccl	*Pro Ecclesia*
SVTQ	*St. Vladimir's Theological Quarterly*
SBET	*Scottish Bulletin of Evangelical Theology*
SJT	*Scottish Journal of Theology*
SBLDS	Society of Biblical Literature Dissertation Series
SBLStBL	Society of Biblical Literature Studies in Biblical Literature
SNTSMS	Society for New Testament Studies Monograph Series
SBT	Studies in Biblical Theology
SCHT	Studies in Christian History and Thought
VTSup	Supplements to Vetus Testamentum
TGST	Tesi Gregoriana Serie Teologia

TMSJ	*The Master's Seminary Journal*
TDNT	*Theological Dictionary of the New Testament*
TS	*Theological Studies*
ThSc	*Theology and Science*
ThTo	*Theology Today*
TynBul	*Tyndale Bulletin*
VC	*Vigiliae Christianae*
WTJ	*Westminster Theological Journal*
WBC	Word Biblical Commentary
WUNT	*Wissenschaftliche Untersuchungen zum Neuen Testament*
WEC	Wycliffe Exegetical Commentary
ZNW	*Zeitschrift für die neutestamentliche Wissenschaft*

1

Introduction

THE LAY OF THE LAND

THE TIMES ARE A-CHANGING. That might be the understatement of the millennium. Both philosophically and theologically, the landscape in the first decades of the twenty-first century is shifting. Philosophically, the world is becoming more multicultural, postmodern, and informed. The modern mindset is being replaced with a collection of posts: post-modern, post-colonial, post-critical, post-Christian, and so forth. Theologically in the West, thanks to the work of Karl Barth, Karl Rahner, and a host of others, the doctrine of the Trinity has been freed from its centuries-long exile on the island of Enlightenment rationalism.[1] In theological reflection on the life of God, theologians have likewise resurrected a long-dormant term to describe the inner relations of the Godhead, *perichoresis*. Western Christianity, both Protestant and Roman Catholic, is rediscovering the relational roots of the faith emanating from the eternally-relational Godhead.

The roots of the relational paradigm are many, including the aforementioned revival of the Trinity, the rejection of the Enlightenment notion of the autonomous self in favor of an attempt at real community, and the innate human need to relate as social creatures. Human persons are who they are because, as Zizoulas and others say, humans are "beings

---

1. Some of the most influential works that helped bring about a revival of the doctrine of the Trinity include Barth, *CD* I/1; Rahner, *Trinity*; plus several works by Moltmann and Torrance, noted in the bibliography. For good summaries of the modern trinitarian revival, see Thompson, *Modern Trinitarian Perspectives*; and Letham, *Holy Trinity*. There have been many more important works since. This is only a sample. For more of an overview, see the opening of Marshall, "Participating in the Life of God."

in communion."[2] If God and humanity are inherently relational, then salvation—the rescue from sin and eternal fellowship with the relational one—should be relational too. Recently, the doctrine of the believer's union with Christ has gained considerable popularity as a way to unify salvation into a central motif that is relational. It is in the framework of such a relational paradigm that this book is located. In a way, the convergence of eternal relationality within the Trinity, the idea of *perichoresis*, and the believer's union with Christ has formed the proverbial "perfect storm" that has produced this study.

This book will attempt to harmonize these three doctrines, as it will argue that the soteriological union—the union of the believer and Christ—constitutes a third type of perichoretic relationship; that is, Christ and the believer mutually indwell and participate in one another analogously to the way the persons of the Trinity do.[3] This study will offer biblical, historical, and theological evidence that supports the argument that the relationship existing between Christ and the believer may rightly be called a third type of *perichoresis* distinct from both the trinitarian and christological varieties of the term, thus providing a theological foundation to Christian soteriology that is inherently relational in nature and directly flows out of the eternal relationality of the triune Godhead. The way the believer's union with Christ is developed in this work will closely overlap patristic views of *theosis*. Further, this study will argue that the twin elements of mutual indwelling and active participation are present in the union of a believer with Christ in ways analogous to that among the divine persons such that *perichoresis* is an appropriate, accurate, and theologically fruitful way to think of that union. However, it is a *perichoresis* of a third type.

One of the difficulties in describing the terminology describing the believer's union with Christ, such as "mutual indwelling," lies in the limitations of language. So often spatial terminology is used to describe relational reality. This occurs in both the biblical and the contemporary worlds. When two people are "close," it is understood that the meaning of "close" is relational rather than spatial. The Bible repeatedly uses

---

2. See Zizioulas, *Being as Communion*.

3. The first two types of perichoretic relationships are found, first, among the persons of the Trinity, and second, in the hypostatic union of the divine and human natures in Christ. These will be designated in this investigation as the trinitarian and christological *perichoresis*, respectively.

spatial terms in a relational fashion. Sometimes it is not easy to discern if the proper meaning of a spatial term is spatial or relational. For example, even though "the presence of God" is spatial language, its true meaning is relational. One is reminded of hell, where it is traditionally held that the presence of God is absent. Spatially this is not true, since God is omnipresent—unlimited in regard to space—even in hell (see Ps 139). However, the relational presence of God (as far as we know) cannot be experienced in hell. Thus in this study, one must be mindful of a relational meaning of spatial terms.

Therefore, to state that the believer's union with Christ is a perichoretic relationship is to proclaim that there is a mutual relational indwelling of the believer and Christ, that is, that Christ is in the believer and the believer is in Christ. Furthermore, this relationship is neither merely static nor spatial. There must be an active, loving pursuit of this relationship by both parties at all times, ultimately reaching the goal of being one, analogous to the way the Father and Son are one. As Christ partakes of human nature in the incarnation, so analogously does the believer partake of the divine nature in the soteriological union. The purpose of this book is to argue from the pertinent biblical, historical, and theological evidence that this is indeed the case.

Rather than a concept which can only be applied in trinitarian and christological enquiry, the soteriological union, this study argues, is a relationship of the same kind as the trinitarian and christological, although a third type.[4] Though this book will interact with some authors who believe there are other types of perichoretic relationships that exist, mirroring with varying degrees of clarity what exists in sole perfection in the Godhead, there will only be three types of perichoretic relationships discussed.[5] The trinitarian *perichoresis* is the pattern for all relationships in creation that resemble it in mutual indwelling and active participation

---

4. Here, the "same kind" means that the soteriological union has the same elements in the structure of the relationship as the trinitarian or christological *perichoresis*—the elements (which will become more apparent as the book unfolds) of mutual indwelling and active participation in the other. These two elements are historically part of the established doctrines of *perichoresis*. This study will show biblically, historically, and theologically that they are part of the soteriological union as well. Hence, it is of the "same kind" (*perichoresis*), but it is a third type (distinguished from trinitarian and christological).

5. The three types are the trinitarian, christological, and soteriological. The soteriological, when viewed in its corporate dimension may be termed ecclesiological, but this study will be restricted to the individual dimension.

in the other.⁶ This study will argue that the union of Christ and the believer is such a relationship while acknowledging the existence of other relationships that come close to being perichoretic.

In arguing the case that the union of the believer and Christ is a perichoretic relationship, two assumptions must be kept in mind. First is the ontological difference between God and his creation. Since Christians are part of that creation, the analogy between the trinitarian *perichoresis* and the relationship inherent in union with Christ will never be an exact correspondence. As Avery Dulles writes, the correspondence will be "asymptotic" rather than identical. ("Asymptotic" is another spatial term representing relational reality.)⁷ Second is the continuing presence of a relational paradigm for understanding not only soteriology but all Christian theology as a whole. A relational paradigm must be maintained for this argument to remain coherent. The rationale behind the relational paradigm comes directly from Scripture and theology. The triune God is inherently relational, and he is love (1 John 4:8). One may rightly argue that God is also holy, just, powerful, and a host of other biblical attributes. But these latter attributes are all adjectives, while love is a noun. Adjectives are descriptive, while nouns are definitive. Thus while holy, just, and powerful are certainly proper words to accurately describe God, he *is* love in his very being. Thus this study operates within the relational framework for understanding God.

Finally, it is extremely tempting to begin discussing the perichoretic ramifications for the union of Christ to all believers, which is the corporate aspect of *perichoresis*. This approach, while appearing to be a highly fruitful area of research, will not be discussed in this study in order to allow the focus to remain as much as possible on the relationship between Christ and the individual believer.⁸

6. The term "trinitarian *perichoresis*" will be used consistently in this study to denote the *perichoresis* that the persons of the Godhead enjoy. Often, the adjective "ontological" will be used in other literature, but because "ontological" can be used in different contexts, "trinitarian *perichoresis*" may avoid potential misunderstanding.

7. Dulles, "Trinity and Christian Unity," 75. An asymptote is a plane geometric figure (usually a line) to which a mathematical function approximates but never completely equals. For example, the line $y = 0$ is an asymptote for the algebraic function $f(x) = 1/x$. As x gets larger, $1/x$ gets very close to zero, but never equals it. The asymptotic qualities of the Christ-Christian relationship to the intra-trinitarian relationship should be fairly obvious. The creature can never be the Creator; and the finite can never be the infinite. Given these differences, the relationships still come asymptotically close to one another.

8. This area of research has been explored, though not exhaustively. See Buxton,

OVERVIEW OF THE WORK AS A WHOLE

This first chapter of this work is the introduction. It includes definitions and clarifications of terminology, a statement of purpose, and an overview of the project as a whole. It provides a brief introduction to the doctrines of *theosis, perichoresis,* and union with Christ. A brief history of the formation of the doctrine of *perichoresis* will also be discussed. Finally, some possible objections to the idea that the soteriological union may be called a third type of *perichoresis* will be surveyed.

The second chapter is an examination of the biblical evidence for the union of Christ and the believer as a perichoretic relationship. The two main biblical authors surveyed are Paul and John. The survey of John analyzes some of the key passages in the gospel with explicit perichoretic content. The survey of Paul analyzes some of his key phrases and ideas, such as "in Christ," "with Christ," and "Christ in you." Again, special attention is given to the phrases that exhibit perichoretic ideas. Finally, 2 Peter 1:4, describing Christians as "partakers of the divine nature," is examined, followed by a summary of the chapter's main ideas.

The third chapter is a historic overview of how the doctrine of union exhibits perichoretic overtones. The chapter begins with a close look at some writings from the patristic era, followed by the medieval and Reformation periods.[9] The patristic era is heavily oriented toward the concept of *theosis,* so the connection between this doctrine and *perichoresis* needs to be explained. Some attention is given to the views of Martin Luther and John Calvin on union. Finally, the last portion of the chapter closely surveys some modern and contemporary authors who more explicitly connect the union with Christ and a perichoretic relationship. Key figures here include E. L. Mascall, Jürgen Moltmann, Colin Gunton, and T. F. Torrance.

The fourth chapter focuses on three biblical and theological pictures of the soteriological union and how these pictures point to the perichoretic relationship present in the union: the new covenant, marriage, and adoption. Although marriage is usually presented as a picture of the

---

Trinity, Creation, and Pastoral Ministry, and Volf, *After Our Likeness* for two good approaches.

9. The medieval and Reformation periods are combined because, aside from the mystical theologians of the medieval period, there was little original contribution on the doctrine of union during that time. Since this investigation focuses on more mainstream theological thinkers, the mystical theologians will not be included.

church as a whole, the individual members who make up the church are also part of that marriage, so the topic is relevant. This chapter draws from both biblical and systematic theological works to show that the three pictures of the soteriological union noted above contain perichoretic overtones, so that the relationship of Christ and the believer can be seen more fully as perichoretic as well. Finally, this chapter includes two additional theological arguments that point toward the soteriological union as a third type of *perichoresis*.

The fifth chapter discusses some of the ramifications of looking at the believer's union with Christ as a perichoretic relationship. One is a brief examination of how the acceptance of the thesis would impact systematic theology. A second is a survey of other implications, such as the proposal of a third way in the justification debates between the traditional Reformed view and the New Perspective on Paul,[10] a trinitarian basis for Christian ethics, and some personal implications for Christians and the church. The book concludes with a restatement of the thesis and areas for possible further research.

This topic is important for at least two reasons. First, it provides a constructive proposal for understanding what constitutes the believer's union with Christ. Instead of reacting against what the union is not, it begins with what the union actually is. Second, if the thesis is correct, it would allow the doctrine of soteriology to be foundationally grounded in the eternal, loving relationship found in the triune Godhead. Hence, salvation would flow smoothly and logically from the being of the triune God, to the incarnation of the Son, through the Spirit to humanity. With the tremendous revival in trinitarian and christological thought over the last quarter of the twentieth century, this topic fits securely, offering a bridge between the doctrine of Christian salvation and that revival.

---

10. For more information on the debates over justification, see Piper, *Counted Righteous in Christ*; and "John Piper Responds," *Desiring God*, http://www.desiringgod.org/ResourceLibrary/Articles/ByDate/2003/1522_John_Piper_Responds_to_Don_Garlington_on_the_Imputation_of_Righteousness/; Garlington, "Imputation or Union?" *The Paul Page*, http://www.thepaulpage.com/Imputation.pdf.; Wright, *What St. Paul Really Said*; and Dunn, *New Perspective on Paul*. For a scholarly treatment of the issue, see the two-volume series edited by Carson, Seifrid, and O'Brien, *Justification and Variegated Nomism*.

AN EXAMINATION OF THE BELIEVER'S UNION WITH CHRIST

A Brief Discussion of the Doctrine of Union

The believer's union with Christ has been an important theme of Christian salvation throughout church history. Although chapter 3 below will address its importance in detail, two important Protestant theologians who have understood its importance are John Calvin and Karl Barth. Recent scholarship has affirmed that the doctrine of union with Christ is one of the central themes in all of Calvin's thought, and is essential for understanding how the benefits of salvation are applied to the believer.[11] Similarly, Karl Barth addresses the importance of union in part 4 of his *Church Dogmatics*. He states that the union with Christ is precisely what makes a Christian a Christian "whatever our development or experience."[12]

The believer's union with Christ occupies an important part in evangelical circles as well. Some theologians see the believer's union with Christ as the central aspect in Christian salvation, while others see it as an objective part of the *ordo salutis*.[13] Bruce Demarest, in *The Cross and Salvation*, describes the believer's union with Christ as supernatural (the divine indwelling), spiritual (via the Holy Spirit), organic ("an organization similar in complexity to that of living things"), vital (involv-

---

11. See Kennedy, *Union with Christ*, and Tamburello, *Union with Christ* for two good sources of Calvin's view of union with Christ.

12. Barth, *CD* IV/3.2, 548.

13. The most notable recent example is Keathley, "Work of God," 686–764. Keathley's chapter in the Southern Baptist systematic theology text puts union with Christ as the central idea in all of soteriology. Keathley (ibid., 688n3) cites Garrett, *Systematic Theology*, 2:329–30, as saying that H. R. Mackintosh and Lewis B. Smedes may be added to a list that includes Millard Erickson, Wayne Grudem, John Murray, and John Calvin as theologians who see union with Christ as the central truth of salvation. Although both Erickson (*Christian Theology*, 961) and Grudem (*Systematic Theology*, 840) see union with Christ as a central soteriological truth, Erickson only devotes seven pages (961–67) of his 1,253 pages to it. Grudem uses eleven pages of his 1,167 to describe union. Although these volumes are very comprehensive, the doctrine of union receives less than 1 percent of the space in each. Demarest (*Cross and Salvation*, 313–44) devotes a chapter to the doctrine of union, but does not declare it to be the central idea of salvation. Likewise, Horton (*Covenant and Salvation*, 129–30) favors the notion of justification as the ground of union and all its benefits. So while all Christian theologians hold union to be very important, its centrality to salvation is a point of debate.

ing a new quality of life), comprehensive (everything in life is related to Christ), mysterious (alluding to the mystery of marriage in Eph 5:32), and non-sacramental.[14]

Millard Erickson's list of terminology to describe union is similar to Demarest's though not quite as extensive. He includes the descriptive terms "vital" and "spiritual." To these he adds "judicial," as he sees the righteousness of Christ imputed to the believer in an eternal union, so that "the two are now one."[15] While both Demarest and Erickson do admirable jobs of describing the believer's union with Christ, they have not provided a way to define how this union takes place. Before moving to that section, what union is not needs to be investigated.

An Evangelical Discussion of What Union Is Not

Part of the difficulty in defining what the believer's union with Christ is can be seen in the way evangelical theologians seem to be compelled to declare what union with Christ is not. Often, describing what the union does not entail is more fully treated than what it does entail. A good example is Bruce Demarest, who lists faulty views of union such as ontological (absorption into the divine), sacramental (the sacraments are the instruments of the union), covenantal-only, and a moral/filial union (removing the supernatural).[16]

Erickson's list is again similar to Demarest's, including the sacramental and filial views. Instead of Demarest's ontological view, Erickson divides them into the metaphysical (God and creation are one) and mystical (absorption) views.[17] Ken Keathley warns against a mystical view that contemporary Eastern Orthodoxy espouses along with the sacramental view.[18] Evangelical theologians rightly avoid any explanation of union that allows the possibility of the human to be absorbed into God. This study proposes that the concept of *perichoresis*, where there is mutual indwelling without loss of individuality, could help lessen the necessity for the emphasis on this caution.

---

14. Demarest, *Cross and Salvation*, 330–33.
15. Erickson, *Christian Theology*, 965–66.
16. Demarest, *Cross and Salvation*, 314–23. He spends roughly three times the space refuting false views as he does offering positive descriptions.
17. Erickson, *Christian Theology*, 963.
18. Keathley, "Salvation," 691–92.

A Proposal to Define Union

So far, the doctrine of union has been described with various technical and common terms. It has been noted what explanations of union evangelicals deny. A deeper understanding of the doctrine of union at this point would be helpful. Beyond the descriptions above, the theology texts already cited do move toward a more constructive definition. Bruce Demarest cites the believer's participation in the death and resurrection of Christ as well as the state of mutual indwelling between Christ and the believer.[19] Both Erickson and Keathley mention mutual indwelling as well.[20] So does Wayne Grudem.[21] This idea of mutual indwelling will figure prominently in the biblical argument in chapter 2 below.

Demarest, Keathley, and Grudem all discuss the biblical metaphors for the soteriological union, which include the head and body, husband and wife, building and parts, vine and branches, and the corporate races in Adam and Christ.[22] Both Demarest and Keathley note the analogy in John 17:21–23, where Jesus prays that the oneness between Father and Son may be the model for the oneness of Jesus with his disciples and the disciples with each other, although both are careful to affirm the soteriological union is not identical to the trinitarian union.[23] This text is the logical starting point for showing that the union of the believer and Christ is a perichoretic relationship since, as will be more carefully defined below, such a relationship is one where two persons mutually indwell and participate in one another.

In a 1979 dissertation at Boston College, Daniel Helminiak offers a helpful taxonomy for understanding the various ways the believer's union with Christ has been explained.[24] He supplies four general categories for understanding the believer's union with Christ. His first category is the "implicitly kerygmatic approach." This approach, accord-

---

19. Demarest, *Cross and Salvation*, 323. The idea of "mutual indwelling" discussed in this work means that simultaneously the believer is "in Christ" and Christ is "in" the believer. This is the language Demarest and most others use.

20. Erickson, *Christian Theology*, 961–62; and Keathley, "Salvation," 688–89.

21. Grudem, 840–45.

22. See Demarest, *Cross and Salvation*, 327–29; Keathley, "Salvation," 694–95; and Grudem, *Systematic Theology*, 842–45.

23. Demarest, *Cross and Salvation*, 328, and Keathley, "Salvation," 694. Both affirm that the soteriological union is analogous to the trinitarian union, however.

24. Helminiak, "One in Christ."

ing to Helminiak, explains the doctrine of union by repeating and exemplifying. He writes, "Rather than explain the doctrine, the implicitly kerygmatic approach insists again on it or repeats it in another form."[25] Whether utilizing common language and imagery or technical language, or appealing to divine fiat, this approach seems content to reiterate the truth of union in different ways rather than explain how it takes place. Helminiak states, "For at heart this approach does not move toward precise and explicit understanding of a doctrine, but is content with insistent and creative reiteration of it."[26]

A second category of understanding union appeals directly to Jesus's divinity. It is not as helpful for this investigation because the glorified Christ, as God, is everywhere present and therefore, as Helminiak notes, all are "in him" due to his omnipresence. It does not make the union personal or necessarily salvific.[27] A third category, however, is directly important. It is the shared-humanity approach. This approach has two meaningful explanations. The first is the patristic idea that God's assumption of human nature in the incarnation provides a link to the humanity in every person. This is the basis of the patristic doctrine of deification discussed below. Helminiak writes, "When the Word became flesh, he associated himself with all humanity in the very fact of becoming human."[28] The second explanation, which Helminiak calls the relational form, has been since further explored by John Zizioulas and others.[29] Helminiak states that to be human "is to relate to other human beings and that this relationship is the basis for human unity in general and union with Christ in particular."[30] Though the purpose of this study is not a comprehensive definition of union, understanding it in either of these shared-humanity approaches will help form an understanding of the perichoretic nature of union to be examined fully later.

The final category Helminiak employs is the "one in Spirit" approach. He notes how the Spirit unites believers and Christ as he writes,

---

25. Ibid., 114–15.

26. Ibid., 123.

27. Ibid., 124–35. This approach deals with everyone already "in Christ" also because Christ is God and knows everything. Helminiak critiques this view because it fails to give sufficient weight to the doctrine of the incarnation.

28. Ibid., 135–36.

29. See Zizioulas, *Being as Communion*.

30. Helminiak, "One in Christ," 160.

"The one Spirit, the same Spirit, and the whole Spirit dwells in each member of Christ and in Christ himself."[31] Helminiak concludes that the best way to define union is a combination of the third (shared humanity) and fourth (one in Spirit) approaches.

At this juncture, a brief sketch of how the union of the believer and Christ may look should be helpful. Christ, as the eternal Son, upholds all of his creation (Heb 1:3). At the incarnation, the preserver of creation became flesh, contained within his creation. As Baxter Kruger states, "The incarnation is the coming of the One who is already the source and sustenance of all things. He brings his prior relationship with the cosmos and every human being within it with him as he becomes human."[32] Thus all humans share in the humanity of Jesus by virtue of his (creating and preserving) deity—the one in whom "we live, move, and exist" (Acts 17:28). This sort of "shared humanity" is essential to demonstrate that the believer's union with Christ is a third type of perichoretic relationship.

AN EXAMINATION OF THEOSIS

This section is a brief examination of the patristic doctrine of deification, or *theosis*. For the purposes of this discussion, the terms "deification," "divinization," and "*theosis*" will be interchangeable. Emil Bartos writes, "Basically, the concept of deification is expressed in a phrase common to many of the church fathers: 'God made himself man so that man might become God.' Yet Eastern theology says very clearly that 'becoming God' does not mean an identification with God's divine nature (essence) but rather something experienced by adoption, by grace, and by imitation."[33] Bartos states that "deification is a divine gift and the ultimate and supreme goal for human existence. It involves an intimate union of the human being with the triune God."[34] Georges Florovsky continues,

> Man ever remains what he is, that is—creature. But he is promised and granted, in Christ Jesus, the Word become man, an intimate sharing in what is divine: life everlasting and incorruptible. The main characteristic of *theosis* is, according to the

---

31. Ibid., 168.

32. Kruger, "Why I Left Calvinism," http://baxterkruger.blogspot.com/2008_04_01_archive.html.

33. Bartos, *Deification*, 7. This quotation is best known from Athanasius in *On the Incarnation*, 54.

34. Ibid.

fathers, precisely "immortality" or "incorruption." For God alone has immortality (1 Tim 6:16). But man now is admitted into an intimate "communion" with God, through Christ and by the power of the Holy Spirit. And this is much more than just human perfection. Only the word *theosis* can render adequately the uniqueness of the promise and offer. *The term theosis is indeed quite embarrassing, if we would think in "ontological" categories.* Indeed, man simply cannot "become" god. But the fathers were thinking in "personal" terms, and the mystery of *personal* communion was involved at this point. *Theosis meant a personal encounter.* It is that intimate intercourse of man with God, in which the whole of human existence is, as it were, permeated by the Divine Presence.[35]

So *theosis* does not involve either absorption into God or a mingling of ontology, both of which evangelical theologians cannot accept.[36]

Norman Russell begins his work on the development of the doctrine of deification with the words, "All the earlier patristic writers who refer to deification, although sometimes conscious of the boldness of their language, took it for granted that their readers understood what they meant."[37] He continues, "No formal definition of deification occurs until the sixth century, when Dionysius the Aeropagite declares: 'Deification (θέωσις) is the attaining of likeness to God and union with him so far as is possible.' Only in the seventh century does Maximus the Confessor discuss deification as a theological topic in its own right."[38] Russell reasons that deification language was almost always metaphorical with clear implications to the first hearers and readers.[39]

Union with Christ (and therefore God) was a doctrine of immense importance to the fathers. Humanity's creation in the image of God and Jesus's assumption of human flesh are the foundation of their notions of union and *theosis*—much more so than even Jesus's death and resurrection.[40] Nancy Hudson writes concerning *theosis*, "It describes a sote-

---

35. Florovsky, "Father Florovsky on Palamas," http://www.nicenetruth.com/home/2009/05/fr-florovsky-on-palamas.html#more. All italics, capitalizations, and punctuations in original.

36. See, for example, Bartos, *Deification*, 7nn26–28. See also Demarest, *Cross and Salvation*, 315; and Keathley, "Salvation," 691 for other views of deification.

37. Russell, *Doctrine of Deification*, 1.

38. Ibid.

39. Ibid.

40. For the basis of the image of God in the patristic doctrine of deification, see

riology in which the individual not only is saved from death and eternal punishment, but is deified. Instead of merely living in eternal relationship with God, the individual reclaims the union with God that was lost or weakened by his earthly, finite, and sinful life."[41] From the patristic era forward, Eastern Christianity has been noted for its emphasis on the believer's participation in the divine nature as a key to understanding salvation. Two biblical texts that support the doctrine of deification are Psalm 82:6 ("I have said, you are gods and sons of the Most High") and 2 Peter 1:4 ("partakers of the divine nature").[42] Deification refers to "the Christian's union with God in this life and to their becoming partakers of the divine nature after the resurrection."[43] In contrast, Western Christianity has taken a more juridical stance affirming the believer's status before God.[44] This division is not as clean-cut as some would make it, however, since Augustine uses the language of *theosis* in numerous places in his writings. This will be discussed further in chapter 3 below.

Russell provides an insight into the variety of concepts of deification the fathers employed. He writes,

> Deification is expressed through a number of different images: it is God's honoring of Christians with the title of 'gods'; it is the believer's filial adoption through baptism; it is the attaining of likeness to God through gnosis and dispassion; it is the ascent of the soul to God; it is the participation of the soul in the divine attributes of immortality and incorruption; it is the transformation of human nature by divine action; it is the eschatological glorification of both soul and body; it is union with God through participation in the divine energies.[45]

This quotation highlights the difference in terminology between patristic and contemporary Eastern Orthodox views of deification. Contemporary views of deification stress the difference between the essence and the uncreated energies of God, describing deification as

---

Maloney, *Undreamed Has Happened*, 17–60.

41. Hudson, *Becoming God*, 1.

42. For a discussion of deification in the New Testament, see Maloney, *Undreamed Has Happened*, 61–72.

43. Bercot, "Deification of Man," 199.

44. Fairbairn, "Patristic Soteriology," 289.

45. Russell, *Doctrine of Deification*, 1–2.

a participation in the latter.⁴⁶ This division was thoroughly explained by Gregory Palamas in the fourteenth century.⁴⁷ Orthodox theologians have subsequently followed his distinction. In Reformed and evangelical Protestantism, there is some debate whether *theosis* can be incorporated into Protestant thinking without the essence/energies distinction of Palamas and Eastern Orthodoxy.⁴⁸ This debate is not necessarily germane to this study for two reasons. First, there will be little discussion of Eastern Orthodox deification after the patristic era, so the distinction means little to this enquiry. Second, the distinction may not be necessary since, as Myk Habets shows, Western theology already has capable terminology (ontological/economic Trinity) to deal with deification without absorption into the Godhead.⁴⁹

Based on the above discussions, union with Christ and *theosis* go hand in hand. Deification, or *theosis*, seems to involve both the shared humanity and indwelling Spirit concepts in Helminiak's treatment of union with Christ. This enquiry will argue that the "theotic" union, as Michael Gorman calls union in *theosis*, is a valid way of understanding the believer's union with Christ as shown on biblical, historical, and theological grounds.⁵⁰

AN OVERVIEW OF PERICHORESIS

This section will examine the doctrine of *perichoresis*, its biblical foundations, historical development, and some contemporary ways the doctrine is overstated. Finally, it will begin to argue that the union of the believer and Christ is a perichoretic relationship.

---

46. See, for instance, the description of the epistemology of Dumitru Staniloae in Bartos, *Deification*, 57–58. The roots of the "essence and energies" distinction may be traced at least as far back as the Cappadocians.

47. Letham, *Work of Christ*, 244–50.

48. For an overview of each position see both Habets, "Reformed *Theosis*?" and Olson, "Deification in Contemporary Theology."

49. Habets, *Theosis in the Theology of Thomas Torrance*, 494–97. Habets also argues that in the incarnation humanity is able to know God in his essence, rather than in just his uncreated energies.

50. Gorman (*Inhabiting the Cruciform God*) repeatedly uses the adjective "theotic" in describing the effects of *theosis*. This study will show that union is not a result of *theosis*, but *theosis* is a result of union.

The Definition of Perichoresis, Including Its Biblical Foundation

In discussing the recent revival in trinitarian theology and the significance of *perichoresis*, Roderick Leupp writes, "If today's devotees of trinitarian theology learn only one technical term, *perichoresis* should be it. Not only does it go a great distance toward describing the immanent Trinity, it also has implications for personal and social ethics, for family life, for politics and even for aesthetics and the theology of Christian worship."[51] In this work, the attempt will be made to take the term *perichoresis* and investigate if it can be properly used to describe the believer's union with Christ. First, it must be properly defined, and then refined for its use in this investigation.

Miroslav Volf defines *perichoresis* as "the mutually internal abiding and interpenetration of the trinitarian persons."[52] T. F. Torrance, in explaining Athanasius's conception of what would later be called *perichoresis*, states it is "a completely mutual indwelling in which each person, while remaining what he is by himself as Father, Son, or Holy Spirit, is wholly in the others as the others are wholly in him."[53] James Womack states, "*Perichoresis* comes from the Greek word χωρέω meaning 'to go, extend, or contain.' When combined with the prefix περί, the verb expresses a sense of complete interpenetration or coinherence."[54] S. M. Smith adds, "Trinitarian *perichoresis* begins with the unity of natures or a strict consubstantiality and affirms a reciprocal interrelation."[55] In other words, it stresses "coinherence without confusion."[56] Colin Gunton adds that *perichoresis* "implies that the three persons of the Trinity exist only in reciprocal, eternal relatedness. God is not God apart from the way in which Father, Son, and Spirit in eternity give to and receive from each other what they essentially are."[57] The scholars noted in this subsection discuss *perichoresis* in its trinitarian context only. The ques-

---

51. Leupp, *Renewal of Trinitarian Theology*, 71–72.
52. Volf, *After Our Likeness*, 208.
53. Torrance, *Christian Doctrine of God*, 169.
54. Womack, "Comparison of *Perichoresis*," 2.
55. Smith, "*Perichoresis*," 907.
56. Fiddes, *Participating in God*, 71. Patristic scholar Prestige (*God in Patristic Thought*, 298), describes *perichoresis* as "co-inherence in one another without any coalescence or commixture."
57. Gunton, *One, the Three, and the Many*, 164.

tion is whether its meaning can be expanded to a soteriological context as well.

Some have misinterpreted the meaning of *perichoresis* in recent years. In a personal interview with Peter G. Heltzel, T. F. Torrance states, "*Perichoresis* is spelled with an omega not an omicron. With the omega (*chora*), *perichoresis* means 'making room or space,' 'mutual containing,' or 'coinhering' within one another. When the omicron (*chori*) is used, *perichoresis* means 'dancing' as in a Greek chorus. So these people today talk about the cosmic dance. I think that is foolishness."[58] Heltzel goes on to state that many authors utilize the idea of *perichoresis* as a "divine dance."[59] Robert Sherman and Paul Fiddes are among them. Sherman describes *perichoresis* as "a wonderfully evocative term that some scholars say is derived from the same root as the word 'choreography.' It speaks to the mutual interaction or 'dance' of the three persons of the Trinity. If you have one, you have the other two, even while you cannot reduce or merge one into any other."[60] Paul Fiddes writes, "In this dance the partners not only encircle each other and weave in and out between each other as in human dancing; in the divine dance, so intimate is the communion that they move in and through each other so that the pattern is all-inclusive."[61] While "dance" is not etymologically correct, it does provide a helpful metaphor to explain how *perichoresis* functions in the Godhead.

The Gospel of John contains the biblical foundation for the doctrine of *perichoresis*. Statements such as "I am in the Father and the Father is in me" (John 14:11) from the lips of Jesus show that there is a sense of mutual indwelling that exists among the persons of the Trinity.

---

58. Heltzel, "*Perichoresis*," 28. The interview took place on February 7, 1997.

59. Ibid. Heltzel's primary example is Zizioulas, *Being as Communion*, 27–66. Lawler, "*Perichoresis*," 53, traces the etymological error to Kress, "Church *Communio*," 140. It is a position Kress later retracted. See Kress, *Church*, 18.

60. Sherman, *King, Priest, and Prophet*, 62.

61. Fiddes, *Participating in God*, 72. Over the next several pages, Fiddes compares the Eastern and Western views of *perichoresis*, noting the difficulties that come with each. In the East, with its tendency toward order within the Godhead, there is the possibility that some may try to find the utterly transcendent in God, as in the "dark side of the moon," in Fiddes's words. In the West, the relative lack of order in the Godhead, with the Spirit as the bond of love that unites Father and Son, might indicate to some that the "divine dance" is closed to all but the Three. Fiddes attempts to resolve these difficulties by looking at *perichoresis* as the relations among the Persons, rather than the Persons as subjects in their own right.

Köstenberger and Swain argue that this "in" language should not be understood as an influence from the ancient mysteries or as a "mystical" relationship in general, but "their relationship is one of intimacy, love, and trust."[62] Other Johannine passages supporting *perichoresis* include John 10:38; 14:10; 17:3; and 17:21–23. Jürgen Moltmann notes that "Jesus and God the Father are not *one and the same*, they are *at one*—a unity—in their mutual indwelling."[63] The concept of *perichoresis* in the Bible does not denote absolute identity, but a union in indwelling and interpenetration. Stephen Seamands argues that Paul's interchangeable use of Father, Son, and Spirit in Romans 8:9–11 points toward the doctrine of *perichoresis*, as he states that the interchange of the divine persons "implies their mutual indwelling and participation in one another."[64]

The doctrine of *perichoresis* is understood differently depending on the Eastern or Western orientation of trinitarian theology. Paul Collins notes that in the Orthodox tradition, since trinitarian theology starts from the three persons, "*perichoresis* is to be understood in terms of a dynamic and reciprocal penetration. By contrast, the Latin tradition, beginning with the unity of the deity, suggests that the reciprocal coinherence of the persons is to be understood in terms of their relation to the single divine essence."[65] Robert Letham notes how the persons of the Trinity occupy the same "space" and mutually indwell each other.[66] R. Matthew Lytle notes that the guarantee of unity in diversity present in the doctrine of *perichoresis* forms a safeguard between the dual heresies of modalism (Sabellianism) and tritheism, the tendencies to heresy in the West and East, respectively.[67] *Perichoresis* therefore serves as an important safeguard to help avoid trinitarian heresy.

*The History of the Development of the Doctrine,
Both Christological and Trinitarian*

According to S. M. Smith, the eighth-century Greek theologian John of Damascus used *perichoresis* to describe "the mutual indwelling or,

62. Köstenberger and Swain, *Father, Son, and Spirit*, 71.
63. Moltmann, *Experiences in Theology*, 316.
64. Seamands, *Ministry in the Image of God*, 141.
65. Collins, *Trinitarian Theology*, 209–10.
66. Letham, *Holy Trinity*, 382. Again there are not sufficient relational words to describe such a reality. Therefore, spatial terminology again represents relational reality.
67. Lytle, "Perichoretically Embodied Ethics," 26.

better, mutual interpenetration" of the persons of the Godhead.[68] John writes, "The subsistences dwell and are established firmly in one another. For they are inseparable and cannot part from one another, but to keep to their separate courses within one another, without coalescing or mingling, but cleaving to one another. For the Son is in the Father and the Spirit; and the Spirit in the Father and the Son; and the Father in the Son and the Spirit, but there is no coalescence or commingling or confusion."[69] Many scholars today believe sixth-century Pseudo-Cyril was the first to use *perichoresis* with its present meaning, while others think that John of Damascus preceded the one whose writings are attributed to Pseudo-Cyril.[70]

Gregory of Nazianzus, nearly two centuries earlier, utilized *perichoresis* to describe how the divine and human unite in Christ, ultimately leading to the teaching of the *communicatio idiomatum*.[71] Gregory of Nazianzus, writing against Apollinarians, claims that the names of Christ are "mingled (περιχωρουσων) like the natures, and flowing into one another, according to the law of their intimate union."[72] James Womack believes that Gregory's use of *perichoresis* is the result of the maturation process of his thinking allowing him to use extra-biblical language to describe the biblical way the natures unite in Christ.[73] Gregory's use of the term is called "christological *perichoresis*" in this work.

T. F. Torrance traces the idea of *perichoresis* back to Athanasius, though he notes that Hilary uses perichoretic language without using the terminology.[74] The Alexandrian bishop derived his understanding of the doctrine from his exegesis of the Gospel of John, although he

---

68. Smith, "*Perichoresis*," 906.

69. John of Damascus, *On the Orthodox Faith* 1.14 (*NPNF2* 9:17b).

70. Fiddes, *Participating in God*, 71. Letham notes that Joseph the Philosopher may have been the one responsible for the *perichoresis* used in Pseudo-Cyril. See Letham, *Holy Trinity*, 366. Agreeing with Letham is Womack, "Comparison," 7–8. For earlier scholarship accepting John's dependence on Pseudo-Cyril, see Heltzel, "*Perichoresis*," 31, and Harrison, "*Perichoresis*," 60.

71. Otto, "Use and Abuse of *Perichoresis*," 368. For a good overview of the history of the development of both the word *perichoresis*, see Torrance, *Christian Doctrine of God*, 168–71. Womack ("Comparison," 25) notes that Gregory was not the first theologian to use the term *perichoresis*, but he was the first to use the term in a theological manner.

72. Gregory of Nazianzus, *Epistle 101* (*NPNF2* 7:439).

73. Womack, "Comparison," 19–24.

74. Torrance, *Trinitarian Faith*, 206.

never used the term *perichoresis* itself.[75] Torrance bases his view of *perichoresis* largely on the work of Athanasius and the connection between *perichoresis* and salvation.[76] R. Matthew Lytle argues that language that anticipates the orthodox doctrine of *perichoresis* is present as far back as Irenaeus and Origen.[77] In any event, its biblical basis goes back to the Gospel of John.

To summarize the patristic and Eastern medieval usage of *perichoresis*, James Womack writes,

> From the time of Gregory until John [of Damascus] each theological use of *perichoresis* was in reference to the two natures of Christ. John follows the common theological understanding of *perichoresis* in his day to refer to the natures of Christ, but also expands his understanding of the term to include the mutual interpenetration of each member of the Trinity into the lives of the others by building upon the Christological language of Chalcedon which stressed unification without loss of personhood. In the same way that *perichoresis* helped to show the relation between the two *hypostases* and one *ousia* of Christ, John also used the term to refer to the individual *hypostases* that make up the Trinity that share one *ousia*. In doing so, John is able to denounce Arianism, Nestorianism, and Monophysitism.[78]

In the West, the idea of *perichoresis* is translated into two terms distinguished by a single letter, *circumincessio* and *circuminsessio*. These Latin words show the two meanings inherent in the richer Greek term *perichoresis*. According to Womack, the former verb denotes "the dynamic circulation of the trinitarian life" while the latter emphasizes "the abiding reality" of that life.[79] Moltmann sees the "enduring, resting

---

75. See Torrance, *Trinitarian Perspectives*, 10. See also Torrance, *Christian Doctrine of God*, 168–71; and Heltzel, "Perichoresis," 32–35.

76. Heltzel, "Perichoresis," 35–36. This idea will be further developed and explained in chapter 3 below.

77. Lytle, "Perichoretically Embodied Ethics," 51–62.

78. Womack, "Comparison," 37.

79. Ibid., 52. The "abiding reality" here is mutual indwelling, while the "dynamic circulation" is the mutual participation in the other. Thus the two Latin terms show these two elements of a perichoretic relationship as found among the persons of the Trinity and in the natures of Christ. According to Buxton (*Trinity, Creation, and Pastoral Ministry*, 131) *circuminsessio* (from *circuminsedere*) means "to sit around" and has a static quality, while *circumincessio* (from *circumincedere*) means "to move around, a state of doing rather than being."

indwelling" in *circuminsessio*.[80] The Latin terminology is used infrequently today, especially with the recent revival of the older Greek *perichoresis*. In English, the term most often used for *perichoresis* is "coinherence," which is quite popular in the works of early- to mid-twentieth century authors such as Charles Williams and G. B. Verity.[81] For the purposes of this investigation, the above terms of *perichoresis* and coinherence will be synonymous.[82]

The doctrine of *perichoresis* was officially recognized by the Roman Catholic Church at the Council of Florence in 1442. The statement issued there is, "The three persons are one God not three Gods, because they share one substance, one essence, one nature, one divinity, one immensity, one everything where there is no opposition of relation. Because of this unity, the Father is entirely in the Son, entirely in the Holy Spirit, the Son is entirely in the Father, entirely in the Holy Spirit, the Holy Spirit is entirely in the Father, entirely in the Son."[83]

As mentioned above, there has been a revival of the doctrine of *perichoresis* in the latter half of the twentieth century. Several theologians make the doctrine an important part of their theological program, including Catherine Mowry LaCugna, Jürgen Moltmann, and T. F. Torrance.[84] Although much of their work on *perichoresis* does not directly intersect with this present investigation, some of their points are important for the believer's union with Christ and will be discussed in chapter 3 below.

Some Contemporary Overstatements of the Doctrine

Randall Otto notes some of the ways in which the doctrine of *perichoresis* has been misconstrued in recent theology. He believes the only way the doctrine can be rightly employed is from a starting point of the unity of the divine essence, which effectively removes any other possible starting

---

80. Moltmann, *Experiences in Theology*, 317. See also Buxton, *Trinity, Creation, and Pastoral Ministry*, 130.

81. The works of these two men will be more diligently explored in chapter 3 below.

82. Turner ("Coinherence," 112) equates *perichoresis*, *circumincessio* and *circuminsessio*, and coinherence as synonyms in Greek, Latin, and English, respectively.

83. Quoted in Otto, "Use and Abuse," 372.

84. See n2 above.

point.⁸⁵ He writes that the doctrine "has suffered in some recent theology from its appropriation to describe relationality apart from mutually shared being."⁸⁶

Otto criticizes Jürgen Moltmann's use of *perichoresis* on three counts. First, Otto shows that Moltmann's starting point for his doctrine of *perichoresis* is not the requisite unity of divine essence; rather Moltmann begins with the three divine persons.⁸⁷ Moltmann writes, "The unity of the Father with the Son and the Holy Spirit lies in their personal community rather than in a common divine substance or in the identification of one, absolute, divine subjectivity."⁸⁸ Otto's criticism here is well founded. The definition of *perichoresis* requires both a unity and a community. Without the divine unity, their relationship may not be properly perichoretic.

Otto's second criticism of Moltmann's concept of *perichoresis* involves Moltmann's ideas of "a mutual *perichoresis* between eternity and time" and "the perichoretic concept of space."⁸⁹ Moltmann proposes a perichoretic union between God and the world in the eschaton but fails to ground this *perichoresis* in the hypostatic union, thereby giving it no ontological basis.⁹⁰ Similarly, Moltmann's concept of perichoretic space, the idea that God is in creation and creation is in God, has the same lack of ontological foundation. Without the proper foundation of *perichoresis* in the divine essence, Moltmann's dreams of eschatological hope are groundless. John Cooper adds,

> Jürgen Moltmann offers the most fully articulated, explicitly panentheistic Christian theology in history. It is panentheistic because the perichoretic mutuality of God and the world is ontologically constitutive for both. It is trinitarian because Father, Son, and Holy Spirit develop in identity and unity through their

---

85. Otto, "Use and Abuse," 377.

86. Ibid., 366.

87. Ibid., 366–67. This criticism is echoed by Cooper, *Panentheism*, 249–51.

88. Moltmann and Moltmann-Wendel, *Humanity in God*, 88, quoted in Otto, "Use and Abuse," 372.

89. Otto, "Use and Abuse," 367. Moltmann is certainly not the first to see perichoretic-type relationships in creation and time. Although it is not important to this work to discuss this topic, Buxton (*Trinity, Creation, and Pastoral Ministry*, 130) notes that the idea of a perichoretic makeup of all creation goes all the way back to the seventh century and Maximus the Confessor.

90. Ibid., 381.

involvement in the world. It is eschatological because the fullness and unity of the Trinity coincide with the complete *perichoresis* of God and creation in the consummation of the kingdom.[91]

Otto's article highlights a danger that this investigation must heed. It is tempting to look for *perichoresis* everywhere and see every relationship as perichoretic. While it would be reasonable to assume that the triune, perichoretic God who created the universe would have built relationships into his creation that mirror his own to some extent, one must be careful not to read too much into what may be observed from the world. Moltmann's emphasis on *perichoresis* that is not grounded in the divine ontology serves as a warning to the excessive use of *perichoresis* and its explanatory power.

A Third Type of Perichoresis?

This study attempts to show that the union of the believer and Christ is a perichoretic relationship, albeit of a third type beside the trinitarian and christological. To do so will require proof that the term *perichoresis* can be applied to wider contexts than the solely trinitarian or christological. It would seem that the incarnation of Christ, in which the christological variety of *perichoresis* finds its full and orthodox expression, would show that a perichoretic relationship between the divine and human would at least be possible—the union of two natures in the person of Jesus Christ shows that both a divine and a human nature can indwell the same physical person simultaneously. In addition, humanity is created in the image of the triune, perichoretic God. Therefore, creation and the incarnation guarantee the possibility of such a relationship.[92] This study seeks to demonstrate its existence. Emile Mersch writes,

> As Christ is in the Father because he is the Son, Christians will be in the Son and the Father because they will be in Christ. The unity which the Son has with the Father will embrace them in their own way. They will be one as the Father and Son are one; they will be one in the Father and the Son; they will be one with a perfect unity: "that they might be made perfect in one." Theology will have to explain and distinguish; it will have to discuss participation, grace, and the finite divinization that is inherent in the Christian. But it cannot blot out or minimize a word. If the divine

---

91. Cooper, *Panentheism*, 257.
92. For more on this, see Mersch, *Theology of the Mystical Body*, 363–66.

gift were not integral, infinite, un-heard of, would it still be truly divine? Our own explanation will come later; for the moment we should note that Jesus Christ does not comment or restrict; he has not the slightest intention of toning down his expressions or making them more credible. At this hour he carries everything to extremes, and he makes no exceptions for unity.[93]

Some contemporary theologians believe this to be the case as well. Jürgen Moltmann explains that there are three different meanings of *perichoresis*, depending on its context. First, in trinitarian thinking, *perichoresis* means "the mutual indwelling of the homogeneous divine Persons of the Father, Son, and Holy Spirit."[94] Second, in Christology, *perichoresis* "describes the mutual penetration of two heterogeneous natures, the divine and the human, in Christ the God-human being."[95] Third, in the world in general, "*Perichoresis* means the full community of different human persons in the presence of the Holy Spirit. It is necessary to distinguish between these three levels of perichoretic existence in order to avoid equivocations."[96]

Moltmann is not the only scholar to see the distinct levels of *perichoresis*. James Fowler, building on the work of E. L. Mascall and others, identifies three "divine onenesses": the trinitarian, christological, and Christian (ecclesiological).[97] The perichoretic relationship between the believer and Christ for which this investigation will argue will be nuanced slightly differently than Moltmann's or Fowler's definitions. In this study, the focus will be on the union of the individual believer and Christ rather than all Christians and Christ together. That is, this study will argue for the individual aspect of Fowler's proposal.[98] Moltmann, in his somewhat panentheistic approach, does not seem to make the distinction between those in the church and those outside of it.

---

93. Ibid., 339.

94. Moltmann, "God in the World," 373.

95. Ibid.

96. Ibid. This book, while making Moltmann's view explicit, does not endorse his view.

97. Fowler, "Three Divine Onenesses." In this article, Fowler follows the work of Mascall, *Christ, the Christian, and the Church*, 92–96.

98. Therefore, the distinction for which this study will argue is not a "fourth type" of *perichoresis*. Rather, it will investigate the individual aspects of the third type of *perichoresis* in Fowler's proposal.

Another nuance is the recognition that the perichoretic nature of the believer's union with Christ is not exactly like the trinitarian *perichoresis*. The Godhead is uncreated, and the *perichoresis* the three persons enjoy is one of underived essence. The union of the believer with Christ, on the other hand, entails a union of the creature with the Creator. This union must be derived, since the human is a creation of God.[99] Thus there is always an "ontological gulf" between creature and Creator.[100] Furthermore, the divine persons are omnipresent, where created persons are spatially finite. This difference also keeps the analogy of the perichoretic union from being identical to the trinitarian *perichoresis* in that it is impossible for humans to physically indwell God or one another.[101] Gunton summarizes thus: "When used of the persons of the Godhead, [*perichoresis*] implies a total and eternal interanimation of being and energies. When used of those limited in time and space, changes in the intension of the concept necessarily follow."[102] Therefore, there is a sense in which any discussion of *perichoresis* outside of the trinitarian context is analogical at best, since all other perichoretic relationships are but copies of the original. That is why this study continually stresses it is arguing for a *perichoresis* of a *third* type.

POSSIBLE OBJECTIONS TO THE SOTERIOLOGICAL UNION AS PERICHORESIS

This section will formulate some anticipated objections to the thesis that the soteriological union of Christ and the believer constitutes a perichoretic relationship and attempt to answer them. This list is certainly not exhaustive but may serve to ease some misgivings readers may have concerning the thesis, as well as potentially clarify some issues and terminology.

The Creator/Creature Distinction

Describing the union of the believer and Christ is difficult because a delicate balance must be maintained. As has been discussed above,

---

99. This language of "underived" and "derived" comes from Fowler, "Three Divine Onenesses."
100. Scoutieris, "People of God," 408.
101. Buxton, *Trinity, Creation, and Pastoral Ministry*, 151.
102. Gunton, *One, the Three, and the Many*, 170.

the believer and Christ are joined in a real union, but the distinction between them always exists. Christ as God is uncreated while the human is a finite creature, thus the "ontological gulf" between them. This ontological gulf guarantees that there can never be a complete absorption of the believer into the divine, since that which is derived can never become underived.[103]

At this point, it may be helpful to observe the different levels at which one may discuss the concept of *perichoresis*. Here, Justin Thacker is quite helpful as he discerns at least three levels of perichoretic activity present in God and the world. First, there is a complete, mutual *perichoresis* in the Trinity *ad intra* (that is, what this investigation calls the trinitarian *perichoresis*). Here there is free and unlimited mutual indwelling and participation.[104] The other two forms of *perichoresis* Thacker discusses, therefore, must be related analogically to the trinitarian *perichoresis*.[105]

Second, he notes that *perichoresis* involving the Trinity *ad extra* (that is, the triune God interacting with creation, of which the christological *perichoresis* is the prime example) is "neither symmetrical nor complete."[106] In the incarnation, the humanity of Christ did not become infinite as his divinity is, showing the asymmetrical quality of even the christological *perichoresis*.[107] Regarding the relationship between God and humans, that relationship is likewise asymmetrical because God is ontologically different than humans. Also, humanity participates in what Christ has become in the incarnation rather than in the preexistent deity. Thacker writes, "We do not enter into what Christ *was*, but rather enter into what he *has become* on our behalf."[108] Regarding the completeness of the *perichoresis*, Miroslav Volf notes that when human beings are involved, the Spirit may indwell the believer, but the believer cannot internally indwell the Spirit. The analogy does not go both ways. In Volf's

---

103. For more, see Son, "Implications of Paul's 'One Flesh' Concept," 121, and Pannenberg, *Systematic Theology*, 2:452–53.

104. Thacker, *Postmodernism*, 44.

105. Ibid.

106. Ibid. It is therefore analogical to the trinitarian *perichoresis*.

107. Though theologians throughout history have differed over how much the human nature of Christ took on divine properties (Luther claimed that Christ's human flesh was omnipresent, for example), one area where there is general agreement is the finite temporal existence of Christ's human flesh. That is, his human existence had a beginning.

108. Thacker, *Postmodernism*, 54. Italics added for emphasis.

words, "This personal interiority is one-sided. The Spirit indwells human persons, whereas human beings by contrast indwell the life-giving ambience of the Spirit, not the person of the Spirit."[109] Recognizing this distinction is a safeguard against the error of humans becoming God by nature. Finally, the third level of *perichoresis,* existing in the human sphere of operations, is only partial but still mutual.[110]

William J. Hill, speaking of the analogous relation of words and propositions to the true object of faith which is God, uses a description of the difference of the two that could be applied equally to the difference between the trinitarian *perichoresis* and the soteriological union. He writes, "And in this there is implicit how far the similitude falls short of being a perfect imitation. Not only is the knowledge proper to God alone and in the creature only by reason of a totally gratuitous participation; but the very concept of faith, indicating the obscurity in which it assents to what it cannot behold, involves an intrinsic imperfection in no wise to be sought in God's vision of his divine essence."[111] In other words, using Hill's ideas, the soteriological *perichoresis* is both derived through the grace of God and experienced by faith rather than full awareness that the Trinity enjoys. Even though the believer's union with Christ falls far short of the trinitarian relationship in this manner, this study will show it is still permissible to call it *perichoresis.*

Likewise, David Cunningham acknowledges that the distinction between Creator and creature makes the exact reproduction of the divine intra-trinitarian life in humans impossible.[112] Yet he states, "But we should not underestimate the power of the Spirit, working in us, to do infinitely more than we can ask or imagine—such that we too might dimly reflect, however inadequately, the complete mutual participation within God."[113] The "complete mutual participation" of which Cunningham speaks, though humans reflect it "dimly and inadequately," is the idea of *perichoresis.*

---

109. Volf, *After Our Likeness*, 211.

110. Thacker, *Postmodernism*, 44.

111. Hill, "Proper Relations," 13–14.

112. See the distinctions in the usages of the term *perichoresis* in Thacker, *Postmodernism*, 53–54. For this study to proceed, *perichoresis* must have explanatory power beyond the trinitarian context only.

113. Cunningham, *These Three Are One*, 169. Cunningham bases the possibility of such a perichoretic union between God and humanity on the Incarnation (ibid., 182).

Bridging the gap between the essential trinitarian *perichoresis* and the derived oneness between Christ and the believer is the hypostatic christological *perichoresis*.[114] Fowler argues, following Athanasius, that the hypostatic union in the incarnation is necessary to bring the perichoretic divine life into the world of human beings.[115] In the hypostatic union, Oliver Crisp notes that "the divine nature of Christ interpenetrates the human nature of Christ in virtue of divine omnipresence."[116] What then is the relationship of the nature of divine interpenetration (in the indwelling of the Holy Spirit) into the Christian's human nature? He answers, "Christ's human nature may be interpenetrated in such a way in the hypostatic union that the difference between it and my nature on the question of interpenetration by the divine nature, whilst only a difference of degree, is nevertheless a significant degree of difference."[117] The interpenetrating divine life is of the same quality though in less "quantity."[118] Crisp maintains the "ontological gulf" because Christ is the Word incarnate,[119] but his argument does lend credence to the thesis that the union between the believer and Christ is a perichoretic relationship. Thus there is not necessarily a creator-creature difficulty because the two were united in Christ. Therefore the creator-creature distinction

---

114. Again, this makes use of Fowler's terminology. To refresh, the trinitarian *perichoresis* is one of underived essence, the Christological *perichoresis* is hypostatic, and the ecclesiological oneness is derived.

115. Fowler, "Three Divine Onenesses." See also Athanasius, *On the Incarnation* 54.

116. Crisp, "Problems with *Perichoresis*," 132.

117. Ibid. Crisp would do well to refine the "degree of difference" and make it more precise. For example, utilizing the work of Fowler, there are some things that the Christian cannot do in her union with Christ that Christ could (and can) do in human flesh. For example, the name "I AM" is off limits to the Christian, as is the essential nature of the indwelling divine. For the Christian, the indwelling of the divine is derived, rather than part of his created essence, although the "new creature" language of the New Testament deserves a closer look.

118. "Quantity" may not be an adequate word choice here, but this underscores why seeing the soteriological union as a third type of *perichoresis* is important. On the one hand, Christians do not become "God-men" as Jesus is, but on the other, the life indwelling Christians is the genuine divine life. Because both of these truths must be maintained simultaneously, terminology that preserves the balance, such as "a third type of *perichoresis*," becomes necessary.

119. Crisp, "Problems with *Perichoresis*," 134. Thus both a "qualitative" (due to the uniqueness of the incarnation) and "quantitative" (akin to the anointing of the High Priest in Exod 28–29 as compared to that of the regular priests) difference exists between the divine in Jesus and the divine in the believer.

does not pose a problem to a doctrine of the perichoretic union of the believer and Christ, but it does qualify it in the sense that *perichoresis* operates on different levels.

The most important corollary following from the distinction between God and his creation that is maintained within the soteriological union is that the possibility of the believer being absorbed into God is eliminated. Thus the inadequate descriptions of union with Christ as absorption into the divine are not possible if salvation is viewed as a third type of *perichoresis*. Both the trinitarian and christological varieties of *perichoresis* are able to maintain unity without sacrificing diversity. Using perichoretic language to describe union with Christ thus becomes a safeguard against the possibility of divine absorption.

Is the Traditional Theological Meaning of Perichoresis Compromised?

This is a valid question. The trinitarian and christological varieties of *perichoresis* are standard Christian orthodoxy. Does extending *perichoresis* beyond these two unique instances jeopardize or cheapen the meaning of the word beyond acceptable limits? Bruce McCormack thinks so, accusing many contemporary theologians of "creeping *perichoresis*," wrenching the word from its trinitarian context and applying it incorrectly.[120]

This study argues that it does not for several reasons. First of all, *perichoresis* was an existing Greek word adapted by the fathers centuries after the apostles to describe the ideas of mutual indwelling and interpenetration of the two natures in Christ (christological) and the relationships among the persons of the Godhead (trinitarian).[121] It is a word that, in theological history, describes the union of natures and persons. It does not need to be confined to divine persons in order to be operative. The trinitarian and christological are the historical expressions

---

120. McCormack, "Crisis of Protestantism in the West," 111.

121. See n78 above, where Womack ("Comparison of *Perichoresis*," 37) describes how John of Damascus modified the existing term (*perichoresis*) that described the interpenetration of the two natures in Christ to fit trinitarian reality. It would seem that John took an existing word and saw an orthodox, biblical application of the same principle in another area of theology. Gregory of Nazianzus did the same centuries earlier as he used an existing Greek word to describe the incarnation.

of perichoretic relationships, but they need not be the only varieties.[122] Both covenants and human marriage display vestiges of *perichoresis* too, as chapter 4 will discuss. This study will show a perichoretic relationship exists between the believer and Christ as well.

Second, Colin Gunton and Jürgen Moltmann argue that *perichoresis* exists in all of creation, as we will see in in chapter 3 below.[123] Though Moltmann lapses into panentheism, by all accounts Gunton does not. It would be reasonable to assume that if God exists perichoretically in three persons, his creation would reflect at least some of that nature, albeit with all the limitations of finitude and creatureliness.[124] Humans, made in the very image of God, should reflect the perichoretic God even more clearly, in both original creation and the re-creation in Christ. Again, finitude and the residual effects of sin will mar the clarity of the reflection, but it should not be surprising that created vestiges of *perichoresis* are found in human institutions that God has ordained to establish relationships—covenants, marriages, and families. It would frankly be more surprising if the creation did not exhibit some of the traits of the Creator.

Third, explaining salvation biblically is far more difficult if the relationship between Christ and the believer were *not* perichoretic.[125] If the soteriological union were not perichoretic, then the promises that the Christian possesses the divine life, though it is derived, could never be

---

122. This study will argue that the intimacy in the biblical language describing the soteriological union implies that it is a perichoretic relationship, consisting of both mutual indwelling and active participation in the other. Full and complete indwelling only exists in the Godhead. Here the objection of McCormack ("Crisis of Protestantism," 111) carries some weight. *Perichoresis*, as is eternally enjoyed in the intra-divine relations, or by the full interpenetration of human and divine in Christ, is impossible to reproduce. That is not what this study is arguing. There is a degree of difference in symmetry and completeness, as Thacker, *Postmodernism*, 44, notes, but the relationship is still perichoretic, albeit one of a third type.

123. See Moltmann, *History and the Triune God*, 132–33, and Gunton, *One, the Three, and the Many*, 167–72.

124. Gunton (*One, the Three, and the Many*, 167) argues this very point.

125. Peter J. Leithart ("Making Room," March 3, 2008, http://rdtwot.wordpress.com/2008/03/03/making-room-by-peter-j-leithart/) writes, "Yet, Jesus clearly highlights the *similarities* between divine *perichoresis*, the church's relationship with him and the Father, and Christians' relations with one another on the other. What else are we to make of John 17:21ff: 'that they all may be one, even as Thou, Father, art in Me, and I in Thee, that they also may be in us'?" This text is the strongest biblical foundation for arguing the believer's relationship with Christ is perichoretic. If that relationship is not perichoretic, what is to be said of that between Father and Son?

an experiential reality. Moreover, without a perichoretic soteriological union, it becomes difficult to explain how believers possess the benefits of salvation. Election, justification, sanctification, security, and more are found "in Christ."[126] The life of faith that believers live daily is a direct result of the indwelling and working of Christ in their lives through the Spirit.[127] The organic terminology the New Testament uses to describe the relationship between Christ and the believer(s) (head/body, husband/wife, body/members, Adam/posterity, vine/branches) suggests that Christ and the believer are so closely united that they are inextricably bound together from now on.[128] John Murray waxes eloquently about how the union has poles in both eternity past and eternity future. There will always be an "ontological gulf" between the human and the divine (since the human can never be ontologically God), but believers are able to experience full communion with the triune God. Even Murray, though he denies believers are incorporated into the life of the Trinity, still affirms the existence of three great mysteries—the Trinity, the incarnation, and the believer's union with Christ.[129] If the Trinity and the incarnation are each described as a *perichoresis*, does it compromise the meaning of *perichoresis* if the "greatest mystery of creaturely relations" is one as well?[130]

The meaning of *perichoresis* is not compromised. The replication of divine life in humans almost demands the presence of perichoretic relationships among the redeemed and Redeemer, if all that is biblically proclaimed is to be true. *Perichoresis* need not be confined to the Trinity *ad intra*. God's life is the pattern that he has chosen to replicate in his re-creation of humanity in Christ. Its explanatory power is just beginning to be investigated.[131] Subsequent research will doubtless find perichoretic

---

126. See Eph 1:4, 1 Cor 1:30, and Rom 8:29–39 for examples.

127. See Gal 2:20 and Col 3:4 for examples.

128. Murray, *Redemption Accomplished and Applied*, 161–73.

129. Ibid., 169. He writes, "The greatest mystery of being is the mystery of the Trinity—three persons in one God. The great mystery of godliness is the mystery of the incarnation, that the Son of God became man and was manifest in the flesh (1 Tim 3:16). But the greatest mystery of creaturely relations is the union of the people of God with Christ. And the mystery of it is attested by nothing more than this: that it is compared to the union that exists between the Father and the Son in the unity of the Godhead."

130. Ibid. See the previous footnote.

131. See, for example, Buxton, *Trinity, Creation, and Pastoral Ministry*, esp. chaps.

relationships throughout creation not because *perichoresis* is being taken completely out of context but rather because God is the creator and has chosen to reflect his perichoretic self in the universe he made.

Does Perichoretic Union Imply Universalism?

A final objection to the union of the believer and Christ as a perichoretic relationship is the possibility of universal salvation. Jesus and the rest of the New Testament have far too much to say about eternal punishment for hell not to be real, so universal salvation does not seem biblically possible. Yet two great patristic minds, Origen and Gregory of Nyssa, affirmed it, utilizing much of the same argumentation this chapter has. How could universalism be a problem in the perichoretic union, and how can it be effectively answered?

Arriving at universalism in the argument this study outlines would not be difficult. If in Jesus Christ the eternal Son joined himself permanently to human flesh, and if human nature is one, then all humanity is joined to Jesus Christ. The ensuing process of deification will lead all to salvation. This was Gregory's reasoning, at least.[132]

John of Damascus answers the universalism objection in his *On the Orthodox Faith*. He appeals to the distinction between nature and person, noting that Jesus did not take on every human *hypostasis* when assuming human nature.[133] Thus it is possible for the nature to be deified without every single person possessing that nature to be so deified. Jules Gross summarizes John's teaching as he writes, "The φύσις common to all individuals is deified once and for all in the incarnation due to contact with divinity. Persons, on the contrary, must gain their deification by the imitation of Christ."[134] Such imitation includes following Christ's teach-

---

5–6; as well as Simmons, "Quantum *Perichoresis*."

132. Burns, "Economy of Salvation," 224–25, 229. For a rebuttal, see Letham, *Work of Christ*, 79

133. John of Damascus, *On the Orthodox Faith* 3.11 (NPNF2 9:54–55). Gross (*Divinization of the Christian*, 261n28) describes John's discussions of the nuances of meaning of φύσις, Greek for "nature." The two most important are the nature common to all individuals, and the nature belonging solely to each individual.

134. Gross, *Divinization of the Christian*, 263. This study affirms John's distinction between nature and person, but does not hold that deification is attained solely by the imitation of Christ.

ing, participating in the sacraments, and the application of the "fruits of Christ's work" by the Spirit to the individual.[135]

John's important distinction shows that universalism does not have to be the result of the union of Christ and the believer as discussed in this investigation. Salvation remains a free, not mandatory, gift. Hopefully, some initial questions concerning the use of *perichoresis* of a third type to describe the soteriological union have been answered.

CHAPTER SUMMARY

This chapter has provided a foundation to explore whether the soteriological union might be seen as a third type of *perichoresis*. The concepts of union with Christ, *theosis*, and *perichoresis* have been surveyed. Some possible objections to the thesis have been raised and answered. The next step is to take a close look at the biblical evidence that helps show that the believer's union with Christ is a third type of *perichoresis*.

As noted above, Jesus's prayer in John 17 is the logical starting point for showing that the union of the believer and Christ is a perichoretic relationship. He prayed that his disciples "may all be one; even as You, Father, are in Me and I in You, that they also may be in Us, so that the world may believe that You sent Me" (John 17:21–23).[136] There are many passages in John's Gospel that portray the special perichoretic relationship Jesus enjoys with the Father, but the John 17 text is likewise one of several that depict the same type of relationship between Christ and his disciples (such as John 10:14–15 and 15:1–8).[137] The relationship between *theosis* and *perichoresis* will be developed more in chapter 3 below as well. This introductory chapter has set the stage for a biblical examination of the believer's union with Christ as a perichoretic relationship. The first text discussed is John 17.

---

135. Ibid.

136. This work retains the capitalization of pronouns from the NASB. The capitalization is omitted otherwise.

137. See the discussion in Köstenberger and Swain, *Trinity in John*, 176–80. See also Moule, *Origin of Christology*, 64–65.

2

Biblical Evidence

THE PURPOSE OF THIS chapter is to provide biblical evidence that supports the thesis that the believer's union with Christ is a perichoretic relationship, albeit of a third type. The vast majority of the evidence surveyed comes from the Gospel of John and the letters of Paul. The section on John will provide exegesis of and commentary on key texts showing the validity of the thesis. The section on Paul will examine some key phrases Paul repeatedly uses that support the thesis as well. The final section will provide evidence from 2 Peter 1:4, which is the text that best supports the idea of *theosis*.

EXEGESIS OF TEXTS IN JOHN

John's Gospel is the logical place to begin because he provides the clearest exposition of the doctrine of *perichoresis* found in the Bible (John 14:10–11, 20; and 17:21–23). The latter text is the most direct textual basis for the thesis of this study. This section will examine texts in John that support the idea that the believer's union with Christ is a perichoretic relationship. All texts in this section are located in the "Farewell Discourse" of John 13–17, because, as Herman Ridderbos writes, the Farewell Discourse is the place where "the church is learning to understand itself in terms of union with Christ."[1]

Recall that a perichoretic relationship is a relationship between two parties encompassing both mutual indwelling (again, spatial terminology to describe relational reality) and active participation in the other. The two traditional varieties of *perichoresis* in theological history, the trinitarian and the christological, both demonstrate these two traits.

---

1. Ridderbos, *Gospel of John*, 489.

The persons of the Trinity mutually indwell each other and are actively participating in each other. The human and divine natures in the person of Christ are, in the language of Chalcedon, joined without confusion or change (mutual indwelling while preserving the identity of both natures) and without division or separation (active participation in the other).[2]

Based on the key components of the trinitarian and christological perichoretic relationships discussed above, the same components need to be present in the soteriological union if it can properly be called perichoretic. They are (1) the believer indwells Christ; (2) Christ indwells the believer; (3) the believer actively participates in Christ; and (4) Christ actively participates in the believer. This section will argue that these four conditions are met in the texts surveyed below. Since these conditions that have historically described the two perichoretic relationships will be shown to be present in the believer's union with Christ, it may be implied that the soteriological union is a *perichoresis* of a third type, since it displays the definitive elements of *perichoresis* discussed above.

John 17:21–23: Mutual Indwelling Introduced

In Jesus's prayer in John 17, he prays that all of his disciples "may all be one; even as You, Father, are in Me and I in You, that they also may be in Us, so that the world may believe that You sent Me. The glory which You have given Me I have given to them, that they may be one, just as We are one; I in them and You in Me, that they may be perfected in unity" (John 17:21–23).[3] What did Jesus mean by these words? How will the disciples be in the Father and Son and also have Christ in them?

The Farewell Discourse and prayer of Jesus (John 13–17) repeatedly emphasize that the Father and Son are "in" one another—the trinitarian *perichoresis*. The text above shows plainly that the believers, and by extension each individual believer, will be "in" the Father and Son. Moreover, the Son and Spirit will be "in" the disciples. Given that the Son is in the Father and the Father is in the Son, the entire Trinity will be

---

2. See Kress, "Unity in Diversity," 67, and Dearborn, "God, Grace, and Salvation," 286–87.

3. All biblical citations are from the New American Standard Version (Nashville: Holman, 1985). Again, capitalization of the pronouns with divine antecedents is retained.

"in" the disciples.[4] Directly from the text, mutual indwelling is evident.[5] The rest of this subsection discusses the likelihood that such indwelling is more than merely symbolic, and may be rightly seen as *perichoresis* in a sense different than but analogous to trinitarian *perichoresis*.[6] The conclusion that real indwelling is present will wait until the discussion of John 14 below.

D. A. Carson writes concerning the unity of John 17:21–23, "Some measure of unity in the disciples is assumed, but Jesus prays that they may be brought to complete unity, sharing richly in both the unity of purpose and the wealth of love that tie the Father and Son together."[7] Leon Morris cautions that the unity the believers share with God is not the same as the unity the Father and Son enjoy. Rather, it is an analogy that holds because the Father and Son are in one other yet remain distinct. The believers are all in both the Father and the Son, yet they retain their identities.[8] C. K. Barrett claims that there is a "strict analogy" between the unity of the church and the unity of the Father and Son, as they remain distinct from God and each other "yet abiding in God and themselves the sphere of God's activity."[9] George Beasley-Murray notes that believers become one by participating in the *koinonia* of the Father and the Son.[10] Since the union of the Father and Son is perichoretic (John 14:10, 20), the believer's participation in that selfsame union is a perichoretic event as well. The above writers all mention the analogy present in relating the union of Christ and the believer to the trinitarian *perichoresis*. This point, made in the previous chapter, is important. But it needs some further clarification, which will be shown below.

Commenting on the importance of the unity between the Godhead and the believers, Herman Ridderbos writes, "We may conclude, there-

---

4. Sherman, *King, Priest, and Prophet*, 62. For a good overview of the indwelling language in John, see Mealand, "Language of Mystical Union."

5. Thus conditions (1) and (2), the mutual indwelling, from the top of this page are already fulfilled.

6. One of the main differences in the soteriological union is that it involves the creation, rather than the trinitarian *perichoresis*, which only consists within the creator.

7. Carson, *Gospel according to John*, 569.

8. Morris, *Gospel according to John*, 649. That is, it is a direct analogy to the trinitarian *perichoresis*.

9. Barrett, *Gospel according to St. John*, 512. The "sphere of God's activity" is yet another example of relational truth couched in spatial language.

10. Beasley-Murray, *John*, 302.

fore, that the unity intended here is not an additional and separate blessing Jesus asks of the Father but the great object that Jesus aimed for during his life on earth and now desires from the Father for the future as well."[11] Ridderbos rejects the absorption of the church into God. Instead, he sees the unity as "the church's participation and incorporation in the work accomplished by Christ in unity with the Father."[12] For Ridderbos, the existence of the unity between the Father and Son is the reason for the unity of the church and, by extension, each individual within the church. All of the writers quoted so far note the obvious implications of Jesus's words. But it remains to be seen in what sense the relationship between the believer and Christ is perichoretic.

Rekha Chennattu sees the direct connection between redemption and union. As she states, "The oneness among the disciples is modeled on the intimate relationship of the Father and Jesus revealed in the redemptive works of God in Jesus (John 17:22, 26; 10:30)."[13] Marianne Meye Thompson writes, "The relationship between Father and Son is the reality in which those who have faith participate and dwell. This is the relationship or reality in which one finds 'life,' and whose fundamental commitment can be summarized in terms of 'love.'"[14] The language moves from the relationship as a "model" in Chennattu to one that is "reality of participation and dwelling" in the Godhead in Thompson. Here the evidence for a perichoretic relationship becomes stronger, since Thompson's sentence could almost be reworded to state, "*Perichoresis* is the reality where believers participate and dwell."

Mark Appold makes the direct connection between salvation and union. As he writes, "Man's integration into this projection of heavenly oneness constitutes the saving event."[15] Here is "integration into" heavenly oneness. He continues, "The goal is incorporation into God's reality, into truth, into glory, into the presence of Christ. In short, to be bound in a relation of oneness with Jesus ('they in us' 17:21; 'I in them' 17:23) is for John the essence of salvation."[16] Appold describes the oneness in John as something "which can only be understood within the context of Jesus's

11. Ridderbos, *Gospel of John*, 559.
12. Ibid., 561.
13. Chennattu, *Johannine Discipleship*, 135.
14. Thompson, *God of the Gospel of John*, 100.
15. Appold, *Oneness Motif*, 284.
16. Ibid.

Biblical Evidence   37

oneness with the believers and his prior oneness with the Father."[17] Since Jesus's oneness with the Father is perichoretic, any oneness with the person of Christ would imply a perichoretic oneness with the Father but of a type that recognizes the inherent difference between a unity of divine persons and the unity of a human person with divine. Köstenberger and Swain identify the Holy Spirit as the one responsible for bringing people "into the perichoretic fellowship of the triune God."[18]

Thus John 17:21–23 guarantees that the trinitarian *perichoresis* provides the pattern for the oneness of the believer and Christ. Protestant Christianity has been historically hesitant to say more than this, preferring to use language like "pattern" or "model" when describing how the believer's union with Christ follows from the trinitarian *perichoresis*. The theological hurdle has been the fact that God is God and humans are not. That "ontological gulf" has always formed a barrier for speaking too "perichoretically" about John 17. The commentaries cited above are all examples of the hesitancy. The discussion near the end of the previous chapter shows that the creator/creature distinction is upheld in the language of *perichoresis*, so it need no longer be a concern. Jürgen Moltmann pushes the thinking of *perichoresis* forward. As he writes, "*Perichoresis* does not merely link others of the same kind, it links others of different kinds, too."[19] If he is correct, then perichoretic relationships are possible outside the Godhead, even though they may not be as perfectly complete as the trinitarian *perichoresis*. The hypostatic union, perichoretically joining two natures in the one person of Christ, is the template for *perichoresis* in different kinds.

It is important to note that the Gospel of John builds to the prayer of Jesus discussed above. What follows is an examination of key texts in John's Gospel that flesh out the sense in which there is a perichoretic relationship between the believer and Christ that take place before Jesus's prayer of John 17. In this way, the rest of the Farewell Discourse is a kind of "foreword" to the prayer of Jesus and it sets the stage for what he prays.

---

17. Ibid., 285.
18. Köstenberger and Swain, *Father, Son, and Spirit*, 177.
19. Moltmann, *Experiences in Theology*, 323.

John 13:1–20: Active Participation in Christ

John 13 begins by announcing that Jesus knew his hour had come, and he loved his own even to the end. Mary Coloe notes how the disciples have become Jesus's own (John 1:12), the ones to whom he will give power to become the sons of God.[20] The idea of adopted sonship itself implies a union, though not a union of the same nature as between Jesus and his Father.

While John 13:4 describes the footwashing, the reasoning behind it lies in the preceding verse.[21] John 13:3–4 reads, "Jesus, knowing that the Father had given all things into His hands, and that He had come forth from God and was going back to God, rose from supper, and laid aside His garments; and taking a towel, He girded Himself about." Verse 3 seems to clearly imply that Jesus bases his act of footwashing on what he possesses, whence he has come, and where he is going. Fernando Segovia notes that Jesus's hour begins with the footwashing.[22] Therefore, as Coloe writes, "Footwashing is an invitation to the disciples to become participants with Jesus in his 'hour.'"[23] Ruth Edwards notes the verb τιθέναι never means the laying aside of a garment elsewhere in the New Testament, but John uses it to describe how the Good Shepherd lays down his life for the sheep in John 10.[24] C. K. Barrett likewise sees the laying aside of the garments as foreshadowing the laying down of Christ's life.[25] Combining the themes of participation and Jesus's death will become important later in this chapter when the doctrine of participation

---

20. Coloe, "Welcome into the Household," 406. The idea of sonship and adoption as perichoretic relationships will be developed in chapter 4 below.

21. Carson (*John*, 462) notes here that since the disciples saw themselves as under Jesus, they would have been happy to wash His feet, as it would be their reasonable service. However, they would not have been so happy to wash one another's feet, since this is the job of a servant. They did not see themselves as servants of one another at this time. He states there is no instance in the Greco-Roman world of a superior washing the feet of an inferior.

22. Segovia, "John 13:1–20," 40.

23. Coloe, "Household of God," 409. As this investigation progresses, the idea of participation in Christ will become important in establishing the case for a perichoretic relationship.

24. Edwards, "Christological Basis," 372. In n14 on the same page, she describes several other words that could be used to lay aside a garment. There is no other use of τιθέναι in either the New Testament or Septuagint that is in the context of laying aside a garment.

25. Barrett, *John*, 366.

in Jesus's death in Paul is discussed, for Paul argues for the participation of the believer in the death and resurrection of Christ.

When Jesus comes to Peter to wash his feet, Peter objects with the words, "Lord, do *you* wash *my* feet?"[26] Peter is chastising Jesus because he feels Jesus, as his master and Lord, is too good to wash his feet. When Peter replies harshly to Jesus that he would never wash his feet, Jesus replies to him that if He does not wash Peter's feet, Peter will have no part (μέρος) in Jesus. According to Lenski, the emphatic denial by Peter is equivalent to "forever," and is the grounds for Jesus's rebuke.[27]

The word μέρος has importance to the doctrine of union. George Beasley-Murray notes the idea of a "part" to the Jews meant "an inheritance, first in the promised land, and then eschatologically in the kingdom of God."[28] Raymond Brown concurs by adding that μέρος is used in the Septuagint to translate the Hebrew *heleq*, originally referring to the children of Israel's inheritance in the land of Canaan, and later to eternal rewards.[29] According to John Thomas, the word can mean a share in eternal life, a share in a person's identity or destiny, a share in one's mission, and, as applied to Jesus, a share in his martyrdom and resurrection.[30] Here is "part" together with "participation." Carson sees the idea of an inheritance and eschatological blessings.[31] John Thomas adds, "Simply put, it appears that μέρος here denotes continued fellowship with Jesus, and a place in his community which ultimately results in uninterrupted residence in the Father's house (14:1–4)." Such a view of μέρος dovetails neatly with John 15:1–7, where remaining in Jesus is the key to life."[32] Craig Koester notes how the μέρος is what Jesus prays his disciples may possess in John 17, connecting Jesus's prayer for the believers' union with himself and the "part with Jesus."[33] Thus the entire ritual of footwashing

26. Italics added to reflect the emphasis noted by Edgington, "Footwashing as an Ordinance," 428. The word order "σύ μού" is the key, according to him. Morris (*John*, 616–17) agrees.

27. Lenski, *Interpretation of John's Gospel*, 917.

28. Beasley-Murray, *John*, 234. See also Witherington, *John's Wisdom*, 236, and Lincoln, *Gospel according to Saint John*, 368–69.

29. Brown, *The Gospel according to John*, 2:565–66.

30. Thomas, *Footwashing*, 93–94.

31. Carson, *John*, 464. He links this verse to John 14:1–3 and John 17:24 as well. Keener (*Gospel of John*, 2:909) concurs, saying it is an "eternal fellowship."

32. Thomas, "Footwashing," 178.

33. Koester, *Symbolism in the Fourth Gospel*, 117.

symbolizes the death of Jesus and the inheritance based upon union that those for whom he died would enjoy with him forever. The footwashing is a symbol of Jesus joining into union with his disciples.

When Jesus had finished washing the disciples' feet, he put his clothes back on and joined them at the table. Then he instructed the disciples about what he did: "Do you know what I have done to you? You call Me Teacher and Lord; and you are right, for so I am. If I then, the Lord and the Teacher, washed your feet, you also ought to wash one another's feet. For I gave you an example that you also should do as I did to you" (John 13:12–15). Ruth Edwards notes that the word for "taking up" garments is λαμβάνω, which is the same word Jesus used in John 10 to mean taking up his life again. She draws the connection of Jesus's clothing with the christological hymn of Philippians 2.[34] Chennattu states, "It seems that sharing a μέρος with Jesus is best paraphrased as entering into a covenant relationship with Jesus characterized by mutual belonging, intimacy, and commitment."[35] Now the perichoretic nature of the believer's union with Christ is becoming clearer, as her language seems to almost require some sense of a perichoretic relationship.

The way Jesus describes footwashing also describes his union with the believer, showing an eschatological dimension to footwashing that upholds the thesis that union with Christ is in view.[36] Arlan J. Hultgren

---

34. Edwards, "Christological Basis," 372–74. As with τιθένι, the use of λαμβάνω to put on a garment is also biblically unique.

35. Chennattu, *Johannine Discipleship*, 96. Maybe a better phrase here would be "perichoretic relationship" instead of "covenant relationship." More will be said of covenant in chapter 4 below.

36. There are at least three other elements in the footwashing that have a possible connection to the believer's union with Christ. First, as Culpepper ("Johannine 'Hypodeigma,'" 137) argues, Jesus's footwashing is a symbol of his death, which in turn implies his disciples must be willing to die also. This is close to Paul's participation language concerning baptism in Romans 6. Likewise, Weiss ("Footwashing in the Johannine Community," 304) argues that footwashing was a preparation for meeting God. Second are the ethical implications in footwashing based on "ought." See Hauck, "οφειλω," in *TDNT*, 5:559–66. Third is Culpepper's ("Johannine 'Hypodeigma,'" 142) argument that the ὑπόδειγμα (example) Jesus gives is his exemplary death. Based on the context of the word in apocryphal literature 2 Macc 6:28 and 6:31; 4 Macc 17:22–23; and Sir 44:6, the statement seems to point to participatory union, since believers are participants in that death. As Jesus marks his death as exemplary, in the washing of his disciples' feet, the disciples are called to do the same that their potential death may be likewise satisfying to God.

notes that footwashing is introduced in Genesis 18, where Abraham participates in a Christophany.[37] He continues,

> In washing the disciples' feet, he does an act of hospitality, receiving the disciples into the place to which he is going, the very house of the Father (14:2). Jesus is the servant of a rich and generous host, the Father in heaven, who welcomes the disciples into the Father's house to rest and stay, although they will not understand this until after Jesus is glorified (13:7). (Compare Luke 12:37, which speaks of the coming of the κύριος to his servants at the end-time: 'he will gird himself and have them sit at table, and he will come and serve them.') Because he and the Father are one, the Son is able to offer such hospitality on behalf of the Father and to share his own destiny of going to the Father with those whom he washes. The act of washing is spoken of in a specifically Johannine way (ο□έψω□ποίω, 13:7); the verb ποίειν is a Johannine expression for Jesus's eschatological work in union with the Father. Moreover, the setting for the act is a meal, and that also has symbolic eschatological overtones of intimacy and fellowship with the Son after his glorification; those who washed are clean and are therefore in union with the Son unto eternal life.[38]

If Hultgren is correct, then the μέρος that Jesus is offering is participation in his own self. The footwashing passage has shown that the believer participates in Christ.

The evidence for the believer's participation is abundant. Mary Coloe adds, "For the disciples, footwashing is a proleptic experience of the welcome into the Father's household that will be accomplished at the cross."[39] Hence the use of the term "children" is a powerful symbol of familial union.[40] Royce Gruenler writes, "Also present is the theme of participation that is essential to hospitality and accounts for the essential unity of the participants, who nonetheless do not lose their individuality. The two essential elements of the divine society, unity and individuality, are reflected in the relationship of Jesus to the disciples and they to him."[41] When Peter objects to Jesus washing his feet and

---

37. Hultgren, "Johannine Footwashing," 541.
38. Ibid., 542.
39. Coloe, "Household of God," 412.
40. The idea of children and adoption again will be further developed in chapter 4 below.
41. Gruenler, *Trinity in the Gospel of John*, 90.

Jesus rebukes him, Gruenler observes, "By [Jesus's rebuke] he indicates that the believing community is constituted through participation in him. The disciples participate in Jesus, as Peter is invited to do, by making themselves available to the generosity of Jesus. One gives, the other receives, in mutual hospitality and disposability that make interpersonal communion and the new community possible."[42] Ample evidence has been given to show the footwashing as a real, active participation of the believer in Christ. This active participation of the disciples in Christ is of an intimacy and intensity such that it is best seen as an element of a genuinely perichoretic relationship, but one of a third type.

John 14:1–2, 23: Mutual Indwelling Confirmed

Jesus says in John 14:2–3, "In My Father's house are many dwelling places; if it were not so, I would have told you; for I go to prepare a place for you. And if I go and prepare a place for you, I will come again and receive you to Myself; that where I am, there you may be also." This subsection attempts to show that certain language in John 14 is evidence for the real mutual indwelling of Christ and the believer, connecting the "dwelling places" in the Father's house in 14:2 with the "abode" in 14:23. The mutual indwelling in these texts is a kind so intimate that it could best be described as perichoretic, as it mirrors how the persons of the Godhead indwell one another.

The imagery of the Father's house with many dwelling places was a familiar one in the first century. Köstenberger writes, "In Jesus's day, many dwelling units were combined to form an extended household. It was customary for sons to add to their father's house once married, so that the entire estate grew into a large compound (called *insula*) centered around a communal courtyard."[43] The Greek word for house is the commonly used οικία, so there are no exegetical clues in the word itself.

The first question that may arise in this passage is about the location of the Father's house. This presupposes that the word οἶκος is properly interpreted to be a physical dwelling. At first glance, one may think that since the Father dwells in heaven, Jesus is going to heaven to prepare a place for his disciples. Many commentaries on John interpret the text in

---

42. Ibid.
43. Köstenberger, *John*, 426.

this manner.⁴⁴ Thus heaven is one option for the location of the Father's house, although it is not the only option.

There are contextual clues in John that cast some doubt that the Father's house of which Jesus speaks is the heavenly home. First, James McCaffrey notes that the idea of "house" in the Old Testament does not constitute a building, but rather a family.⁴⁵ Second, in John 2:16, Jesus calls the temple his Father's house. John 2:17 quotes Psalm 69:9, that the zeal for his Father's house will consume him. In John 2:19, he refers to his death and resurrection by telling the Jews that if they destroy this temple, he will raise it up in three days. The temple in this instance is his body, as John 2:21 clarifies. The dwelling, or house, of God changes in the Gospel of John; it starts as the temple, and progresses to Jesus of Nazareth and finally to the indwelling of all who believe.⁴⁶ When this theme of replacement is combined with Jesus's words to the Samaritan woman in John 4:21–24, it seems as though the physical place of worship is unimportant. If this is the case, then heaven may not be the Father's house after all. Possibly, Jesus goes to prepare not a spiritual home in heaven but a dwelling in the Father.⁴⁷ He wants believers to be in union with the Father and him. Ron Kangas writes concerning the last clause of John 14:3,

> The Lord's word here does not mean that he is in heaven and that we will be with him in heaven where he is. The Lord is in the Father, and it is his desire, as the expression of the Father's desire, that we would be with him where he is—in the Father. Through his death and resurrection, he has brought the believers into himself. Since he is in the Father and we are in him, we also are in the Father by being in him. Surely, to be in the Father is much better than being in heaven. Through the Lord as the

---

44. For an extensive list of commentaries with citations that interpret the Father's house as heaven, see Kerr, *Temple of Jesus' Body*, 276n24. Köstenberger, *John*, cited above and published after Kerr's monograph, also states the Father's house is heaven.

45. McCaffrey, *House with Many Rooms*, 49–54.

46. Kerr (*Temple of Jesus' Body*, 277) notes that a large part of the gospel of John presents Jesus as the replacement of the Jewish temple and its festivals. The idea of replacement is one of the major themes of his entire book. For a fuller treatment of Jesus as the temple replacement, see Thettayil, *In Spirit and Truth*, 348–471, and Hoskins, *Jesus as the Fulfillment*. See also Hamilton, *God's Indwelling Presence*, 147–54. For a treatment of the church as the temple in the rest of the Bible, see Beale, *Temple and the Church's Mission*.

47. Kangas, "In My Father's House," 26.

way to the Father, we are now in the Father. His word has been fulfilled: where he is, we also are.[48]

Though Kangas does not touch upon the idea of the return of Christ in his article, there is a sense in which the "coming again" is partially fulfilled in the indwelling and completed in the return of Christ to the earth.[49]

The next word of interest is "dwelling places." The Greek word here is μόναι.[50] It only appears in the New Testament twice, both times in John 14. It does not appear in the Greek version of the Old Testament at all.[51] The other appearance is in John 14:23, where Jesus says to Judas, "If anyone loves Me, he will keep My word; and My Father will love Him, and We will come to him, and make Our abode [μόνην] with Him." This is a real instance where Christ indwells the believer. This indwelling, where Christ is "at home" (making his "abode") in another person, is language that resembles the closeness of the trinitarian and christological *perichoresis*, where the persons and natures, respectively, are "at home" in the other. Therefore, it may be implied such an intimate indwelling that John 14:23 describes is constitutive of a third type of perichoretic relationship.

The promise of John 14:2, the many dwelling places in the Father's house, is now connected to the indwelling of John 14:23. Therefore, divine disclosure is the union of the Father and Son to one that loves Jesus. Beasley-Murray equates the manifestation of Jesus to his followers to the "coming" of the Father and the Son to dwell with the believer.[52] Kangas concludes that the indwelling in each believer is the "many dwelling places" Jesus promised in John 14:2.[53] God intends his union with the believer to be not only a future event but also a present reality to be enjoyed now.[54] Barrett states that the idea of God dwelling with humanity

---

48. Ibid., 28.

49. Chennattu (*Johannine Discipleship*, 103) discusses the exegetical difficulties resulting from the tension between a future and realized eschatology in this passage.

50. The word μόναι is the verbal noun corresponding to μένω, which will be discussed in detail below.

51. McCaffrey (*House with Many Rooms*, 62) notes that it does appear in the apocryphal book of 1 Macc (7:38).

52. Beasley-Murray, *John*, 260.

53. Kangas, "Father's House," 27.

54. Bernard, *Critical and Exegetical Commentary*, 2:551.

realized in John 14:23 is the primary concern of the entire Old Testament as well as the goal of many ancient pagan religions.[55] Therefore, the coming of Christ to finally accomplish the true union between God and man is the completion of the desire of many of the religions of the world—the experience of union with the divine.

If the better interpretation of "the Father's house" is not heaven, then more work remains. Jesus says he is going to prepare a place (τόπος) for his disciples. There are two important issues in this text, the idea of going and a place he will prepare. Concerning the first, is his departure his death or his resurrection and ascension?[56] John 13:1 states that he is going to depart out of this world to return to the Father. From the context, it seems that his resurrection and ascension are in view. Concerning Jesus's departure, John Pryor writes, "[It] serves the purpose of enabling the people of God to be brought into union with God. It is not a departure resulting in loss or absence, but is in fact full of potential for the community."[57]

Concerning the second idea, that of preparing a place, McCaffrey notes that the verb for "prepare" (ετοιμάζω) in the Septuagint denotes the ordinary preparation of a house or room but also describes God's preparation of the promised land and the rooms of the second temple.[58] Royce Gruenler adds,

> The Father's house of many rooms is the central image in the ecology (literally, "a study of the house") of the new community the triune society is calling into being. Jesus's nature is to speak the absolute truth; He describes the reality of a dwelling place for the new family of God, and the fact that at the cost of great suffering he is going to prepare a place for them in the Father's house. Jesus the Son together with the Father is opening their home in supreme hospitality to those who believe the promise is true.[59]

Alan Kerr sees temple imagery in τόπος, though the word is very common in the Septuagint. He notes that the formula of Deuteronomy

---

55. Barrett, *John*, 389–90.

56. For a full discussion of this question, see DeBoer, "Jesus' Departure," 1–20.

57. Pryor, *John*, 61–62.

58. McCaffrey, *House with Many Rooms*, 88–89. He adds that the Targum tradition of ancient Israel identifies the Messiah as the one who builds the eschatological temple.

59. Gruenler, *Trinity in the Gospel of John*, 96.

repeatedly refers to "the place (τόπος) where YHWH has chosen to establish/place his name (Deut 12:5, 11)."[60] McCaffrey believes that the eschatological temple is a theme that represents unity for Israel, as the last book of the Pentateuch refers repeatedly to the "place where Yahweh has chosen to establish/place his name."[61] Brown adds concerning the preparation, "If by his death, resurrection, and ascension Jesus is to make possible a union of the disciples with his Father, he must prepare his disciples for the union by making them understand how it is to be achieved."[62] In other words, he prepares the place by preparing them.

In the final clause of the passage, Jesus promises that by coming again and receiving the disciples to himself, they would be where he is. This language sounds like the second coming.[63] The key phrase here to convey the second coming seems to be that the disciples will be where he is, rather than him being where they are, as an indwelling would indicate. So in a sense both interpretations are correct. Jesus, as God, returns both at the giving of the Holy Spirit (as an invisible indwelling) and at his visible second coming. At some future point, either Pentecost or *parousia* (or both), Jesus will come and join himself to his followers so that they will always be where he is. According to McCaffrey, Jesus's passion and resurrection effect the new temple of the risen Jesus; his departure through this passion and resurrection effect the place prepared, which is the new temple, which is also the Father's house with many accessible rooms.[64] The believer's indwelling of Christ here is both real and permanent. Such indwelling seems to share some of the qualities of the trinitarian indwelling of Father and Son, especially the "abodes" and "being at home" in the other, and furthers support for seeing soteriological union as a *perichoresis*, albeit of a third type. It remains to show that John describes Christ actively participating in the believer, which will be done in the next subsection.

The perichoretic idea embodied in John 14 is summed up well by Jey Kanagaraj. He writes, "The idea of mutual union is described in 14:2–3 and 14:23 with a different but complementary emphasis: whereas

---

60. Kerr, *Temple of Jesus' Body*, 303. He continues to trace the τόπος idea throughout the Old Testament.

61. McCaffrey, *House with Many Rooms*, 103–4.

62. Brown, *John*, 627.

63. Köstenberger, *John*, 427.

64. McCaffrey, *House with Many Rooms*, 191.

in 14:2–3 the Father becomes the spiritual sphere in which all believers dwell individually in union with Jesus, in 14:23 each believer individually becomes the spiritual sphere in which the Father dwells in union with Jesus."[65] The believer makes room for Christ while Christ makes room for the believer.[66] This spatial language describing relational reality is remarkably similar to T. F. Torrance's definition of *perichoresis* as "making room or space" from chapter 1 above.[67] The theme continues in John 15.

John 15:1–16: Perichoretic "Abiding" and Christ's Participation

Jesus's discourse in John 15 concerning "abiding" is another important piece of evidence showing that the relationship the believer enjoys with Christ is perichoretic in nature. The chapter begins with Jesus describing himself as a vine. He says, "I am the true vine, and My Father is the vinedresser."[68] Beasley-Murray comments on why Jesus calls himself the true vine. He notes that often in the Old Testament, Israel is represented as a vine or vineyard.[69] He writes, "It seems likely therefore that the description of Jesus as the *true* vine is primarily intended to contrast with the failure of Israel to fulfill its calling to be fruitful for God. That the vine is *Jesus*, not the Church, is intentional; the Lord is viewed in his representative capacity, the Son of God–Son of Man, who dies and rises that in union with Him a renewed people of God might come into being and bring forth fruit for God."[70]

Therefore Jesus is the head of the true people of God, the one promised to Israel, the type of the vine, all along. As branches on a vine cannot live without the vine, so must the Christian feed off the divine life supplied by Christ. The Father, as the vinedresser, cuts away the

---

65. Kanagaraj, "'Mysticism' in the Gospel of John," 266.

66. See the quotation of Torrance in chapter 1 above, as he lists "making room" as the root meaning of *perichoresis*.

67. See Heltzel, "*Perichoresis*," 28. For more, see n58 in chapter 1 above.

68. For a comprehensive study on the "I Am" sayings in the gospel of John, see Ball, *"I Am" in John's Gospel*. For the significance of "true" and its usage, see Segovia, *Farewell of the Word*, 135; and Pink, *Exposition of the Gospel of John*, 395. For a discussion of the "vine" imagery in the Old Testament, see Bernard, *Critical and Exegetical Commentary*, 477–78. For comments on Jesus contrasting himself with Judaism, see Pryor, *John*, 63.

69. This may be seen most clearly in Hos 10:2 and Isa 5.

70. Beasley-Murray, *John*, 272. Italics in original. See also Hanson, *Prophetic Gospel*, 183–85.

fruitless branches and prunes those that bear fruit so that they will bear even more fruit. The disciples are the branches, while the fruit is living the life of a Christian disciple.[71] Thomas Brodie writes, "The image in question, the vine and its branches, is particularly effective in suggesting unity, for unlike other trees where one may distinguish clearly between trunk and branches, such a distinction is not clear. The vine consists of its branches; all flow together into one."[72] Thus the image of the vine and branches contribute a picture where all are indeed one. Even more so, Jesus as the vine shows his active participation in the life of the believer, as he is the supplier of life.[73] The idea of supplying his own life implies an active participation of Christ in the believer that is so intense it may best described as perichoretic. In the Farewell Discourse, John has described both of the main conditions that are present in the trinitarian and christological forms of *perichoresis*—mutual indwelling and active participation in the other.

Jesus continues his word picture of the vine, "Abide in Me and I in you. As the branch cannot bear fruit of itself, unless it abides in the vine, so neither can you, unless you abide in Me" (John 15:4). The word translated "abide" is μένω, a prominent word in John, used some forty times in the Gospel alone. Its various translations include "abide," "remain," "dwell," and "tarry." Jesus instructs the disciples, represented as branches, to abide "in Me." Carl Laney writes, "To 'abide' is to maintain a vital, life-giving connection with Christ, the vine, the source of life. Belief is the connection that unites the vine and branches. Without belief there is no abiding."[74] Again here is the picture of union portrayed as "mutual abiding." Beasley-Murray comments on the deeper significance of "abiding" in Jesus:

> It connotes continuing to live in association or in union with him. "Μείνατε" (aorist tense), could signify "Step into union with me,"

71. Segovia, *Love Relationships*, 101. See also Barrett, *John*, 395.

72. Brodie, *Gospel according to John*, 479.

73. See the argument in Erickson, *God in Three Persons*, 234–35, where he argues that the doctrine of trinitarian *perichoresis* implies that the persons of the Trinity cannot live apart from the others. The vine and branches would certainly be analogous to Erickson's idea, since the branches cannot live without the nourishment the vine supplies, but neither can the vine live without branches and leaves.

74. Laney, "Abiding Is Believing," 65. For a comprehensive analysis of metaphor in John, especially the metaphor of the vine, see Van der Watt, *Family of the King*, esp. 26–54.

which would be a suitable injunction for readers of the gospel, and not wholly unsuitable for the group in the upper room in prospect of the new relationship with the Lord about to be initiated through his death and resurrection. "And I in you" may be viewed as the apodosis of a conditional sentence: "*If* you remain in me, I shall remain in you"; but the emphasis of the passage is on *Jesus*, the vine, hence it is more likely that a note of encouragement is intended here.... In the divine relationship grace is alike the source and support of faith.[75]

Gary Derickson sees "abiding in Jesus" as maintaining close fellowship with him.[76] Chennattu, commenting on the "mutual abiding," writes, "One cannot ignore the intimate, binding relationship implied here and separate the fruitful branches from the true vine. Just as there can be no branches without the vine, one cannot talk about the vine and its fruitfulness without its branches. The mutual and abiding covenant relationship between Jesus and the disciples is underlined."[77]

Looking back to Jesus's statements concerning the dwelling place of God in John 14, Keener writes, "Most likely it [the 'abide'] develops here the prior image of believers as the dwelling place of the Father, Son, and Paraclete and that believers also would have dwellings in the Father's presence (14:2–3, 23)."[78] Rudolf Schnackenburg comments that the vine and branches are a metaphor to show the organic nature of the believer's union with Christ, calling the "Abide in me and I in you" a "reciprocal immanence formula."[79] He notes the connection between the "reciprocal immanence formula" of John 15 and the earlier descriptions of the perichoretic relationships between the Father and Son in John.[80] R. Matthew Lytle argues this verse explicitly teaches a perichoretic relationship between Christ and the believer.[81]

---

75. Beasley-Murray, *John*, 272.

76. Derickson, "Viticulture," 40–41.

77. Chennattu, *Johannine Discipleship*, 114. Again, this study argues that "perichoretic relationship" is a more-encompassing term than "covenant relationship."

78. Keener, *John*, 2:999.

79. Schnackenburg, *Gospel according to St. John*, 3:99.

80. Ibid.

81. Lytle, "Perichoretically-Embodied Ethics," 153–56. Lytle is correct here as far as the definition from chapter 1 goes. It is fairly evident that "abiding in" each other contains both indwelling and active participation.

Jesus continues utilizing the picture of the vine to reinforce what He said earlier. John 15:5 says that "mutual abiding" will bear much fruit. This "mutual abiding" also occurs interestingly in John 6:51–58, a passage with great covenantal applications.[82] In John 15:5, Jesus also says, "Apart from Me you can do nothing." Brown discusses how this clause has figured prominently in Christian history concerning the doctrines of grace and merit in union with Christ.[83] D. A. Carson writes concerning John 15, "It deals with the union between Christ and his followers, a union apart from which they can bear no fruit. Whatever is involved in this intimacy between Christ and Christians, it stands at the heart of spiritual vitality. So important is this fruit-bearing that every productive branch is pruned to make it more fruitful."[84] John 15:6–7 shows the contrast between abiding and not abiding. Those who do not abide are cast away and destroyed. Those who do abide inherit the promise that anything they ask will be done for them.[85] Donald Guthrie remarks, "The branches become useless unless they abide in the vine. Fruit is impossible and the branches must be stripped off and burnt. In no more vivid way could Jesus have expressed the centrality of his own life in the on-going life of his people."[86]

John 15:8 equates bearing fruit with glorifying the Father and proving to be true disciples. John 15:9 underscores the type of love Jesus displays for his disciples is exactly the same love that the Father has for him. As Victor Furnish writes, "Love is first of all that which unites the Father to his Son and then the Son to his own who are in the world (John 17:20–26; 15:9). This is not just a static unity between Father and Son, and Son and disciples; it is a living and moving unity."[87] He also notes that in the same vein, "abiding" is not static, but is played out in the functions of obedience as the Son obeys the Father.[88]

---

82. Appold, *Oneness Motif*, 41–42. This is Schnackenburg's "reciprocal immanence formula" mentioned above; and the covenantal applications will be discussed in detail in chapter 4 below.

83. Brown, *John*, 678.

84. Carson, *Farewell Discourse*, 91.

85. For more on asking in Jesus's name is related to being "in Christ," see Mitchell, "Praying 'In My Name,'" 27–32; as well as Guthrie, *New Testament Theology*, 642.

86. Guthrie, *New Testament Theology*, 642.

87. Furnish, *Love Command*, 145.

88. Ibid.

To summarize this subsection, Jesus's illustration of the vine and the branches is a call for the disciples to remain (abide) in him. The branches find their source of life in the vine. Therefore, it shows how necessary the believer's union with Christ is. Moreover, the idea of "abiding" is the same as what the Father and Son enjoy together. Thus, there is no textual distinction between the "abiding" of Father and Son and the "abiding" of Christ in the believer or the believer in Christ. D. Moody Smith captures the essence of the passage well: "When Jesus speaks of the disciples' abiding in him and uses the parable of the vine to portray that relationship (15:1–8), the key to that unity is again love (15:9–10), and Jesus immediately defines love as the kind of self-sacrifice that he himself will display (15:12–13). There is a wonderful coherence between unity and love."[89]

The idea of "abiding" in John 15 is evidence for the union of the believer and Christ being perichoretic. George E. Ladd comments,

> The idiom of abiding is usually called mysticism, but it is difficult to define. There is a mutual abiding of the believer in Christ (16:56; 14:20, 21; 15:5; 17:21) and Christ in the believer (6:56; 14:20, 23; 15:5; 17:23, 26). This is analogous to the Son abiding in the Father (10:38, 14:10, 11, 20, 21; 17:21) and the Father abiding in the Son (10:38, 14:10, 11, 21; 17:21, 23). Once it is said that believers are in both the Father and the Son (17:21); and once it is said that both Father and Son will come to make their abode in believers (14:23).[90]

Ladd sees the obvious connections between the trinitarian *perichoresis* and Christ's union with the believer. So does G. B. Verity, who boldly says the meaning of "abide" is "coinherence," one of the synonyms for *perichoresis*.[91] Thus the evidence is compelling that the "abiding" of John 15 is a perichoretic abiding where Christ and the believer are "reciprocally immanent" with one another.

Summary of John's Gospel

In the preceding pages, it has been shown that the main texts depicting the believer's union with Christ in John's Gospel portray that union as a perichoretic "mutual indwelling" of Christ and the believer on par with

---

89. Smith, *Theology of the Gospel of John*, 145.
90. Ladd, *Theology of the New Testament*, 313–14.
91. Verity, *Life in Christ*, 20.

the relationship the Father and Son have enjoyed from eternity. Jesus's prayer in John 17:21–23 both summarizes John's message and sets the table for this discussion. The footwashing passage of John 13 shows that Jesus's "part" is shared by the disciples. The many abodes of John 14 become the place where both the Father and the Son make their dwelling place. The vine imagery of John 15 clearly states the mutual indwelling of Christ and the believer that is directly connected to the mutual indwelling of the Father and Son. These three passages, when combined with others such as John 6:51–58 and 10:14–15, show that the union of the believer and Christ share many of the elements of the union of Father and Son and thus may properly be called a third type of *perichoresis*.[92]

Not only do the texts themselves show the perichoretic relationship of the believer's union with Christ, but so do the recurring themes of knowledge, love, and seeing in John. The Father loves the Son (John 10:17–18); the Son loves the Father (John 14:31); the Father and the Son love the believers (John 14:23); the believers love the Father (John 5:42, implicitly); and the believers love the Son (John 8:42).[93] Similarly, the Father knows the Son, and the Son knows the Father (John 10:15); believers know both the Father and the Son (John 17:3); and the Son knows believers (John 10:15).[94] The mutual abiding of John 15 leads to the mutual "seeing" of Christ and the believer in John 16:16–22.[95] Kanagaraj states that "seeing" is "experiencing indwelling."[96] Furthermore, in John, "seeing" roughly equals "knowing," which roughly equals "loving," which is eternal life and mutual indwelling. It is interesting that the verbs "know," "see," and "love" constitute some of the closest possible relationships in the English language today. It would seem a deeper word is needed that embraces all of these concepts. Perhaps *perichoresis* is that word. Both

---

92. That salvation is expressed by John as *perichoresis* is argued explicitly by Crump, "Re-examining the Johannine Trinity," 409–12. This study will return to Crump at the beginning of chapter 3, where it makes the connection between the perichoretic relationship of the believer's union with Christ and deification.

93. Van der Watt, *Family of the King*, 305–13. Maloney (*Entering into the Heart of Jesus*, 148) states that the love of the Father for the Son and the love of the Father for the disciples is "the selfsame love."

94. Ibid., 323–31. See also Staton, "Vision of Unity," 296. For a deeper discussion of perichoretic knowing as the foundation for Christian epistemology, see Thacker, *Postmodernism*.

95. See both Kanagaraj, *Mysticism*, 267, and Brodie, *John*, 494–95.

96. Kanagaraj, *Mysticism*, 275.

knowledge and love are elements in the perichoretic relationship within the Trinity as well as the soteriological union between Christ and the believer. The textual and theological evidence in John indicates that the believer's union with Christ may be called a third type of perichoretic relationship.

ANALYSIS OF PHRASES IN PAUL

The perichoretic language in John's writings has been discussed above. Now such language in the work of Paul will be examined. This section will utilize a different approach. While the Johannine study proceeded in a verse-by-verse, exegetically-based manner, the Pauline investigation will be more theological, utilizing a broad survey of some of Paul's key themes, including "in Christ," "with Christ," and "Christ in you/me." These phrases themselves show mutual indwelling and participation. The following discussion investigates the extent of their usage to show that Paul describes the relationship between Christ and the believer in ways that may best be seen as perichoretic.

Paul's Use of "In Christ"

The phrase "in Christ" is often repeated in the writings of Paul.[97] Adolf Deissmann, a pioneer in the research of Pauline "in Christ" usage, counted 164 occurrences of the phrase in the Pauline epistles.[98] Although Paul's usage of "in Christ" is so widespread,[99] literature discussing it directly is relatively sparse—especially when compared to contemporary discussion on the doctrine of justification, for example, a topic which occupies far less space in the Pauline corpus.[100] Its prominence, combined with the idea of a person being "in" Christ, makes it a good starting point to argue for a perichoretic relationship between Christ and the believer.

---

97. Albrecht Oepke, "εν," in *TDNT*, 2:543. See also Stewart, *Man in Christ*, 147–203, and Harris, "Appendix," in *NIDNTT*, 3:1192–93.

98. Deissmann, *St. Paul*, 128. Deissmann tabulated all of the occurrences of "in Christ" and "in the Lord" in the Pauline epistles, not counting Ephesians, Colossians, and the Pastorals. His original dissertation was published in German, which is Deissmann, *Die neutestamentliche Formel*.

99. George, *Galatians*, 275. Here George states there are 172 instances of "in Christ" in Paul's letters, though he offers no further elaboration. Son (*Corporate Elements*, 187–88) lists 165 occurrences.

100. See Dunn, *Theology of Paul*, 397.

Consequently, this subsection will focus on two main ideas. First is to discover how the phrase "in Christ" may be interpreted. For the purposes of this study, what needs to be investigated is whether the Pauline "in Christ," in any or all of its usages, draws any parallels to the Johannine usage of "in" in the sense of a real indwelling of Christ in the believer. Second is to discuss a few key passages where "in Christ" seems to imply such a real indwelling.[101] Then it will be argued that this real indwelling is of such a nature that it is most adequately described as perichoretic.

Studying Paul's use of "in Christ" is a very difficult enterprise for several reasons. First, the phrase is so common that a detailed systematic investigation becomes difficult.[102] Second, scholars have noticed a range of multiple meanings. Third, there has been little scholarly consensus in studies in the past century as to the precise meaning of the "in Christ" phrase.

One can scarcely read a page in Paul without encountering "in Christ," "in the Lord," or some other related phrase.[103] Deissmann believed it to be the characteristic expression of Paul's Christianity.[104] As seen in the discussion of Johannine literature above, the idea of a person being "in" Christ (and reciprocally, Christ in the believer) is a key component in arguing for a perichoretic relationship. Does the same relationship of mutual indwelling exist in the Pauline corpus? The discussion below will utilize selections from Paul's epistles that seem to point toward a real indwelling of Christ in the believer that may justifiably be seen as perichoretic.

Interpreting the "in Christ" phrases has become a thorny issue in the last century.[105] Deissmann, the pioneer in the field, believed all of the

---

101. Because of the sheer volume of passages involving "in Christ," this study will be quite selective in the passages chosen and will by no means be exhaustive in its search. The point of surveying the passages is to show how the phrase helps to show a perichoretic union between Christ and the believer.

102. To add to the numbers of occurrences discussed above, Ziesler (*Pauline Christianity*, 50–51) notes that there exists little, if any, difference in the meanings of the phrases "in Christ," "in the Lord," and even "in the Spirit" in the writings of Paul.

103. Dunn (*Theology of Paul*, 396–97, esp. nn29–30, 37) gives a helpful breakdown of the phrases Paul uses that seem to be equivalent in meaning.

104. Deissmann, *Paul*, 128. For a review of Deissmann's argument, see Spivey, "Scope of the Phrase 'In Christ,'" 8–12.

105. For a fuller account on the history of interpretation of "in Christ" since

phrases could be interpreted equally in a "locative" sense.[106] Likewise, he believed that "locative" sense to be mystical at its foundation, which allowed critics to charge him with teaching the loss of personality in Christ.[107] These critics, as critics often do, overreacted and rejected or minimized the importance of the locative sense of "in Christ."[108] Contemporary scholarship now sees that Deissmann's original idea was not precise enough. For instance, Frank Porter writes, "In the great majority of the occurrences of the phrase 'in Christ' we do not find the mood of mysticism, and in none of them, I believe, do we find the suggestion of a semi-physical or metaphysical process. We are not in the region of elements and their interactions, of substances and their blending; we are in the regions of persons and their relationships."[109]

Currently, following the pioneering work of E. P. Sanders, Pauline scholarship is taking a keen interest in a participatory model of salvation, where the "in Christ" phrase connotes the believer's participation in Christ and Christ's work in the believer.[110] This model has perichoretic implications in its "reciprocal immanence," to borrow from

---

Deissmann, see Reid, *Our Life in Christ*, 11–31; Best, *One Body in Christ*, 8–19; and Wethington, "Paul and John," 35–48. Ziesler (*Pauline Christianity*, 51) states, "The main difficulty in examining this language is that nowhere does Paul explain himself, but assumes that his readers will readily understand it." For an earlier difference of interpretation between "in Christ" and "in the Spirit," see Wickenhauser, *Pauline Mysticism*, 54.

106. Barcley, *"Christ in You,"* 6. Barcley gives an excellent summary of not only Deissmann's interpretation of "in Christ," but those who followed him as well (7–13). The term "locative" above denotes "location," that is, for Deissmann, the believer is "mystically" located in Christ. The history of interpretation of the phrase is not germane to this study, but Best, Reid, and Barcley provide excellent summaries.

107. Best, *One Body in Christ*, 9. Not all contemporary scholars see the locative idea as central. For an example, see Seifrid, "In Christ," 436. For two other criticisms of Deissmann, see Schreiner, *Paul*, 157; and Forsee, "Role of Union," 32–36.

108. For an example of mid-twentieth century reaction against Deissmann, see Wahlstrom, *New Life in Christ*, 93. He wants to redefine "in Christ" as "in dependence upon Christ" or "belonging to Christ," which he believes captures the phrase "in Christ." There is no mystical sense of participation in Wahlstrom's phrases, and no hint of a perichoretic relationship. One wonders how he would redefine the Johannine "in," especially in relation to the Father and Son.

109. Porter, *Mind of Christ in Paul*, 283. This underscores the importance of seeing soteriological union as a third type of *perichoresis*.

110. See Sanders, *Paul and Palestinian Judaism*, esp. 505–8. More recently the work of Gorman (*Inhabiting the Cruciform God*) argues thoroughly for a participatory view of salvation in Paul. Fee (*Paul, the Spirit, and the People of God*, 52) adds the eschatological element of this participation as well.

Schnackenburg, as well as participation. To quote Michael Gorman, "To be in Christ is a corporate reality, but it is experienced as such by individuals."[111] The individual aspect is the one with which this investigation is concerned.[112]

William Barcley and James Dunn provide the clearest categories for interpretation among current scholars. Dunn sees three broad categories for interpretation, including an "objective usage," which describes the redemptive act which has happened or will happen in Christ; a "subjective usage" that is akin to Deissmann's locative sense above; and a usage that describes actions or attitudes.[113] Barcley has similar categories, adding to Dunn's list only a category stressing the benefits to believers who are in Christ.[114] Both Barcley and Dunn emphasize that these categories have considerable overlap. Here Barcley writes, "This lack of specificity, though it has often been troublesome for interpreters of Paul, reveals the flexibility, as well as the beauty and the power of this metaphor in Paul's writings. 'In Christ' at times defies categorization and stands as an all-encompassing metaphor for the Christian life."[115]

Thanks to the work of Barcley and Dunn, there are four broad, though not necessarily distinct, categories for the interpretation of "in Christ."[116] They are, in order of logical, if not temporal sequence, objec-

---

111. Gorman, *Inhabiting the Cruciform God*, 56.

112. This study will not examine the corporate aspects of union with Christ, that is, the union of all believers with Christ. While an important topic, and one that is treated extensively elsewhere, the focus here will remain the individual relationship, while in no way denying the corporate aspects. There are many good treatments of the corporate idea of union. Best, *One Body in Christ*, and Son, *Corporate Elements*, are two excellent examples from among many, as is Powers, *Salvation through Participation*, and Moule, *Origin of Christology*, 47–96. Articles with a corporate emphasis include Wedderburn, "Some Observations," and Helminiak, "Human Solidarity," 34–59. For a balanced treatment of various interpretations, see Colijn, "Paul's Use of the 'In Christ' Formula," 9–26. Son (*Corporate Elements*, 27–28) sees the meaning of "in Christ" best explained in a corporate context. While it is outside of the aim of this study to critique his assertion, even the corporate Christ is made up of individuals. Another corporate treatment includes Gundry, Soma *in Biblical Theology*.

113. Dunn, *Theology of Paul the Apostle*, 397–98.

114. Barcley, *Christ in You*, 106–11.

115. Ibid., 106–7.

116. Moo, *Romans 1–8*, 409–10. Here Moo states the original thesis of Deissmann has been largely abandoned in favor of other interpretations, such as "a sacramental approach (communion mediated through a cultic experience); an ecclesiastical approach (incorporation into the church as the body of Christ); and a strictly forensic approach

tive/redemptive, subjective/locative, beneficial, and ethical/modal.[117] It is the subjective/locative sense of "in Christ" that needs investigation because if it can be shown that Paul taught a believer is "located" in Christ without losing his or her own identity, then he will be describing a kind of indwelling that is remarkably similar to the type of indwelling that constitutes the trinitarian or christological *perichoresis*—one that may itself be described as a third kind of *perichoresis*.

What does the locative sense of "in Christ" entail? E. L. Mascall argues that a Christian should be defined by what he is, or rather, what God "has made him to be." He writes, "Being a Christian is an ontological fact, resulting from an act of God."[118] Paul agrees: "Therefore if any man is in Christ, he is a new creature; the old things passed away; behold, new things have come" (2 Cor 5:17). Scripture plainly states a new creation for the person in Christ, and that creation is found precisely in Christ.[119] Timothy George adds that the phrase "in Christ" is used "to describe that participation in and union with Jesus Christ that is effected for every believer by the indwelling of the Holy Spirit."[120] Richard Longenecker writes that "the phrase 'in Christ' is a favorite of Paul's to sig-

---

('in Christ' speaking of the 'historical' and 'indicative' fact that Christians have had their destinies determined by Christ)." Also is the approach Moo favors, which is an interpretation that takes into consideration Paul's concept of "salvation history," which emphasizes Christ as the "representative head of the new era, or realm, who incorporates within himself all who belong to that new era. For us to be 'in Christ' means, then, to belong to Christ as our representative, so that the decisions applied to him apply also to us." This study does not try to evaluate the strengths and weaknesses of these various approaches, but rather seeks to combine the perichoretic aspects of all of them into a loosely-titled "perichoretic approach."

117. The "objective," "subjective," and "ethical" are Dunn's categories, the first two being his own words. The redemptive, locative, beneficial, and modal are Barcley's categories, the last being his own words. It is important to note that Barcley sees the third and fourth of his categories (the beneficial and modal) as flowing directly out of his second (locative), which is itself a direct result of the first (redemptive). Thus a logical, and possibly temporal, sequence is involved.

118. Mascall, *Christ, the Christian, and the Church*, 77. In context, Mascall is describing a real change that has taken place in the Christian. He describes a Christian as "a man who has been re-created in, and into, Christ."

119. Forsee ("Role of Union," 163) notes the creation motif, that is, the new creation God is enacting through Christ, is not an "isolated concept" in Paul. The new creation always exists "in Christ." On his next page, Forsee notes that this new creation is partly now, and partly eschatological. See also Powers, *Salvation through Participation*, 70–71.

120. George, *Galatians*, 275.

nal the personal, local, and dynamic relation of the believer to Christ."[121] Again, he adds that the phrase "appears frequently in Paul's letters to signal the sphere within which the believer lives and the intimacy of personal fellowship that exists between the believer and Christ."[122] Here Longenecker describes the locative usage of "in Christ" clearly as "the sphere in which the believer lives." Emile Mersch comments that the repeated usage of "in Christ" in Ephesians is a "supernatural inclusion in the savior."[123] Therefore, "in Christ" signals a new, personal mode of existence for believers that carries with it the sphere of living and inclusion in Christ as well as overtones of *theosis*.[124]

Paul makes the distinction between humanity that descends from Adam and the humanity that is recreated "in Christ." In 1 Corinthians 15:22, he draws explicit connections between being "in Adam" (causing death) and being "in Christ" (bringing life).[125] It is easy to see that being "in Adam" means all humanity in its natural birth. Thus all humanity is part of Adam, since he is the father of the human race. Similarly all who are believers united with Christ are part of Christ because he is the head of the new, re-created humanity and will share in his life.[126] Herman Ridderbos explains the Adam-Christ comparison as two heads of humanity, so that Adam is representative of all who are born from him and is therefore representative of all humans, just as Christ is with those who are his.[127] This idea elicits a comparison with John 17:21–23 mentioned above.[128]

As D. E. H. Whiteley notes, the participations in both Adam and Christ are real, as "Christ shared our life in order that we might share his."[129] Contrary to Deissmann, the humanity of Christ is necessary to

---

121. Longenecker, *Galatians*, 41.

122. Ibid., 89.

123. Mersch, *Whole Christ*, 107.

124. For more on *theosis* in 2 Cor 5:17, see Gorman, *Inhabiting the Cruciform God*, 6. Here again (sphere of living) is spatial terminology with relational meaning.

125. See Powers, *Salvation through Participation*, 152–56.

126. Fee, *First Epistle to the Corinthians*, 751. See also Stepp, *Believer's Participation*, 99–100, and Son, *Corporate Elements*, 43–47.

127. Ridderbos, *Paul*, 63–64. Forsee ("Role of Union," 71–87) provides a list of the four interpretations of man's solidarity in Adam, settling on the representative view as the best explanation.

128. That is, "that they all may be one in us."

129. Whiteley, *Theology of St. Paul*, 133. Whiteley notes that there was one side of

provide the "in Christ" ontology. In other words, as Adam is necessary for a person to experience humanity, Christ had to become and remain human in order for believers to be "in Christ."[130] In his incarnation, Christ united himself with humanity, thereby becoming the head of the redeemed human race as the last Adam.[131]

Galatians 3:26–29 is a passage of Scripture that utilizes the phrase "in Christ" and close derivatives several times. It speaks of "faith in Christ Jesus" (3:26), being baptized into Christ (3:27), being clothed with Christ (3:27), all believers existing as one in Christ (3:28), and belonging to Christ (3:29). Certainly a locative interpretation makes sense in at least three of these phrases, particularly in 3:27–28.

Commenting on the relationship present in these verses, Richard Longenecker writes,

> As Jesus is reported to have spoken of his relationship with the Father as being "in the Father," all without diminishing the concept of the real personality of God, so Paul with his high Christology could speak of being "in Christ" without softening or dissolving the fixed outlines of personality for either Christ or the Christian. To have been forced to give a definite psychological analysis of this relationship would have left Paul speechless.[132]

He continues, "Being 'in Christ' is, for Paul, communion with Christ in the most intimate relationship imaginable, without ever destroying or minimizing—rather, only enhancing—the distinctive personalities of either the Christian or Christ. It is 'I-Thou' communion at its highest."[133] The highest "I-Thou" communion in all of Christian theology exists among the persons of the Godhead. By his choice of words, Longenecker implies the Christ-Christian relationship is of the same order because it occurs "in Christ." Thus he makes a powerful argument for the Christian to be "located" in Christ in a real indwelling. Moreover, the perichoretic idea of union-without-absorption seems to be what Longenecker is describing.

---

human life Jesus did not know, and that was sin.

130. Reid, *Our Life in Christ*, 73.

131. Letham, *Work of Christ*, 79. This ties in closely with the argument of Helminiak ("One in Christ, 135–36) discussed in chapter 1 above.

132. Longenecker, *Galatians*, 153.

133. Ibid., 154.

Perhaps the most direct Scripture pointing toward a perichoretic union between Christ and the believer is in Romans 8:39. This verse culminates Paul's triumphant eighth chapter. He writes that nothing "shall be able to separate us from the love of God which is in Christ Jesus our Lord." Commenting on this phrase, C. E. B. Cranfield writes, "The love of Christ is not truly known until it is recognized as being the love of the eternal God himself, and it is only in Jesus Christ that the love of God is fully manifest as what it really is."[134] Porter believes that love is the proper answer to the question of how a person simultaneously can be in Christ and have Christ in him. He writes,

> The new commandment is that we love one another. But to command love is to ask what we cannot give. Paul found that Christ gives men the capacity to become that which they see in him to be divine. If there is a secret or a mystery in Paul's phrase 'in Christ Jesus' its solution is surely to be found in the nature of love. When love in one becomes a like love in the other, it is as if the persons had created themselves in each other. The eighth chapter of Romans ends with the exultant affirmation that no evil powers on earth or in heaven can separate us from the love of Christ, the love of God which is in Christ. This is the consummation of Paul's exposition of what it means to be in Christ. We are lifted up into a region where there is nothing that is perplexing, though we are filled with wonder because we are in the presence of something infinitely great.[135]

Contained within the trinitarian *perichoresis* is the active, loving indwelling and participation that exists reciprocally among the Father, Son, and Spirit. That love of God is present in Christ, as both Paul and John testify. If anyone is "located" in Christ, he or she is surrounded by the trinitarian love of God that is also present in Christ. Further, Paul writes that there is no power strong enough to separate the believer from that love.

The love of God is not the only benefit shared with the Christian due to being located "in Christ." Adolf Deissmann provides a list of gifts that are available to those "in Christ," including righteousness, joy, love, peace, and sanctification.[136] All of these properly belong to God alone,

---

134. Cranfield, *Critical and Exegetical Commentary*, 1:444.

135. Porter, *Mind of Christ in Paul*, 296.

136. Deissmann, *Paul*, 126–27. This is only a short sampling from Deissmann's list. For another such list of the benefits of the believer's union with Christ, see Mueller,

which are communicated to the believer through the God-man. It would be difficult to see how such personal characteristics of the Trinity could be given to human beings in any real way without also communicating the personal divine relationship in which they reside. Also, since the benefits are Christ's, they become the possession of the believer due to her location in Christ.

Ernest Best develops the "local" argument from benefits further. He writes, "Believers are 'in Christ' because they are 'in his corporate personality.'" He continues, "This explanation also affords us an interpretation of the link connecting the formula with the fact and experience of redemption; redemption is in Christ; believers are in Christ; so redemption passes over to them."[137] If believers are actually located in the corporate personality of Christ, it would suggest the idea that one person can indwell another, which points toward the perichoretic relationships in the Trinity and the person of Christ. The exchange of benefits Best mentions, while not exactly a *communicatio idiomatum*, does parallel the patristic christological teaching in striking ways.[138] Moreover, the *communicatio* and *perichoresis* are closely related, though distinct, concepts.[139]

"Mystical Union." Wickenhauser (*Pauline Mysticism*, 82–83) gives a comparison of benefits of "in Christ" and "in the Spirit."

137. Best, *One Body in Christ*, 20–21.

138. The *communicatio idiomatum* is a patristic teaching concerning the incarnation, which holds that because the divine and human natures of Christ are joined in the hypostatic union, properties that are intrinsically divine are communicated to the human, and vice versa. The simplest of these is that the flesh of Christ is the flesh of God, which led to the *theotokos* controversy, as well as Acts 20:28, where God purchased the church with his own blood. If, due to the believer's incorporation into Christ, Christ assumes all that we are and we are given by grace all that he is, this is almost like the *communicatio*. 1 Corinthians 1:30 is a biblical example of the communication of what Christ possesses to the believer, including sanctification, righteousness, and redemption. Perhaps this idea is seen more clearly in a quote in chapter 3 below from Martin Luther. The reference is Luther, "Freedom of a Christian," 603. For patristic resources on the *communicatio*, see Leo, *Tome*, in Bindley, *Ecumenical Documents*, 226–27; and Cyril of Alexandria, *On the Creed* 14, in Wickham, *Cyril of Alexandria*, 111. For further discussion, see Prestige, *God in Patristic Thought*, 292–96, and MacLeod, *Person of Christ*, 193–99.

139. For the distinction, see Crisp, *Divinity and Humanity*, 4–27, as well as his "Problems with *Perichoresis*"; Heron, "*Communicatio Idiomatum* and *Deificatio*"; and Dragas, "Exchange or Communication."

This has been a very brief survey of Paul's usage of "in Christ." It has been shown that in at least some of Paul's usages of "in Christ," he intends a "locative" sense. The "locative" idea implies a real presence of the believer in Christ, or equivalently, the believer indwelling Christ. Not all instances of "in Christ" imply a "locative" sense, for the phrase has a wide range of meaning. But the existence of a locative interpretation of "in Christ" in a significant number of its uses shows that there is a real indwelling where a person is "located" inside Christ without being absorbed by him. The parallels are evident with the trinitarian or christological *perichoresis* as the persons and natures, respectively, indwell (or are "located in") the other without damage. Therefore, it may be said that such an indwelling leads to the idea that the soteriological union is likewise a form of *perichoresis*, albeit a third type. The texts surveyed above also stress active participation in a way that points to *perichoresis*, but do so indirectly. For active participation, the next subsection is crucial.

Paul's Use of "With Christ"

Another important theological expression in Paul's letters is "with Christ," although it does not appear nearly as often as "in Christ." It is interesting to note that unlike "in Christ" and its counterpart "Christ in you/me," the phrase "Christ with me" never occurs in the writings of Paul. Ernest Best believes the reason is because "Christ with me" would imply that the person is the leader and Christ the follower, which of course is not the case.[140] This subsection will argue that Paul's "with Christ" language, in various forms, shows an active participation of the believer in Christ. The previous subsection has demonstrated the striking parallels between the indwelling of the believer in Christ and the standard views of *perichoresis*, suggesting that such indwelling may be a third type of perichoretic relationship due to its intensity. Now the writings of Paul that describe the active participation of the believer in Christ must be examined.

Some of the most theologically rich passages in Paul are those that describe the believer and Christ in action together. Many of these passages contain compound nouns or verbs beginning with σύν.[141] Dunn

---

140. Best, *One Body in Christ*, 60.

141. For lists of these compound nouns and verbs, see Dunn, *Theology of Paul the Apostle*, 402–3, as well Cerfaux, *Christian in the Theology of St. Paul*, 338, and Grundmann, "σύνμέτα," in *TDNT*, 7:786–87.

notes that there are two notable clusters where several of these compound words appear together. They are Romans 6:4–8 and 8:16–29.[142] The first passage concerns how believers participate in Christ, while the second notes some of the benefits of that participation. Both passages deserve a closer look.

The "with Christ" language appears several times in Romans 6. Believers have been buried with Christ through baptism (Rom 6:4), united with him in the likeness of his death (Rom 6:5), crucified with him (Rom 6:6), and they have died with him (Rom 6:8) and shall live with him (Rom 6:8).[143] All but the last in the "with Christ" list here are past tense.[144] Scholars are agreed that Paul is describing a participation of the believer with Christ that goes far beyond the symbolic. For instance, Thomas Schreiner writes, "We died to Christ in baptism in that we were united with him in his once-for-all death. Because we are incorporated into Christ, his death becomes ours. At baptism (i.e., conversion) the death of Christ becomes ours because we share the benefits of his death by virtue of our incorporation into him."[145] The language of "what is his becomes ours" is an active participation in the life of Christ.

Richard Gaffin adds, "Baptism signifies and seals a transition in the experience of the recipient, a transition from being (existentially) apart from Christ to being (existentially) joined to Him."[146] Christ's death and resurrection is both an actual event and an analogy, as he views them as an event happening to the church and an analogy to the individual.[147] Because Christ and the believer are existentially in union, Christ's death becomes the believer's death experientially.[148] Cranfield explicitly adds, "Our fallen human nature was crucified with Christ in our baptism in the sense that in baptism we received the sign and seal of the fact that by God's gracious decision it was, in his sight, crucified with

---

142. Dunn, *Theology of Paul the Apostle*, 403.

143. Stepp, *Believer's Participation*, 100–2, notes the participatory language in the Greek term for "united with," ὁμοίωμα.

144. Carlson, "Role of Baptism," 258. Carlson states that the tense of "live with" means that the Christian lives in the expectation of a resurrection like Christ's.

145. Schreiner, *Romans*, 310.

146. Gaffin, *Resurrection and Redemption*, 50.

147. Ibid., 55.

148. Ibid., 123.

Christ on Golgotha."[149] John Fischer writes, "The Christian's experiential death and resurrection is not a little reproduction of Christ's physical death and resurrection; it is an event that somehow actually happened to Christians as it happened to Christ."[150] The participation language is both evident and explicit.

Finally, Ernest Best writes, "How are we to explain this close relationship between believers and Christ? There is some kind of identity between the believer and Christ." He continues that the believer "is connected to Christ by a bond similar to that which links together two parts of an organism, or similar to that which links husband and wife. He shares in the actual experiences of Christ, or at least in those experiences of Christ which are most significant for Paul, viz., his sufferings, death, burial, resurrection and exaltation. He is 'with Christ'; it is not Christ who is with him."[151] Best certainly affirms active participation in Christ. Could it be that the description Best is trying so hard to grasp is one of *perichoresis*?

Baptism is the symbolic act that denotes that a person has entered into union with Christ.[152] Immersion under water is a sign of burial, which certifies that death has occurred.[153] Although the analogy between going under water, submerging, and emerging from water and death, burial, and resurrection is one that scholars debate,[154] there is a fairly clear consensus that the baptismal act is symbolic of the believer's union with Christ due to the believer's participation in his death, burial, and resurrection. Robert Tannehill writes, "If the believer dies and rises with Christ, as Paul claims, Christ's death and resurrection are not merely events which produce benefits for the believer, but also are events in which the believer himself partakes. The believer's new life is based upon his personal participation in these saving events. Furthermore, these events continue to give their stamp to the life of the believer, for he continues to participate in Christ's death and resurrection in his daily

---

149. Cranfield, *Romans*, 134.

150. Fischer, "Identification with Christ," 17. He also states on pages 65–66 that the death of the Christian represented by baptism in Romans 6 implies "an actual participation and not imitation."

151. Best, *One Body in Christ*, 55.

152. Moo, *Epistle to the Romans*, 360.

153. Mounce, *Romans*, 149. For a discussion of why Paul refers to water baptism rather than Spirit baptism, see Schreiner, *Romans*, 306–7.

154. Schreiner, *Romans*, 308–9.

life."¹⁵⁵ Because the believer is "with Christ" in these events, what happens to Christ happens to the believer because the believer is somehow present in the action.

In Christian theology, the union of the believer to Christ precedes the benefits derived from the union. The death and resurrection of Christ, in which the believer at some level participates, follows the joining of Christ and the believer. As Gert Pelser writes concerning this union,

> It further seems that this incorporation is something more than the believer's transition to Christ's ownership or domain, or entering into a special relationship with Christ. It is rather the coming about of a totally new form of existence, an existence of being fully controlled by Christ, of living through Christ living in the believer. It is the coming about of a new personality in which Christ can be identified, yet without the believer losing his/her identity.¹⁵⁶

Thomas Weinandy writes, "The Pauline corpus places before us a Christian life that is integrally trinitarian. We, who are baptized, participate in the same transformation that Christ himself underwent through his death and resurrection."¹⁵⁷ He adds, "Therefore, like the risen Christ, we now live a whole new life directly initiated by, and expressly lived in, the Holy Spirit."¹⁵⁸ Both Pelser and Weinandy use language resembling a perichoretic relationship, especially when discussing union-without-absorption and an "integrally trinitarian" life, respectively, though they never imply the believer's becoming part of the trinitarian *perichoresis*. What they are struggling to articulate seems to be a third type of *perichoresis* to describe the soteriological union of the believer and Christ.

The relationship enacted by participation in Christ's death and resurrection constitutes more than a shift of allegiance for the believer. As Tannehill writes concerning dying and rising with Christ, "This motif is used to indicate the decisive transfer of the believers from the old to the new aeon which has taken place in the death of Christ as an inclusive event."¹⁵⁹ He continues, "It takes place only once—in the death and

---

155. Tannehill, *Dying and Rising*, 1.
156. Pelser, "'Formulas' *Dying* and *Rising with Christ*," 132.
157. Weinandy, *Father's Spirit of Sonship*, 33.
158. Ibid., 33–34.
159. Tannehill, *Dying and Rising*, 70.

resurrection of Christ, and it is to the believer's participation in these eschatological events that dying and rising with Christ refers."[160] Here is the participation theme again, but there is more evidence from Romans 8, where the Christian is "fellow heir with," "suffers with," and is "glorified with" Christ.

James Dunn makes a further comment concerning the language Paul uses in his emphasis on participation. He writes,

> We simply need to underline the tremendous sense of "togetherness" implicit in Paul's language. This again can hardly be reduced to a merely literary motif, a feature of Pauline style. Here the more mystical dimension comes into focus primarily in the decisive salvation-effecting events of Christ's death and resurrection. And here too the language cannot be reduced simply to a description of baptism or of membership in the believing community. Paul's language indicates rather a quite profound sense of participation with others in a great and cosmic movement of God centered on Christ and effected through his spirit. Here again a term like "mysticism" is only an attempt to indicate that profundity and to signal that there are depths and resonances here which we may not be able fully to explore, but for which we need to keep our ears attuned.[161]

Like so many other authors this chapter surveys, Dunn is grasping for a word that encompasses the depth of the soteriological union. This sense of participation, this sense of "mysticism," is better seen as a component of a third type of perichoretic relationship, where persons may live within another's sphere of existence without contradiction or absorption.

The gulf of time that exists between the believer today and the act of Christ two thousand years ago does not pose a problem. Perichoretic relationships do not need to be bound by time.[162] Gary Deddo summarizes this well: "We are so joined that what has happened to Christ 2,000 years ago has actually included us. So in the letter to the Colossians we

---

160. Ibid.

161. Dunn, *Theology of Paul the Apostle*, 404.

162. Smedes, *Union with Christ*, 103–4, notes, as a parallel, that Israelites who lived centuries after the Exodus could still affirm that God brought them up out of Egypt. While the believer's union with Christ is different than Israel's union with God through the Mosaic covenant, the events of the Exodus seem to apply to all who share in that covenant.

hear that we have 'co-died' with Christ and have been 'co-raised' with Christ (Col 2:12–13; 3:1). Paul announces this fact as a completed action which is actually true of all the members of the body of Christ."[163]

While, as it has been shown, "in Christ" and "with Christ" are remarkably similar, they are not completely interchangeable. That is, they show two different components of a relationship best described as perichoretic—indwelling and participation, respectively. Ernest Best summarizes the difference well:

> The "with Christ" passages emphasize the fact that it is Christ's life, his risen life, in which they share; the "in Christ" passages emphasize the nature of the new life and the relationships which it implies between one Christian and another. The Christian does not hope, work, or believe "with Christ," but "in Christ"; he does not die and rise to new life "in Christ" but "with Christ." The "with Christ" formula describes the origin of the Christian life; the "in Christ" formula describes that life as it is lived from day to day.[164]

Best concludes by saying that "Christ is a personality who includes believers."[165] This aptly summarizes what has been shown in Paul's writings so far. Believers both indwell and participate in Christ. Taken together, "in," "into," "through," and "with Christ" show how the believer participates in and indwells the person of Christ.[166] But the believer in/with/through Christ is only one side of the coin. Christ in the believer, creating the idea so familiar in John of "mutual indwelling," must complete the argument.

---

163. Deddo, "Our Participation," 139.

164. Best, *One Body in Christ*, 62.

165. Ibid.

166. Due to the limited usage of "into Christ" beyond the idea of baptism that is pertinent to this study, "into Christ" is not discussed here. Other authors treat its usage with respect to being "baptized into Christ" and show it has a meaning similar to "in Christ." For more on this usage, see Best, *One Body in Christ*, 65–73, and Dunn, *Theology of Paul the Apostle*, 404–5. Again, the survey of usage of "through Christ" is omitted from this study. Dunn (*Theology of Paul the Apostle*, 406) notes that "through Christ" carries much of the same meaning as "in Christ" and "with Christ," with a further nuance, namely "His most regular formation envisages the saving or commissioning or final action of God as happening or coming to effect 'through Christ.'" Dunn further notes that the use of διά with the genitive case shows "his conception of Christ was of an open channel between God and his people, a living intermediary through whom God acted and through whom his people could approach him."

Paul's Use of "Christ in You/Me"

Paul does not employ the terminology of "Christ in you/me" nearly as often as he does "in Christ." There are only a half-dozen references in his letters, though this is still a highly significant number of occurrences. It is significant because it seems to complement the "in Christ" passages in a way that is reminiscent of Johannine "reciprocal immanence" language. Whether this is true remains to be seen. Since there are only six texts to examine, all will be investigated. Moreover, there are many more references to the indwelling Spirit than "Christ in you."[167] But, as Bruce Forsee argues, "The Holy Spirit does his work in such a way that, as far as the practical experience of the believer is concerned, it is as if Christ himself were the only indwelling influence mediating the benefits of redemption to believers."[168] Thus there is little experiential difference between "Christ in you" and the indwelling Spirit.[169] This subsection will show that despite its small number of occurrences, "Christ in you" shows both the indwelling of and the active participation of Christ in the believer, which are ideas that imply that the believer's union with Christ is a third type of *perichoresis*.

William Barcley, in his monograph *Christ in You: A Study in Paul's Theology and Ethics*, provides an excellent historical overview of the history of interpretation of the "Christ in you/me" texts. He notes that Deissmann equated "Christ in you/me" and "in Christ."[170] Although he noted some differences in expression, Albert Schweitzer believed the phrases "we in Christ" and "Christ in us" functioned in an equivalent manner in his understanding of Paul's "mysticism."[171] Even some contemporary authors see the two phrases as "complementary."[172] Lewis Smedes calls "Christ in you/me" the other side of the coin, as it involves personal transformation to make believers resemble what they are "in Christ," that is, in the new order of life that began at the death and res-

---

167. Guthrie, *New Testament Theology*, 653.

168. Forsee, "Role of Union," 292.

169. Since this study is limited to the relationship between Christ and the believer, the texts containing the Spirit's indwelling will not be surveyed.

170. Barcley, *Christ in You*, 5–6.

171. Schweitzer, *Mysticism of Paul the Apostle*, 125.

172. For example, see Dunn, *Theology of Paul the Apostle*, 400, and Moo, *Romans 1–8*, 523.

urrection of Christ.[173] Smedes states that three meanings exist for the phrase "Christ in you/me." They are an infusion of the divine life, the reality of "Christ for us," and the fact that Christ rules within the lives of believers.[174] These categories will be helpful when investigating the individual passages below.

In Galatians 2:20, Paul boldly asserts that "It is no longer I who live, but Christ lives in me." Barcley notes that Paul's language denotes a "radical break" from the past when the person's participation in the death, burial, and resurrection of Christ has been fully realized.[175] The new life in Christ is made real because of the real, living presence of Christ in Paul. He is at once both "in Christ" and Christ is "in him." This is the mutual indwelling language so common in John's writings. Furthermore, this mutual indwelling does not result in the loss of one or more of the personalities. No one is absorbed into the other. Just as in the trinitarian *perichoresis*, mutual indwelling occurs without any loss of personality.[176] Moreover, Paul's words imply an active participation of Christ in him because the very life he lives is "by the faith of the Son of God."

In Galatians 4:19, Paul states that he "is again in labor until Christ be formed in you." The imagery here is Christ as a fetus needing more time to be fully formed.[177] As Timothy George points out, Paul did not want the Galatians to suffer a "spiritual miscarriage."[178] Barcley notes a common theme running through both usages of "Christ in you/me" in Galatians, which is the beginning of the life of faith. He writes, "It indicates that a transition and transformation has taken place in believers' lives, and that the entirety of the life of faith is to bear the imprint of their initial experience of Christ."[179] The transition could perhaps be the indwelling of Christ in the believer. The transformation then becomes Christ's active participation in the believer.

---

173. Smedes, *Union with Christ*, 112. Dunn (*Theology of Paul's Letter to the Galatians*, 118–19) agrees.

174. Ibid., 115–28.

175. Barcley, *Christ in You*, 25.

176. For a discussion, see Longenecker, *Galatians*, 92–93, and George, *Galatians*, 200–1.

177. Longenecker, *Galatians*, 195.

178. George, *Galatians*, 330.

179. Barcley, *Christ in You*, 31.

In Romans 8:9, Paul is in the midst of a passage where he uses the terms "Christ" and "Spirit" almost interchangeably. More precisely, "Christ and the Spirit are so closely related in communicating to believers the benefits of salvation that Paul can move from one to the other almost unconsciously."[180] Barcley writes, "For Paul, the Spirit is the sign that the age to come has broken into the present age."[181] Smedes notes that the proof of the indwelling Christ is the presence of the Spirit and of power—power that is able to transform lives.[182] This power does not come from within the individual believer. It comes from the indwelling presence of the Godhead, for both Christ and the Spirit are present. The power is the active participation of the indwelling Christ and Spirit. The idea of God dwelling in humanity is the hope of the eschatological age, a point Barcley notes as Paul blends his discussion of the Spirit as well as Christ in you/me.[183] Similarly, the occurrence of "Christ in you/me" in 2 Corinthians 13:5 has many of the same overtones discussed above, such as a return in thought to the basics of the faith as well as the eschatological dimension present in Romans and Galatians.[184]

In Colossians 1:27, Paul affirms "Christ in you, the hope of glory." Barcley notes that the major themes of "Christ in you/me" are again present, such as the introduction to the life of faith, the conformity to the image of Christ, and especially here the eschatological promise of the end of the life of faith.[185] The glorification believers have "with Christ" will be fully realized. It points to a time when the soteriological union believers enjoy will be fully manifest, when those who are in Christ will no longer see through the dark glass, but face to face (1 Cor 13:12).

In Ephesians 3:17, Christ and the Spirit are again linked together, except this time the order is reversed. Here, the Spirit dwells in the believer's heart in order that Christ may dwell there. Harold Hoehner sees a different interpretation than that reached by both Smedes and Barcley. He states that Christ dwelling in the heart through faith does not refer to the initial experience of salvation. Rather it is the result of the life of faith, so that "Christ may 'be at home in,' that is, at the very center

180. Moo, *Romans 1–8*, 523.
181. Ibid., 34.
182. Smedes, *Union with Christ*, 130.
183. Barcley, *Christ in You*, 37.
184. Ibid., 38–43.
185. Ibid., 47.

of or deeply rooted in believer's lives."[186] In other words, it is a deeper realization and growth of the indwelling and participation rather than the initiation into it. Hoehner's use of "at home in" language parallels the ideas developed in John above that point to the indwelling Christ as part of a relationship that may rightly be described as perichoretic.

This concludes the section on "Christ in you/me." Although much more may be said about the phrase "Christ in you," it has been shown that it denotes a real indwelling presence of Christ in the believer. In addition, that indwelling is augmented by an active participation of Christ through the Spirit in the believer as well. While some have seen these Pauline phrases as pointing to something mystical, seen in the light of the Johannine teaching surveyed earlier they may be better described as pointing to a third type of *perichoresis*. "In Christ" denotes that Christ indwells the believer. "With Christ" shows the active participation of the believer in the life of Christ. "Christ in you" is the basis of Christ indwelling and actively participating in the life of the believer. Therefore, the Pauline phrases outlined in this section follow in step with the perichoretic language of the Father/Son relationship in John and the expected repetition of that relationship between Christ and his disciples.[187]

Other Pauline Phrases

Space does not allow a close examination of other Pauline phrases, such as "in the Spirit," the indwelling Spirit, and the indwelling God. A brief summary is given below, which also serves as a starting place for more research.

When Paul refers to the Holy Spirit, he often does so in language that mirrors the phrases he uses concerning Christ. Thus the phrases "in the (Holy) Spirit," "with the Spirit," and "through the Spirit" are present, just as "in Christ," "with Christ," and "through Christ," surveyed above. For every category discussed in the section on "in Christ," a parallel discussion of Pauline use of "in/by/with the Spirit" is present as well. To briefly summarize, in both Romans and Galatians, Paul urges believers

---

186. Hoehner, *Ephesians*, 481.

187. Son (*Corporate Elements*, 18) notes that there is not textual evidence to conclude that a complete reciprocity exists between the Pauline "in Christ" and "Christ in you/me" and the Johannine "mutual immanence," as he states it is "probably the Spirit rather than Christ who dwells in believers." This seems to ignore the direct statement to the contrary in Gal 2:20, however.

to "walk after/in the Spirit"; believers receive spiritual blessings in the heavenlies in Christ. As Paul creates a dichotomy between a person "in Adam" and a person "in Christ," he likewise creates one between one "in the flesh" and one "in the Spirit." The parallels Paul constructs in his writings show the almost fluid interchange between the Sprit and Christ while maintaining their distinctions.

Commenting on the interchangeability in Paul of the phrases "in Christ" and "in the Spirit," Eric Wahlstrom writes, "It is clear that in his thinking the activity of the Spirit is firmly connected with the person of Christ. The quality and nature of the Spirit's work are determined by the quality and nature of the person of Christ. The formula 'in the Spirit' must, therefore, be understood from the formula 'in Christ' rather than the opposite."[188] Gordon Fee likewise notes the close relationship between the two phrases but does not think the two are interchangeable.[189] Though it is beyond the scope of this study, a similar argument for a perichoretic relationship between the believer and the Spirit could possibly be made.

Summary of Paul and Union

The second section of this chapter has surveyed how Paul taught the reality of the believer's union with Christ. Several of his favorite expressions have been briefly examined, and some general conclusions may be drawn.

First, as with the Johannine description of union, there is a strong sense of interpenetration of persons. The language of Jesus in John's writings is paralleled by Paul's description of the persons of the Trinity both being indwelt by and indwelling the believer. Just as the persons of the Trinity indwell one another without a loss of personality, so the believer and Christ indwell one another without loss of distinction.[190] That is, the believer retains his own personality without having it assimilated into

---

188. Wahlstrom, *New Life in Christ*, 90. Ladd (*Theology of the New Testament*, 532) further comments concerning Paul's free exchange of "in Christ," "in the Spirit," "Christ in you," and "Spirit in you," "probably the precise idiom would be 'Christ indwells his people in the Spirit.'"

189. Fee, *God's Empowering Presence*, 593. Fee agrees with Wahlstrom's assessment of precision in the relationship of the phrases in the note above as well (374).

190. Gorman (*Inhabiting the Cruciform God*, 4) suggests that "in Christ" is Paul's "shorthand for 'in God/in Christ/in the Spirit.' That is, his christocentricity is really an implicit trinitarianism."

the Godhead. In addition, the individual believers make up the body of Christ without loss of individual personalities.[191]

Like John, Paul places stress on the idea of knowing God as part of the mutual indwelling.[192] Wethington further observes that in both Paul and John, Christ is not just the cause of life or righteousness. Rather, "Christ *is* the righteousness in the believer's life (for Paul); and Christ *is* eternal life (for John)—and in both cases because Christ is internalized. With Christ internalized we are what he is; inasmuch as he is 'righteous' (in Paul), we partake of that righteousness; inasmuch as Christ is 'life' (in John), we partake of that life. Christ is internalized and what he is we can become."[193] Thus we partake of what he possesses due to the nearly unparalleled closeness of the soteriological union. Only the traditional two contexts of *perichoresis* describe a closeness as intense as the one in the soteriological union.

One of the differences in Paul is the presence of strong participation language that is less common in John. The believer, in some real sense, is present in the death, burial, and resurrection with Christ. The believer is already a participant in the heavenly realms. There is one body with many members. But the participation theme runs in both directions, as Daniel Powers writes: "Paul sees Christ as being actively involved in the life of the believer, he lives through the believer. Christ participates in the life and the fate of the believers in the same way as the believers participate in Christ's fate."[194] Thus the participation is mutually between both Christ and the believer just as in the common explanations of *perichoresis*.

The mutual indwelling and participation of distinct persons in "one" without loss of personal identity describes the key components of the perichoretic relationships within the Trinity and the person of Christ. Thomas Weinandy aptly summarizes, "The contention of the whole Pauline corpus is that we are taken into the intimate life of the Trinity, becoming genuine adopted sons and daughters of God. We enjoy the same rights and privileges as Jesus. We experience a heavenly

---

191. See, for example, Best, *One Body in Christ*, 23.

192. Wethington, "Paul and John," 113–18. He cites 1 Cor 8:23 and 13:12; and Gal 4:9 as evidence (80).

193. Ibid., 110. Italics in original. He further quotes John 14:20 and Gal 2:20 as evidence from both writers showing the "internalization" as a perichoretic relationship.

194. Powers, *Salvation through Participation*, 124.

life analogous to his own."[195] This type of intense, intimate relationship knows no parallels within the created order. The soteriological union Paul describes is so close, so "reciprocally immanent," so participative that *perichoresis* seems to be an apt word to describe it, although it is a third type along with the trinitarian and christological.

OTHER BIBLICAL EVIDENCE

2 Peter 1:4

This verse states, "For by these He has granted to us His precious and magnificent promises, in order that by them you might become partakers of the divine nature, having escaped the corruption that is in the world by lust." The obvious interest to this investigation is the phrase "partakers of the divine nature." Does this phrase help support the thesis of this study?

The answer depends on whom one asks. Eastern Orthodox Christians see this phrase as a solid proof of their doctrine of *theosis*.[196] Western Christians are hesitant to concur.[197] In fact, much of the Western exegetical tradition on 2 Peter 1:4 holds that the phrase is a "kind of alien intrusion" of Hellenistic thought into the New Testament.[198] The idea of participation in the divine nature was common in Greek dualistic thought, especially the idea of escaping the evil, material world and becoming one with the divine.[199]

The evangelical commentaries surveyed for this brief section all deny the connection between 2 Peter 1:4 and any hint of *theosis*. For example, Gene Green, in the newest of the commentaries, goes no deeper into the meaning than moral character, saying that moral transformation only is in order and not "divinization."[200] Peter Davids concurs, stating that neither the indwelling of the Holy Spirit nor of Christ is in view either.[201] He does not believe any ontological change occurs in the

---

195. Weinandy, *Father's Spirit of Sonship*, 35. Believers enjoy the same rights and privileges as a result of the adopted sonship, further explained in chapter 4 below. They obviously do not become members of the Trinity as Jesus is.

196. See, for example Maloney, *Undreamed Has Happened*, 61–72.

197. The discussion of the text immediately following contains several examples of such hesitancy.

198. Wolters, "Partners of the Deity," 28.

199. See Davids, *Letters of 2 Peter and Jude*, 173, and Bauckham, *Jude and 2 Peter*, 180.

200. Green, *Jude and 2 Peter*, 186–88.

201. Davids, *2 Peter and Jude*, 174.

participation of the divine nature: "The dualism in Judaism and in 2 Peter is at root ethical, not ontological."[202] He concludes such an ethical nature eventually leads to immortality.[203] Richard Bauckham concurs, saying it is not likely that the text points to either a participation in God's own essence or the doctrine of deification.[204] Instead, the text leads to a doctrine of immortality.[205]

Thomas Schreiner offers a little more help. Although he believes the verse to point toward moral perfection, as do Davids and Green, he does note that it will be fully consummated at the return of Christ.[206] Al Wolters, noting the fear in the Western tradition of exegesis of the idea of an ontological participation in God, proposes to translate the phrase differently, to "partners of the deity."[207] He believes this will clear up the fears, but his case is not convincing.

Given the evidence in this chapter from Paul and John, there is reason to believe that participation in the divine nature goes deeper than only moral qualities. It would seem from the evidence discussed above that a perichoretic relationship with God through Christ is in view in the Pauline and Johannine writings, but the exegetical works on 2 Peter from the Western tradition do not concur. They are not the last word, however. James Starr asks and answers the question "Does 2 Peter 1:4 speak of deification?" in an article by the same name. After surveying all of the data from Scripture and Hellenism, he answers, "If [deification] means equality with God or elevation to divine status or absorption into God's essence, the answer is no. If it means the participation in and enjoyment of specific divine attributes and qualities, in part now and fully at Christ's return, then the answer is—most certainly—yes."[208] So there is some possibility for perichoretic union in 2 Peter 1:4, but it needs further research. At any rate, the commentators are correct in rejecting that humans are ontologically changed into God, but they are wrong in not seeing a third type of *perichoresis* implied in the verse.

---

202. Ibid., 175.
203. Ibid., 176.
204. Bauckham, *Jude and 2 Peter*, 181.
205. Ibid., 180–81.
206. Schreiner, *1, 2 Peter, Jude*, 294–95.
207. Wolters, "Partners of the Deity," 29–30.
208. Starr, "Does 2 Peter 1:4 Speak of Deification?" 90.

76 PERICHORETIC SALVATION

Other Biblical Support

Although John and Paul are the two main exponents of the idea that the believer's union with Christ is a perichoretic relationship, they are not the only biblical authors to do so. Matthew and Luke show language of mutual knowing between the Father and Son that extends to believers (Matt 11:27; Luke 10:22). A few Old Testament texts demonstrate a union resembling a perichoretic relationship between God and his people. Kanagaraj identifies the "divine presence filling the people in Isaiah 40:22, Proverbs 20:27, Job 32:8, Ecclesiastes 12:7, and Psalm 139, and the idea of Yahweh dwelling among his people in Exodus 25:8 and Ezekiel 37:27."[209] He continues, "The reciprocal relationship between God and his people can be envisaged in Leviticus 26:12, 2 Samuel 7:14, and Song of Songs 6:3. Moreover, the dwelling of Jesus in his disciples and thus of God in them echoes also the Wisdom tradition."[210] Therefore, the introduction of a perichoretic mutual indwelling in the New Testament documents is not a completely new idea. The seed of the doctrine of union, like all other foundational Christian doctrines, is present in the Old Testament. This is a very brief sketch, and certainly more work could be done here.

CHAPTER SUMMARY

The evidence presented in this chapter shows that the Bible presents the believer's union with Christ in ways that may aptly be described as a third type of perichoretic relationship. John, Paul, Peter, and various Old Testament authors reiterate the same idea. Both John and Paul see the believer and Christ mutually indwelling and participating in one another to a degree so intimate that it is on a par with the types of relationships present among the persons of the Trinity, or between the divine and human natures in Christ.[211] Since no other word so accurately describes this type of close relationship, it may be said that the soteriological union is a third type of *perichoresis*. John stresses that the relationship of the believer to Christ will be "as" the oneness of Father and Son.[212] Paul's

---

209. Kanagaraj, *Mysticism*, 271.

210. Ibid., 272.

211. For a brief overview that mentions much of what this chapter discusses in depth, see Smalley, "Christ-Christian Relationship," 95–105.

212. While Ladd (*Theology of the New Testament*, 314) sees some differences in the

participative language incorporates the believer into Christ so that the Christian is taken up into the life of God and, in Peter's words, made a partaker of the divine nature. True knowledge of God can only exist in a world where Christ and the believer mutually indwell and participate in one another. This relationship mirrors the trinitarian *perichoresis* the persons of the Trinity enjoy with one another eternally and therefore may be called a third type of *perichoresis* in its own right.

Finally, Michael Gorman's thesis of *theosis* as a central motif in Pauline soteriology provides a segue into the next chapter.[213] It remains to be shown that the doctrine of *theosis* is the outworking of the perichoretic relationship of the believer's union with Christ. That will be the next idea to explore.

---

indwelling language of Paul and John, Caird (*New Testament Theology*, 221) notes the similarities in approaches and results of the teachings of incorporation into Christ in both Paul and John. Ladd states that the Pauline "in Christ" is theological while the Johannine "abiding" involves more of a personal relationship. After showing how the abiding of John is based on the *perichoresis* of the Persons of the Trinity, one may wonder if it is any less theological than Paul.

213. Gorman is not alone here. See also Finlan, "*Theosis* in Paul?" For a list of theotic texts in Paul, see Gorman, *Inhabiting the Cruciform God*, 6–7, esp. n15. Gorman writes, "For Paul *theosis* takes place in the person and especially the community that is in Christ and within whom/within which Christ resides, as his Spirit molds and shapes the individual and community into the cruciform image of Christ" (93).

3

Historical Development

This chapter will survey the historical development of the union of Christ and the believer. Since much of the language describing this union in Christian history revolves around the language of *theosis*, an explicit theological connection must be made to show that soteriological union as a third type of *perichoresis* is implied in *theosis* language. Once this is complete, a historical survey of both *theosis* and language that implies a perichoretic relationship within the soteriological union can be undertaken. This chapter is divided into the patristic period, the medieval and Reformation period, and finally the modern and contemporary period.[1] The last period contains a great deal of direct language concerning perichoretic union, while the others mostly are represented by *theosis* language.

THE DOCTRINE OF THEOSIS AND PERICHORETIC UNION—HOW THEY OVERLAP

At the end of the previous chapter, a few references to the doctrine of *theosis* were made in the letters of Peter and Paul. The first section of this chapter addresses the direct relationship of *theosis* and the third (soteriological) type of perichoretic union. This is necessary for two reasons. First, the goal of this study is to be as terminologically precise as possible. Second, Christian history has largely favored speaking of *theosis*

---

1. The medieval and Reformation periods are combined because, aside from the mystical theologians of the medieval period, there was little original contribution on the doctrine of union during that time. Since this study focuses on more mainstream theological thinkers, the mystical theologians will not be included. Also, after the end of the patristic era, the chapter will focus solely on Western theologians, which itself is heavily slanted toward Protestantism.

(whether it is called as such or not) rather than perichoretic union when describing either the believer's union with Christ or partaking of the divine nature. Subsequent sections of this chapter will examine the *theosis* language throughout Christian history but only after the proper connection between *theosis* and perichoretic union is made.

Theosis is still a misunderstood and mistrusted doctrine in much of Protestant theology, although some significant inroads have been made in recent years.[2] Much of the theological exploration of the doctrine has been done by either Eastern Orthodox or Roman Catholic writers.[3] The following is a rough sketch of how *theosis* and the idea that the soteriological union is a third type of *perichoresis* are related.

The possibility of *theosis* begins in the incarnation of Jesus Christ. In one person two natures dwell—the divine and the human. It is the blessed intrusion of God into human flesh.[4] The man Jesus Christ was fully God because he was hypostatically joined to the Logos, the Son.

Theosis first entered human history in the deification of Christ's human nature. Because the enhypostatic humanity of Christ was joined to the Logos, the presence of the Logos deified his human nature.[5] Moreover, according to Martin Chemnitz, this deification of Christ's human nature is a direct result of the christological *perichoresis*—the interpenetration of the divine and human natures in one person.[6] The person of Christ is the person of the Logos. Therefore, the human nature must consequently be taken up into the person of the deity while never being absorbed or consumed. As Emile Mersch writes, "It must be a perfecting

---

2. See Christensen and Wittung, *Partakers of the Divine Nature*, and Gorman, *Inhabiting the Cruciform God*. For some recent manuscripts and articles, see the bibliography for some *theosis* works this investigation will reference. See Christensen and Wittung, *Partakers of the Divine Nature*, 294–310, for a comprehensive list of works on *theosis*.

3. See, for example, Russell, *Doctrine of Deification*; Bartos, *Deification in Eastern Orthodox Theology*; Gross, *Divinization of the Christian*; Staniloae, *Experience of God*; and two works by Mersch, *Whole Christ* and *Theology of the Mystical Body*.

4. For more on the divinity of Christ, see McCready, *He Came Down from Heaven*; Erickson, *Word Became Flesh*; and Fee, *Pauline Christology*, 26. On the hypostatic union, see MacLeod, *Person of Christ*, 188–93. For a comprehensive logical defense of the doctrine of the incarnation, see Morris, *Logic of God Incarnate*. For a history of interpretation, see Witherington, *Jesus Quest*.

5. Mersch, *Theology of the Mystical Body*, 361.

6. Chemnitz, *Two Natures in Christ*. This is quoted in Schmelling, "Life in Christ," 103–4.

of the human nature, a new way of existing that the human nature takes on."[7] Therefore the human nature of Christ is deified (or experiences *theosis*) at the hypostatic union.

Theosis for other human beings was therefore made possible because a real human nature, the human nature of Jesus Christ, was deified. Because it has happened to one human, it could potentially be passed to others.[8] There is only one incarnation, and the deification of Christ's human nature is due to the (perichoretic) hypostatic union. But the possibility is present for the deification of others too.[9] Because of the incarnation and the deification of a real human, the possibility, though not the guarantee, of *theosis* has been opened to the rest of the human race.[10]

Since *theosis* came to humankind through the *theosis* of Christ's human nature, the only way *theosis* can come to other humans is by participating in Christ's human nature. Such an active participation (seen in John 13 and Rom 6), as alluded to in chapter 2 above, is part of the soteriological union that may biblically be described as a third type of *perichoresis*. If participation in Christ's human nature may rightly be seen as a sort of prerequisite for *theosis*, then the soteriological union as a third type of *perichoresis* is implied and the two ideas—perichoretic soteriological union and *theosis*—are closely and inextricably linked. Timothy Schmelling states, "*Theosis* (θέωσις) and mystical union (*unio mystica*) are Eastern and Western Christendom's customary terms for essentially the same thing. . . . So what exactly is the relationship between *theosis* and the mystical union? *Theosis* is the verbal idea or action that takes place in the mystical union. Therefore the mystical union is the bond in which *theosis* occurs."[11] He further connects the believer's union with Christ with *perichoresis*:

---

7. Mersch, *Theology of the Mystical Body*, 362.

8. This argument is not one of necessity, but of possibility.

9. Mersch, *Theology of the Mystical Body*, 365. See also Helminiak, "One in Christ," 392–406, 411. Harrison ("*Theosis as Salvation*," 436) agrees that the solidarity of the human race opens the possibility of *theosis* to all humans, though it does not guarantee it.

10. See Habets, *Theosis in the Theology of Thomas Torrance*, 12, as he attributes this idea to John Calvin as well. He writes, "*Theosis* is only possible because human nature has been deified in the theandric person of the mediator. As men and women are united to Christ, his divinity deifies them."

11. Schmelling, "Life in Christ," 71. Schmelling's term "*unio mystica*," or mystical union, is the believer's union with Christ.

Since all the teachings about the mystical union also apply to *theosis*, the following brief schema will be provided for clarification. *Theosis* is best described as that which takes place in the mystical union. When the Sacred Scriptures use *theosis* language, it does not mean that the substance of man is changed into the substance of God or that a third substance is produced. Rather the biblical notion of *theosis* is founded upon the nature of the mystical union, that is, a union of substances (John 17:21–26; 1 John 1:3; 1 Cor 1:9; 2 Pet 1:4). In this union the substance of God and the substance of man interpenetrate (περιχωρήσις) but never become one substance or a new substance. As "the Word became flesh" does not destroy Christ's deity likewise "you are gods" does not destroy the believer's humanity. This is not to say that the personal [that is, hypostatic] union is the same as the mystical union. Rather it is meant to say that God so permeates us with his divinity that we are called sons of God and even gods by adoption. Furthermore the *theosis* of Christ's human nature is also distinct from the *theosis* of man. The *theosis* of Christ's human nature results in one person or hypostasis and also receives divine attributes of God. Furthermore the human nature of Christ does not subsist in itself [*anhypostasis*], but subsists in something else [*enhypostasis*] namely the personality of the pre-incarnate λόγος. In contradistinction to the *theosis* of Christ's humanity, God communicates created grace to man in the *theosis* of man. The effecting cause of this union is the Trinity with whom man has communion via the human nature of Christ.[12]

Thus *theosis* is properly the outworking of the existing soteriological union between Christ and the believer—a union that has been biblically argued as a third type of perichoretic relationship.[13] The existence of such a union allows the believer to participate in the process of *theosis*. Because *theosis* requires the existing mutual indwelling and active participation in the other (that are key elements of the type of perichoretic union found in the biblical teaching surveyed in chapter 2 above), any use of *theosis* language within the church must assume the existence of something very close to a third type of perichoretic relationship analogous to and made possible by the christological *perichoresis*. As Mersch writes concerning Christ, God "is present by way of union and personal

12. Ibid., 71–72.

13. A possible area of further research is exploring the link between *theosis* and the traditional evangelical doctrines of sanctification and glorification, since there seems to be a strong connection here.

unity. He is present in such a way that the ultimate depths of this man are those of God himself, and the inward reality of this man is that of God himself; for this man is a divine person. The presence of God that we Christians enjoy is sharing in that presence, and is a sort of membership in it; for we are members of Christ."[14]

One more source sums up the idea of the overlap, though somewhat imprecisely, of *theosis* and *perichoresis*. Commenting on John 17:21–23, David Crump claims that John's Christology leads to "a distinctively perichoretic soteriology reminiscent of the Eastern Orthodox view of deification."[15] To sum up his point, Crump writes,

> Mutually indwelling the life of God is the heart and soul of John's understanding of salvation. Whether the disciple's indwelling is labeled Johannine mysticism, deification, or perichoretic soteriology, every believer's inclusion within the exchange of divine life and love between the Father and the Son is the essence, the heart and soul, of his message about eternal life. If *perichoresis* is an appropriate description of the Son's interpenetration of the Father, then it equally (and amazingly) describes the disciple's interpenetration of the Son. And since life in the Son is the *summa bonum* of a disciple's salvation, just as the Son's life in the Father is the *summa bonum* of his ministry in the world, then the mutual exchange of divine life circulating among Father, Son, and disciple is both the essence of Johannine salvation and the closest he comes to articulating a perichoretic 'trinity.' Because John's soteriology is a function of his Christology and *perichoresis* is intrinsic to this Christology, John's soteriology is necessarily perichoretic.[16]

Crump thus believes the relationship Christians enjoy is a type of *perichoresis* very close to *theosis*.[17] This section has demonstrated the close relationship between *perichoresis* and *theosis*, both technically and generally. Therefore this investigation will proceed to survey the language of *theosis* in Christian history as support for the third type of perichoretic union argued for in this study.

---

14. Mersch, *Theology of the Mystical Body*, 608.
15. Crump, "Re-examining the Johannine Trinity," 409.
16. Ibid., 410–11. To correct, proper Latin is *summum bonum*.
17. Again, the believer does not participate directly in the trinitarian or christological *perichoresis*, but a third type, the perichoretic relationship of Christ and the believer.

THE PATRISTIC PERIOD

The Patristic Framework

This section examines the doctrines of the deification and perichoretic union during the patristic era. Because the patristic era spans several centuries, three continents, and two primary languages, complete uniformity in doctrine and practice is impossible. Given such diversity, a universal framework existed upon which all in the orthodox faith could agree: the tradition the apostles passed on to their successors, in both oral and written form. John Behr notes that the model of soteriology the fathers derived from the Scriptures is one of "healing and salvation through sharing, solidarity, and exchange."[18]

In addition, the fathers placed great importance on baptism and the Eucharist. Baptism was the mode of initiation into the Body of Christ.[19] Also, some fathers believed the body and blood of Jesus were present in the communion meal.[20] Whenever Christians ate the bread and drank the wine, they were ingesting Christ and becoming one with him. The fathers' views on Scripture, tradition, and the sacraments are important for understanding their approach to *theosis*.

The Ante-Nicene Fathers

Ignatius of Antioch is the first post-apostolic writer to speak of union with Christ. J. N. D. Kelly writes, "For Ignatius, with his intense Christ-mysticism, the essence of salvation seems to consist in union with Christ, through whom new life and immortality flow into us."[21] According to Ignatius, Christians "participate in him."[22] He calls Jesus "our inseparable life" and "our true life."[23] Ignatius does continue at least some of Paul's concept of union, whether or not he writes about all of it in his letters.[24]

---

18. Behr, *Way to Nicaea*, 75.

19. For examples of union in baptism, see Tertullian, *On Baptism* 8 (*ANF* 3:672–73); Gregory of Nazianzus, *Oration on Holy Baptism* 3–4 (*NPNF2* 7:360); and Cyril of Jerusalem, *Catechetical Lecture 20* 3–4 (*NPNF2* 7:147).

20. For evidence, see Justin Martyr, *First Apology* 66 (*ANF* 1:185); Irenaeus, *Against Heresies* 5.2.2–3 (*ANF* 1:528); and Basil of Caesarea, *Letter* 93 (*NPNF2* 8:179).

21. Kelly, *Early Christian Doctrines*, 164.

22. Ignatius, *Epistle to the Ephesians* 4.2 (*ANF* 1:51).

23. See ibid., 3.2 (*ANF* 1:50); and Ignatius, *Epistle to the Smyrnaeans* 3.2 (*ANF* 1:87), respectively.

24. Schweitzer (*Mysticism of Paul the Apostle*, 341), accuses Ignatius of limiting the

Justin Martyr, in the next generation, quotes and interprets Psalm 82:6 in *Dialogue with Trypho,* the passage that would later become a proof text for *theosis*.[25]

Irenaeus, Bishop of Lyons, is the first Christian writer to develop a theology of *theosis*, though it would take several centuries to tease out its full meaning.[26] He writes, "In the New Testament faith has been enhanced by the incarnation of the Son of God, so that man might have a share in the deity."[27] He adds, "The Word of God, our Lord Jesus Christ, who did, through his transcendent love, become what we are, that he might bring us to be even what he is himself."[28] Later in book 5 of *Against Heresies,* Irenaeus lays out his doctrine of salvation:

> So then, since the Lord redeemed us by his own blood, and gave his soul for our souls, and his flesh for our bodies, and poured out the Spirit of the Father to bring about the union and communion of God and man—bringing God down to men by the working of the Spirit, and again raising man to God by his incarnation—and by his coming firmly and truly giving us incorruption, by our communion with God, all the teachings of the heretics are destroyed.[29]

Irenaeus adds,

> The Lord thus has redeemed us through his own blood, giving his soul for our souls, and his flesh for our flesh, and has also poured out the Spirit of the Father for the union and communion of God and man, imparting indeed God to men by means of the Spirit, and on the other hand, attaching man to God by his own Incarnation, and bestowing upon us at his coming immortality durably and truly, by means of communion with God.[30]

Christ-mysticism of the Apostle Paul, because Ignatius never argues from the standpoint that believers "have already died and risen again in Christ." While Ignatius does not use the popular Pauline phrase "in Christ," nor does he continue Paul's notion of explicit participatory union, Schweitzer's critique of Ignatius may be somewhat premature. Ignatius is not writing doctrinal treatises, but letters of encouragement, and doing so in the face of martyrdom. See also Russell, *Doctrine of Deification,* 92.

25. Russell, *Doctrine of Deification,* 99, quoting Justin Martyr, *Dialogue with Trypho* 124 (*ANF* 1: 262). For more on the interpretive history of Psalm 82, see Mosser, "Earliest Patristic Interpretations," and Nispel, "Christian Deification."

26. McGuckin, "Strategic Adaptation of Deification," 96.

27. Irenaeus, *Against Heresies* 4.28.1 (*ANF* 1:501).

28. Ibid., 5, pref. (*ANF* 1:526).

29. Ibid., 5.1.2 (*ANF* 1:527).

30. Ibid., 5:1:1 (*ANF* 1:527).

It is clear from *Against Heresies* that Irenaeus sees the believer's union with God through Christ as a central fact of the Christian faith. One also sees the personal way he approaches participation in God. He concludes his thoughts on the deification of humanity by stating, "The Word of salvation became very man like him who perished, making possible through himself our organic union with him."[31] Commenting on the logical progression of Irenaeus's thinking, Norman Russell writes, "The incarnation is an essential prerequisite for our journey to God, for we need to be mingled with the Logos through the adoption of baptism in order to participate in immortality and incorruption. These attributes belong to God alone; we can only participate in them if God first unites himself to the human race through the incarnation of the Logos."[32] Irenaeus sets the stage for discussing *theosis* terminology for all who come after him.[33]

Origen was able to utilize the foundation Irenaeus laid for *theosis* and place it within the context of the incarnation, which allowed for the elevation of humanity to communion with God.[34] For instance, speaking against Celsus, Origen proclaims, "They see that from him there began the union of the divine with the human nature, in order that the human, by communion with the divine, might rise to be divine."[35] Origen, utilizing as his first principles the Father, Son, and Holy Spirit, teaches that union with the Son is simultaneously union with the entire Godhead:

> As now by participation in the Son of God one is adopted as a son, and by participating in that wisdom which is in God is rendered wise, so also by participation in the Holy Spirit is a man rendered holy and spiritual. For it is one and the same thing to

---

31. Ibid., 5.14.2 (*ANF* 1:541).

32. Russell, *Doctrine of Deification*, 106.

33. For more on Irenaeus and his views of deification, see Schmelling, *Life in Christ*, 120–21; Vishnevskaya, "*Perichoresis* in the Context of Divinization," 63–66; Maloney, *Undreamed Has Happened*, 81–87; Mersch, *Whole Christ*, 227–47; and Kruger, "Irenaeus' Vision of the Incarnation," June 10, 2009, http://baxterkruger.blogspot.com.

34. McGuckin, "Strategic Adaptation," 97. Chronologically, between Irenaeus and Origen lay Clement and Hippolytus. For more on them and their development of the doctrine of deification, see Russell, *Doctrine of Deification*, 112; Vishnevskaya, "*Perichoresis*," 66–69; Maloney, *Undreamed Has Happened*, 87–90; Mersch, *Whole Christ*, 248–62; and Ritschl, "Hippolytus' Conception of Deification," 392.

35. Origen, *Against Celsus* 3:28 (*ANF* 4:475). Origen attaches right ethical behavior as a qualification immediately following this quote. The point is that he is continuing the type of language Irenaeus used.

have a share in the Holy Spirit, which is (the Spirit) of the Father and the Son, since the nature of the Trinity is one and incorporeal. And what we have said regarding the participation of the soul is to be understood of angels and of heavenly powers in a similar way as of souls, because every rational creature needs a participation in the Trinity.[36]

Origen was extremely influential in helping to develop the ideas of union with Christ and deification. Nathan Ng writes that Origen "views the Son as the Logos of the Father through whom rational creatures may participate in the Trinity."[37] Norman Russell says Origen's idea of participation is "living with the life of God."[38] He continues, "Indeed Origen's doctrine may be said to be the re-expression in metaphysical terms of the Pauline metaphors of participatory union with Christ."[39] Finally, Origen sees the Christian's union with the Godhead as something that has its full occurrence in the eschaton, since at that time the "contemplation of God will be their only activity."[40] His grounding of union with Christ through *theosis* in the incarnation and union with Christ implying union with the entire Godhead are two important contributions to Christian thought.[41]

Eastern Theosis in the Fourth and Fifth Centuries

Athanasius of Alexandria is known in church history as the great adversary of the Arians, and he utilizes the language of deification to fight them. The quotation for which he is (in)famous is, "God became man so that man might become God."[42] He certainly did not mean that humans become ontologically God. Instead, Athanasius interprets redemption

---

36. Origen, *On First Principles* 4.1.32 (ANF 4:379).
37. Ng, "Reconsideration of the Use of the Term 'Deification,'" 36.
38. Russell, *Doctrine of Deification*, 154.
39. Ibid.
40. Origen, *Commentary on the Gospel according to John*, 52.
41. For more on Origen and *theosis*, see Vishnevskaya, "Perichoresis," 69–74; and Maloney, *Undreamed Has Happened*, 90–94.
42. Athanasius, *On the Incarnation* 54, in Hardy, *Christology of the Later Fathers*, 107. Athanasius's *On the Incarnation* came early in his career. The fight for Nicene orthodoxy came afterward. He was able to utilize the ideas of *On the Incarnation* to argue for the deity of Christ. In other words, he moves from salvation to the Trinity, instead of the other way around. Athanasius argues that deification is impossible if Christ is not deity. See also Gross, *Divinization of the Christian*, 163.

as a restoration of the God-like qualities Adam lost in the fall; therefore *theosis* is the process of recovery of those qualities.[43] Like Irenaeus, he sees the incarnation as the catalyst for *theosis*. Athanasius writes, "The Word became flesh, that he might make man capable of Godhead."[44] He adds, "For as the Lord, putting on the body, became man, so we men are deified by the Word as being taken to him through his flesh, and henceforward inherit life everlasting."[45] Athanasius spoke of union with Christ as incorporation as well. He writes concerning Christ, "His flesh before all others was saved and liberated, as being the Word's body; and henceforth we, becoming incorporate with it, are saved after its pattern."[46] He adds some language reminiscent of Paul as he states, "For so he is founded for our sakes, taking on him what is ours, that we, as incorporated and compacted and bound together in him through the likeness of the flesh, may attain unto a perfect man, and abide immortal and incorruptible."[47] Also, "We shall be capable of a life not temporary, but ever afterwards abide and live in Christ; since even before this our life had been founded and prepared in Christ Jesus."[48] Athanasius is able to take the seeds Irenaeus provided and grow them into more mature thoughts.

The Cappadocian fathers were successors to both Origen and Athanasius.[49] They further developed *theosis* language as the way to understand the believer's union with Christ. Showing less constraint against using non-biblical terminology than his Cappadocian counterparts, Gregory of Nazianzus uses the term *theosis* more than Basil and Gregory of Nyssa.[50] He modified Athanasius's famous saying to "In order that I

43. Gross, *Divinization of the Christian*, 165.
44. Athanasius, *Against the Arians* 2.59 (*NPNF2* 4:380).
45. Ibid., 3.34 (*NPNF2* 4:413).
46. Ibid., 2.61 (*NPNF2* 4:381).
47. Ibid., 2.74 (*NPNF2* 4:389).
48. Ibid., 2.76 (*NPNF2* 4:390). For more on Athanasius and deification, see Schmelling, "Life in Christ," 121–22; Vishnevskaya, "*Perichoresis*," 74–85; Maloney, *Undreamed Has Happened*, 97–100; and Mersch, *Whole Christ*, 263–87.
49. McGuckin, "Strategic Adaptation," 109. He writes, "The Cappadocians were collectively taken by [*theosis*], led there in no small part by Gregory of Nazianzus' enthusiastic reading of Origen, and his equal determination to take Athanasian theology as a standard on which to build the neo-Nicene settlement in the late fourth century."
50. Alfeyev, "Deification of Man," 111. McGuckin notes, Gregory often pushed the envelope of language (and enjoyed doing so) so far that others (Gregory of Nyssa and

may become God so far as he has become man."[51] Gregory believed, "By becoming like the incarnate Son through the sacraments and the practice of 'philosophy,' human beings can eventually transcend their earthly limitations, with the result that they are transformed by 'mingling'—one of Gregory's favorite expressions—with the divine light."[52] For Gregory, true philosophy is the life lived with God, a life made possible by his union with God in Christ through *theosis*.

The contributions Gregory of Nyssa makes to *theosis* stem from his belief that the created order is good, even after the fall.[53] His view of the inherent goodness of the current world combined with his emphasis on humanity as created in the image of God led him to believe that *theosis* is the true destiny of all creation rather than merely the redemption and "retrieval of a fallen spiritual universe."[54] Because Christ came in the flesh, he is able bring all humanity into the process of *theosis*,[55] which unfortunately leads to a doctrine of universal salvation. Growth in union with God through Christ occurs when the soul reaches a state of freedom from passion, a sign that the divine image has been fully restored in a person's life.[56] Lewis Ayres argues that the theme of participation in the life of God and of human life itself as a mode of that participation is "the heart of Gregory's account of the soul's transformation and the perfected life."[57] H. E. W. Turner writes concerning Gregory, "The deification of the soul is achieved through baptism, that of the body through the Eucharist."[58] Following in the Greek tradition, Gregory emphasizes

---

Maximus the Confessor notably) felt the need to go back and comment on what he "must have meant" (102).

51. Gregory of Nazianzus, *Third Theological Oration* 19.9–10, in Hardy, *Christology of the Later Fathers*, 173.

52. Russell, *Doctrine of Deification*, 214. This study would reject the necessity of participation in the sacraments and the attainment of salvation via ethical behavior. The point of the quote for this study is the idea of "mingling," which points toward the mingling of the two natures in Christ—a perichoretic idea.

53. Hudson, *Becoming God*, 15.

54. Ibid.

55. Burns, "Economy of Salvation," 224–25, 229.

56. Ibid., 230–31.

57. Ayres, "Deification and Dynamics," 385.

58. Turner, *Patristic Doctrine of Redemption*, 93–94. This quotation is included to show Gregory's views on *theosis*. This author does not agree that the physical acts of baptism and Eucharist are the cause of *theosis*. They are certainly symbols of what *theosis* represents, but not the cause.

that union with Christ results due to the incarnation and humankind's identification with the Son of Man. He does not emphasize being united to Christ by faith as much as he does by common humanity. Finally, Gregory's teaches that *theosis* is a process that lasts eternally.[59]

Following in the traditions of his forebears Origen and Athanasius, Cyril of Alexandria gives *theosis* a more mature expression. Norman Russell explains how Cyril understands *theosis*: "The deification of the believer is correlative to the incarnation of the Word, the working out in the individual of the descending and ascending pattern of salvation.... Like Athanasius, Cyril sees in Christ a paradigmatic transformation of the flesh, the promotion of our nature in principle through union with the Word from corruption to incorruption, from human inadequacy to the dignity of deity."[60] He requires the divine life in the incarnation to be present in order that human life may be exalted to deification.[61] Cyril writes,

> The communion and abiding presence of the Spirit has passed even to ourselves. This was experienced first through Christ and in Christ when he was seen to have become like us, that is, a human being anointed and sanctified. By nature however, he was God, for he proceeded from the Father. It was with his own Spirit that he sanctified the temple of his body and also, in a way befitting it, the world of his creation. Through the mystery of Christ, then, sharing in the Holy Spirit and union with God has become possible also for us, for we are all sanctified in him.[62]

Cyril utilized participation language as well. Norman Russell writes, "Cyril's perspective is profoundly Pauline as well as Johannine. We share in the life of Christ because Christ is 'in us' and we are 'in Christ.' Christ emptied himself to accommodate our human nature and by his subsequent exaltation we are exalted too."[63] Cyril builds on a tradition that Irenaeus planted and Athanasius watered.[64] While their ideas are not

59. Hudson, *Becoming God*, 24–26. For more on the Cappadocians' concept of deification, see Schmelling, "Life in Christ," 122–23; Vishnevskaya, "*Perichoresis*," 90–123; Mersch, *Whole Christ*, 307–22; and Maloney, *Undreamed Has Happened*, 100–9.

60. Russell, *Cyril of Alexandria*, 21.

61. Ibid., 45.

62. Cyril of Alexandria, *Commentary on the Gospel of John* 11.11, in Elowsky, *Ancient Christian Commentary on Scripture*, 4b:257.

63. Russell, *Deification*, 197.

64. For more on Cyril and deification, see Schmelling, "Life in Christ," 126–28;

identical to the third type of *perichoresis* advocated in this study, there are a number of important common elements, including the participation in Christ and the mutual indwelling of Christ and the believer.

Western Deification in the Fourth and Fifth Centuries

Theologians in the West during the fourth and fifth centuries had less to say about union with Christ than their Eastern counterparts, though Ambrose, Hilary, and Augustine were the leading voices.[65] Augustine taught the doctrines of union and deification, though not as widely as some of his Eastern counterparts. Augustine bases deification on the incarnation, since Christ as both God and man is the mediator between them.[66] Augustine writes, "The teacher of humility and sharer of our infirmity, giving us participation of his divinity, coming down that he might both teach and be the way, has deigned most highly to commend his humility to us."[67] Elsewhere, Augustine almost quotes verbatim the famous *theosis* statement of Athanasius.[68]

Again, he writes, "Putting away lying, therefore, speak truth, so that this mortal flesh which you have up to now from Adam may, after the reformation of the spirit, itself deserve renewal and transformation in

---

Vishnevskaya, "*Perichoresis*," 123–34; Mersch, *Whole Christ*, 337–64; and Maloney, *Undreamed Has Happened*, 111–17. For a slightly earlier contemporary of Cyril, see John Chrysostom, *Homily 5 on the Epistles of Paul to the Corinthians* (*NPNF1* 12:24). John writes, "God did not just make us wise, righteous, and holy in Christ. He gave us Christ so that we should never need anything else for our salvation."

65. Ambrose, *On the Christian Faith* 4.3.36–38 (*NPNF2* 10:266–67), writes on the nature of the union of the believer and Christ while commenting on John 17:21. He states, "Union is of grace, rather than nature, between Christ and his disciples. The union between Christ and the Father is one of nature." Commenting on the same passage, Hilary of Poitiers (*On the Trinity* 8.5 [*NPNF2* 9:139]) states, "This passage shows that since human beings cannot, so to speak, be fused back into God or themselves coalesce into one undistinguished mass, this oneness must arise from unity of will, as all perform actions pleasing to God and unite with one another in the harmonious agreement of their thoughts. Therefore it is not nature that makes them one, but will." See also Jerome, *Against Jovinianus* 2:19 (*NPNF2* 6:403). Commenting on John 17:21, he writes, "'As we are Father, Son, and Holy Spirit, one God,' [as Jesus might say], 'so may they be one people in themselves, that is, like dear children and partakers of the divine nature.'"

66. Bonner, "Augustine's Conception of Deification," 372.

67. Augustine, "Sermon on Psalm 58." This quotation is Bonner's translation from the original Latin, which appears in *CCSL* 39:734.

68. Augustine, "Sermon 192.1.1," in Rotelle, *Sermons III/6*, 46. That is, "God became man in order that man might become God."

the time of its resurrection; and thus the whole man, being deified, may cleave to the perpetual and unchanging truth."[69] To Augustine, deification, the participation in the divine life of Christ, belongs in the realm of dogmatic rather than speculative theology because "it describes the consequence of the saving work of Christ rather than a mystical state enjoyed by a contemplative."[70]

While Augustine uses *theosis* language, he certainly does not imply that humans attain complete Godhood. He states, "If we have been made Sons of God, we have also been made gods; but this is the effect of grace adopting, not of nature generating. For only the Son of God is God."[71] Russell discusses Augustine's view on participation in God: "Augustine frequently refers to the concept of participation to convey the relationship between the contingent and the self-existent. Thus the ability not to sin is a participated divine quality, a gift dependent on God, not a natural human attribute."[72] Finally, Russell sums up Augustine's view of union with Christ by participation: "'Participation in the divine is for Augustine the heart of redemption.' But such participation is qualified. We cannot be the same as God, even if we can become one with his flesh through the sacraments. 'The creature will never become equal with God even if perfect holiness were to be achieved in us. Some think that in the next life we shall be changed into what he is. I am not convinced.'"[73] Thus Augustine is significantly more guarded in his conception of deification and union than his Eastern counterparts. Given Augustine's influence over Western theology, both Catholic and Protestant, it is easy to see why deification language did not take root as easily in the West as in the East.

Late Patristic Developments

As the patristic era draws to a close, Maximus the Confessor and John of Damascus add to both the doctrines of union with Christ and *theosis*. Although Maximus draws upon the language of both Irenaeus and

---

69. Augustine, "Sermon 166.4.4," in Rotelle, *Sermons III/5*, 210.

70. Ibid., 382.

71. Augustine, "Sermon on Psalm 49" in Russell, *Doctrine of Deification*, 331. He modifies the translation from *The Nicene and Post-Nicene Fathers*.

72. Russell, *Doctrine of Deification*, 332.

73. Ibid. The quotation beginning this citation is via a personal correspondence from Henry Chadwick to Russell. The quote ending the citation is Chadwick's translation of Augustine, *On Nature and Grace* 33.37. For more on Augustine and deification, see Mersch, *Whole Christ*, 384–440, and Schmelling, "Life in Christ," 27, 123–26.

Athanasius when formulating his ideas of *theosis*, he is the first Christian author to explicitly utilize the concept of *perichoresis* as a soteriological concept.[74] Following Gregory of Nazianzus, Maximus uses *perichoresis* to describe the hypostatic union, which he then applies to the union between Christ and the believer. Since in Christ the human and divine natures are perichoretically joined, the assumption of human nature by the Logos allows the christological *perichoresis* to be extended to other humans. This can occur because the perichoretic union in Christ forms a "theandric" energy that is transferable to the Christian.[75] Elena Vishnevskaya writes,

> Maximus's idea of *perichoresis* of Creator and creature confirms that these are relational terms, and each is understood better in the context of the other. The mutual partaking of the other bears witness to, on the one hand, a God who, through the incarnation, is fully invested in the human being, the recipient of the abundance of divine grace, and, on the other, the believer, who is free by nature, to orient his or her being toward God and become like him in divinization. Hence Maximus celebrates the supra-logical reciprocal interpenetration of the ontologically polar.[76]

That is, the idea that the Creator and creation (the "ontologically polar" of the eternal Christ and the created believer) would indwell each other ("reciprocal interpenetration") is beyond anything logically deducible in the human mind.

She goes on to quote Maximus: "It is in this blessed and most holy embrace that is accomplished this awesome mystery of a union transcending mind and reason by which God becomes one flesh and one spirit with the Church and thus with the soul, and the soul with God."[77] Summing up the difficulty in a perichoretic relationship between Christ and the believer, Hans Urs von Balthasar notes the "most decisive contradictions" in such a relationship yet writes, "Because it cannot be self-contradictory, however, these contradictions must be both preserved and overcome within it. . . . Thus the mutual indwelling of natures . . . be-

---

74. Alfeyev, "Deification of Man," 114.

75. Vishnevskaya, "*Perichoresis*," 214. "Theandric" is a combination of the Greek words for "God" and "man." It does not refer to a new energy, but the result of the union of the divine and human energies, though they remain distinct. This extends to the wills also, which is why Maximus was so opposed to monotheletism.

76. Ibid., 220.

77. Maximus the Confessor, *Mystigogia* 5, in *Maximus the Confessor*, 194. This quotation is found in Vishnevskaya, "Divinization as Perichoretic Embrace," 134.

comes an ontological unity of the highest order and accomplishes both a transformation and an assimilation of its two components."[78] Maximus builds on shared love as the basis of the perichoretic relationship, echoing both John 13 and 15.[79] In doing so, he is the first Christian thinker to use explicit *perichoresis* language to describe the soteriological union. Yet Maximus was no innovator. He is utilizing the existing language to show the intensity of the relationship between Christ and the believer.

John of Damascus, in the words of Bishop Alfeyev, harmonizes and systematizes *theosis*.[80] He pays particular attention to the "sacramental and eschatological dimensions of deification."[81] He writes, "For since [Christ] bestowed on us his own image and his own spirit and we did not keep them safe, he took himself a share in our poor and weak nature, in order that he might cleanse us and make us incorruptible, and establish us once more as partakers of his divinity."[82] This quotation lies in John's exposition of the Lord's Table, again a common theme. Also, John does not follow explicitly the thinking of Maximus in calling the union between Christ and the believer a perichoretic one, possibly because for John *perichoresis* represented stability. Instead, participation was the way he described the union of the believer and Christ, though it does seem possible that he may have affirmed the union as a third type of *perichoresis* given the opportunity to do so.[83]

Summary of Patristic Teaching

This section has summarized the patristic teaching of the perichoretic union of Christ and the believer largely through its connection with *theosis*.[84] The perichoretic language of indwelling and participation was

---

78. Von Balthasar, *Cosmic Liturgy*, 258–59, quoted in Vishnevskaya, "*Perichoresis*," 224. Here "ontological" is probably not the best choice of words because it may be confused with the trinitarian *perichoresis*. There is always a danger of equivocation with such a term. What von Balthasar is trying to convey is that the soteriological union is more than symbolic; it is real. In that sense, "ontological" may be the only word to use.

79. Vishnevskaya, "*Perichoresis*," 227–28. Maximus sees the perichoretic relationship in the sacraments of the church as well (ibid., 236–39).

80. Alfeyev, "Deification of Man," 114. McGuckin ("Strategic Adaptation," 98) agrees, noting that John reads the work of Maximus through the lens of Gregory of Nazianzus.

81. Russell, *Deification*, 299.

82. John of Damascus, *Exposition of the Orthodox Faith* 4.13 (*NPNF2* 9:82).

83. Twombly, "*Perichoresis* and Personhood," 164. Twombly sees *perichoresis* and participation in John's thought as strongly analogical, yet distinct (172–73).

84. For more on the later development of *theosis* in Eastern Orthodoxy, see

present long before Maximus articulated it, going back as far as Irenaeus. Nonetheless, the purpose has been to set the stage for both *theosis* and perichoretic union language throughout the Christian era.

THE MEDIEVAL AND REFORMATION PERIODS

The Medieval Period

In the years between the fathers and the Reformation, little advance was made in the doctrines of union and *theosis* among the noteworthy Catholic theologians.[85] Mysticism flourished during this period, however, in the teachings and poetry of those who sought union with God in experience.[86] Often these "mystics" were not in the theological mainstream. A notable exception is Bernard of Clairvaux. His influence has been felt centuries after his lifetime. Some believe he was a serious influence on both Martin Luther and John Calvin generations later.[87]

The preeminent theologian of the medieval era, Thomas Aquinas, continued the patristic doctrine of deification, although he mentions less concerning it than did the fathers. He writes, "It is therefore impossible for any creature to be a cause of grace. Hence it is just as inevitable that God alone should deify, by communicating a sharing of the divine nature through a participation of likeness."[88] Greear makes the case that Aquinas identifies union with God as the goal of salvation.[89] Daniel Keating writes, "Thomas' doctrine of grace is, in fact, a doctrine of divinization whereby God deifies the soul by granting to it (through

---

Mantzaridis, *Deification of Man*.

85. A recent article (Kerr, "*Theoria* and the Doctrinal Language of Perfection") argues that Anselm of Canterbury teaches a form of *theosis* in his *Proslogion*.

86. This study omits the medieval "mystics" purposefully. Notable mystics of this period include Julian of Norwich, Meister Eckhart, John Tauler, Nicholas of Cusa, and Hildegard of Bingen, just to name a few. For reference to the mystics, see Brunn and Burgard, *Women Mystics*; Bullett, *English Mystics*; Szarmach, *Introduction to the Medieval Mystics*; and Windeat, *English Mystics*.

87. See Posset, *Pater Bernhardus, Martin Luther and Bernard of Clairvaux*, and Tamburello, *Union with Christ*. For more on his theology, see Gilson, *Mystical Theology of St. Bernard*, 126. Though Bernard is often labeled a "mystic," Akin ("Bernard of Clairvaux," 219) believes that Bernard's ideas of the believer's union with Christ are essentially evangelical in content.

88. Aquinas, "Summa Theologica 112.1," in Fairweather, *Nature and Grace*, 175.

89. Greear, "*Theosis* and Muslim Evangelism," 90.

Christ) a participation in his very nature,"[90] and, "Aquinas underlines our direct and ongoing participation in the very life of God as the source of all transformation and growth into the image of Christ."[91] While Aquinas upheld the patristic ideas of *theosis* and union, he did not make any significant additions to the doctrine. While the Reformation leaders below likewise add little doctrinally to the teachings of the fathers, they provide an important link to the contemporary discussion on the perichoretic union of the believer and Christ.[92]

Luther, His Followers, and Interpreters

Among Martin Luther's many notable theological contributions was a continuation of the doctrine of union with Christ.[93] Many of his thoughts are found in his 1520 work *The Freedom of a Christian*. The following paragraph of Luther's sums up well his idea that the union between Christ and the believer is like a marriage:

> The third incomparable benefit of faith is that it unites the soul with Christ as a bride is united with her bridegroom. By this mystery, as the Apostle teaches, Christ and the soul become one flesh (Eph 5:31–32). And if they are one flesh and there is between them a true marriage—indeed the most perfect of all marriages, since human marriages are but poor examples of this one true marriage—it follows that everything they have they hold in common, the good as well as the evil. Accordingly the believing soul can boast of and glory in whatever Christ has as though it were his own, and whatever the soul has Christ claims as his own. Let us compare these and we shall see inestimable benefits. Christ is full of grace, life, and salvation. The soul is full of sins, death, and damnation. Now let faith come between them and sins, death, and damnation will be Christ's, while grace, life, and salvation will be the soul's; for if Christ is a bridegroom, he must take upon himself the things which are his bride's and bestow upon her the things that are his. If he gives her his body and very self, how shall he not give her all that is his? And if he takes the body of the bride, how shall he not take all that is hers?[94]

90. Keating, "Justification, Sanctification, and Divinization," 154.

91. Ibid.

92. For more on the medieval period and the "mystical body" of Christ, see Mersch, *Whole Christ*, 441–530.

93. For some of the influences on the background of Luther's thought, see Johnson, "Luther and Calvin," 61–62, and Garcia, *Life in Christ*, 56–68.

94. Luther, "Freedom of a Christian," 603.

In other words, in his union with the believer, Christ takes everything the believer has upon himself. In turn, he gives to the believer everything he has. This sharing is possible because they mutually indwell and actively participate in the other as was demonstrated in chapter 2 above, which argues for the relationship as a third type of *perichoresis*. In chapter 4 below, it will be shown that the biblical analogy of marriage is one of the ways the perichoretic relationship between Christ and the believer is described.

Luther is rightly famous for his treatment of justification, which he grounds in the doctrine of union.[95] Bruce Marshall writes, "Luther sometimes speaks of participation in the divine nature in order to characterize God's gift of righteousness and eternal life to us in Christ."[96] Luther explicitly makes justification dependent on union with Christ, even further reaffirming the Pauline teaching that justification is Christ himself.[97] Luther himself writes concerning justification, "Christ and I must be entirely conjoined, and united together, so that he may live in me, and I in him. And this is a wonderful manner of speech. Because Christ liveth in me, look now what grace, righteousness, life, peace, and salvation is in me, it is his, and yet it is mine also, by that inseparable union and conjunction which is through faith, by the which Christ and I are made as it were one body in spirit."[98] Luther sees the soteriological union as possessing the same elements as those relationships which have historically been labeled perichoretic.[99]

---

95. Martin Luther, *Lectures on Galatians 1535*, in Pelikan, *LW*, 26:168. Concerning Paul's words in Galatians 2:20, which reverberate between living and not living, dying and not dying, sinning and not sinning, and so forth, Luther writes, "But this phraseology is true in Christ and through Christ. When it comes to justification, therefore, if you divide Christ's person from your own, you are in the Law; you remain in it and live in yourself, which means that you are dead in the sight of God and damned by the Law." He continues, "But faith must be taught correctly, namely, that by it you are so cemented to Christ that He and you are as one person, which cannot be separated but remains attached to Him forever and declares: 'I am in Christ.'" These quotations show that union is the basis for justification in Luther's thought. See also Vickers, *Jesus' Blood and Righteousness*, 27.

96. Marshall, "Justification as Declaration and Deification," 9.

97. Ibid.

98. Luther, *Commentary on Galatians*, 89.

99. See the quote from Luther in Schmelling, "Life in Christ," 28–29, concerning the hypostatic union and the believer's union with Christ together. The quote is taken from Luther's commentary on Psalms, but is given without specific reference.

The Lutheran Church continued the emphasis on what this study is calling perichoretic union both in Europe and America.[100] Timothy Schmelling presents some excellent original sources as he quotes Lutheran Abraham Calov, "The form (of the mystical union) is a union (*conjunctio*) with God, not relative but true, not purely extrinsic but intrinsic, not through a bare positioning but through an intimate emanation, not only the operation of grace alone but likewise of a divine substance caused by an approximation to faith with a mystical περιχωρήσις, nearer to a commixture or an essential transformation of man."[101] Schmelling comments on Calov's strong language thus:

> Abraham Calov is only trying to explain how real, true, and intimate this union actually is. . . . In reality, Abraham Calov is borrowing a Greek christological term (περιχωρήσις) used by Luther to explain the sacramental union and even the mystical union via his "one cake" analogy. The purpose of the term was to indicate that Holy Communion is a real union and that the substance of bread, body, wine, and blood still remain even in the sacramental union. Martin Luther also uses the concept of περιχωρήσις to describe the mystical union as one loaf.[102]

Calov is an example of the struggle to find a word deep enough to convey the essentials of the soteriological union. Thus many of the ideas relating to perichoretic union have been a part of Lutheran teaching from the beginning.

There has been a great deal of recent debate concerning Luther's views on union and how the Christian should appropriate it in the understanding of the benefits of salvation. As Mark Seifried notes, those who believe Pauline theology to be more participatory than forensic elevate the doctrine of union.[103] This elevation has been heightened due to the

---

100. For numerous European Lutheran examples, including Melanchthon and Chemnitz, see Schmelling, "Life in Christ," 28–29, 68–71, and 81–86. For an American Lutheran example, see Harkey, *Justification by Faith*, 193. Here Harkey emphasizes the nature of participation in the divine life as the explanation of union.

101. Calov, *Theologia Postiva*, 1.c.8.3, 503. This is quoted in Schmelling, "Life in Christ," 29.

102. Schmelling, "Life in Christ," 30. For the one cake analogy, see Saarinen, "Presence of God," 7–8. For the one loaf analogy, see Luther, *Sämmtlichte Schriften*, 11:616. See also Hoenecke, *Dogmatik*, 3:410 for the use of "interpenetration" to describe mystical union. All of the sources in this note are cited by Schmelling, "Life in Christ," 30.

103. Seifrid, "Paul, Luther, and Justification," 215. Seifrid claims that the either/or

1998 publication of *Union with Christ: The New Finnish Interpretation of Luther*. The book consists of a collection of essays written by a number of Finnish Lutheran scholars from the University of Helsinki, which grew out of Lutheran-Russian Orthodox ecumenical dialogue begun in the 1970s attempting to find common ground between the two ecclesiastical bodies.[104] They found this common ground in Luther's view of union and the Orthodox doctrine of deification, or *theosis*.

The theses of the Finnish essays are that Luther actually held a doctrine of *theosis* highly compatible to Eastern Orthodoxy. As Tuomo Mannermaa writes, "At the very beginning of our studies we came to the conclusion that Luther's idea of the presence of Christ in faith could form a basis for the Lutheran-Orthodox dialogue. The indwelling of Christ as grasped in the Lutheran tradition implies a real participation in God, and it corresponds in a special way to the Orthodox doctrine of participation in God, namely the doctrine of *theosis*."[105] From the works of Luther, the Finnish scholars stress that justifying faith is actual participating in God in Christ's person. This allows the "Happy Exchange" of the sinner's evil and the good gifts of God in Christ. As Mannermaa writes, "Because faith involves a real union with Christ and because Christ is the divine person, the believer does indeed participate in God."[106] Mannermaa ties together other Lutheran teachings with *theosis*, such as Luther's doctrine of the cross, love, Christ as favor and gift, and Christ as the form of faith.[107]

Although these scholars have done some important work in renewing interest in Luther's teaching on union with Christ and *theosis*, they are not without their critics. Carl Trueman attacks their thesis that the doctrine of union is central to Luther's soteriology. Trueman notes that there are different ways of understanding union, among them the marriage union, the legal union, and the ontological union.[108] He also criticizes them for emphasizing Luther's writings of the second decade of the

---

dichotomy between forensic and participatory understanding is due to a flaw in the understanding of Albert Schweitzer.

104. Mannermaa, "Why Is Luther So Fascinating?" 1.

105. Ibid., 2.

106. Mannermaa, "Justification and *Theosis*," 32.

107. Ibid., 33–41.

108. Trueman, "Is the Finnish Line a New Beginning?" 235. Schmelling does much the same with the different levels of union throughout his thesis. Another criticism is Metzger, "Mystical Union."

sixteenth century above his more mature later works.[109] He chides them for an "implausible distancing of Luther from the Lutheran confessional tradition" in that they try to drive a wedge between their conceptions of Luther and even the Augsburg Confession.[110] Schmelling notes that the Palamite essence-energies distinction required for the Russian Orthodox form of *theosis* cannot stand in Lutheranism.[111] While many of Trueman's criticisms have merit, they do not disprove that Luther held a view of the believer's union with Christ that resembles a third type of *perichoresis*, for which this investigation argues. The point here is that the Finnish scholars are correct in showing what Luther said in proper context.

To summarize the Lutheran teaching on the believer's union with Christ, David John Boehmer describes *perichoresis* as an appropriate description for the union of Christ and the believer:

> It is an appropriate term insofar as it implies an "ontologically real" presence of the person of Christ in the Christian, in his or her faith, in a paradoxical union of still separate entities. This understanding of Christ's presence, whereby he both preserves and does away with the "infinite qualitative difference" between God and human beings, allows the maintained use of the total sense of the Lutheran axiom *simil iustius et peccator*.[112]

109. Ibid., 236. While Trueman is correct that the Finns utilize many of Luther's early works, his criticism is not fully warranted. A cursory examination of references to pertinent *theosis* language in the Finnish works shows a great deal of footnotes from the *Lectures on Galatians* from 1535, as well as explicit *theosis* language in a sermon preached only four years prior to his death. Therefore, it is unfair to say the Finns rely only on the early Luther while ignoring his later work. Moreover, Schmelling ("Life in Christ," 81–82), no supporter of the Finnish interpreters, provides several quotes from post-1521 Luther that shows the *theosis* language still present.

110. Ibid., 243. For a response to Trueman, see Jenson, "Response."

111. Schmelling, "Life in Christ," 60–61. Schmelling notes that in Lutheranism, God's essence and attributes (energies) are equated, while Palamite Orthodoxy divides them. Since the Finns' reason for research is dialogue between the Lutheran Church in Finland and the Russian Orthodox, the essence-energies distinction is problematic in using a post-Palamas conception of *theosis* in reading Luther. On page 115, he writes, "The Finnish school under the leadership of Tuomo Mannermaa has brought to light many of Luther's *theosis* citations and has emphasized the continuum of Lutheran theology with the fathers. Unfortunately the Finns did not stop here."

112. Boehmer, "Kierkegaard and the 'Finnish' Luther," 108. "Ontologically real" here does not imply the trinitarian *perichoresis*, but, like the discussion of Maximus the Confessor above, Boehmer is reaching for a term that describes the depth of the union of Christ and the believer at its very foundation. It is what this study argues as a third

Calvin and His Interpreters

Like Martin Luther, John Calvin held a prominent place in his theology for the believer's union with Christ.[113] Like Luther, he taught a version of *theosis* that closely resembled patristic thinking and held a view of the soteriological union similar to that advocated in this study. These will be discussed below.

Whenever Calvin speaks of the believer's union with Christ, faith is usually the key ingredient.[114] For Calvin, election, faith, and union all work together. As Dennis Tamburello clarifies, "The Holy Spirit brings the elect, through the hearing of the gospel, to faith; in so doing, the Spirit engrafts them into Christ."[115] In describing the mystical union between Christ and the believer, Calvin writes,

> Therefore, that joining together of head and members, that indwelling of Christ in our hearts—in short, that mystical union—are accorded by us the highest degree of importance, so that Christ, having been made ours, makes us sharers with him in the gifts with which he has been endowed. We do not, therefore, contemplate him outside ourselves from afar in order that his righteousness may be imputed to us but because we put on Christ and are engrafted into his body—in short, because he deigns to make us one with him. For this reason, we glory that we have fellowship of righteousness with him.[116]

Earlier in the *Institutes*, he writes, "Christ is not outside us but dwells within us. Not only does he cleave to us by an indivisible bond

---

type of *perichoresis*.

113. The extent of Calvin's use of the theme of union with Christ has become a debate in modern Calvin scholarship. All Calvin scholars seem to agree that the theme of union is important. Others go further and try to insist that union is the organizing principle behind all of Calvin's theology. For a good look at both ideas, see the running debate between Johnson and Wenger in *JETS*. See Johnson, "New or Nuanced?"; Wenger, "New Perspective"; and Wenger, "Theological Spectacles."

114. Tamburello, *Union with Christ*, 85.

115. Ibid., 86. On pages 11–13, Tamburello provides an extremely helpful three-page appendix showing all of the references to the doctrine of union in the *Institutes* and other important writings of Calvin, sorted by the language Calvin uses to describe it. Calvin's most popular term for union is "engrafting," used a total of twenty times in the *Institutes* and thirteen times in the Commentaries. Other popular terminology include "communion," "fellowship," and "partakers of Christ." In all, Tamburello cites ninety-nine references to union in the *Institutes* alone.

116. Calvin, *Institutes* 3.11.10.

of fellowship, but with a wonderful communion, day by day, he grows more into one body with us, until he becomes completely one with us."[117] Calvin seems to affirm that a key component of the soteriological union is mutual indwelling.

Calvin connects the benefits of Christ with the existing union with Christ: "It is only when we obtain Christ himself, that we come to partake of Christ's benefits. He is, however, obtained, I affirm, not only when we believe that he was made an offering for us, but when he dwells in us—when he is one with us—when we are members of his flesh, when, in fine, we are incorporated with him (so to speak) into one life and substance."[118] Jim Purves notes that the doctrine of union is important to Calvin because Christ only works through those that are his own, that is, through the church he has united with himself.[119] Commenting on Calvin's theology, Kevin Kennedy writes, "I believe that the solution is in recognizing that, in Calvin's theology, all the elements of our salvation, all of the benefits of Christ's death, are actually embodied in Christ. Our union with Christ, therefore, is the actualizing event where we come to share in all that Christ possesses for us."[120]

W. Duncan Rankin, in analyzing Calvin's correspondence with Peter Martyr in 1555, notes Calvin holds three distinct nuances of the believer's union with Christ.[121] The first is the "incarnational union" (resulting from the hypostatic union) that Christ has with all humanity by virtue of God becoming flesh. The second is the "mystical union," which is a "definitive sacred ingrafting [sic] into the life of Jesus Christ by the action of the Holy Spirit upon faith."[122] The third, the "spiritual union," is the "progressive enjoyment of the Spirit and blessings of Christ's life that flow from mystic union."[123] The spiritual union depends upon the mystical union, which in turn depends on the incarnational union, which itself flows from the hypostatic union. It would seem that Calvin sees the mystical union as an indwelling, while the spiritual union is participatory. If so, both of the key elements of a perichoretic relationship outlined above are present here.

117. Calvin, *Institutes* 3.2.24.
118. Calvin, *Corinthians Vol. I*, 379.
119. Purves, *Triune God*, 87–89.
120. Kennedy, *Union with Christ*, 135.
121. See Rankin, "Calvin's Correspondence."
122. Ibid., 250.
123. Ibid.

Calvin also taught a version of *theosis* that was comparable to the fathers through the fifth century. J. Todd Billings makes the case that Calvin teaches a "doctrine" of deification that is highly qualified. First, the communication of attributes is only reserved for Christ, not for the believer.[124] Second, the language of deification is "hyperbolic," meaning that believers do not ontologically become God, but participate in his divine nature.[125] Third, Calvin does not have a fully developed doctrine of deification with all the intact terminology. Instead, his theology is replete with the themes that are common to *theosis*, such as union, participation, and adoption.[126] All of these qualifications must be kept in mind whenever one looks at Calvin and *theosis*.

Given these qualifications, Calvin can write, "We not only derive the strength and sap of the life which flows from Christ, but we also pass from our own nature into his."[127] In his *Commentary on John*, he writes, "We infer that we are one with the Son of God, not because he pours his substance into us, but because, by the power of the Spirit, he shares with us his life and all the blessings which he has received from the Father."[128] To summarize, Julie Canlis proclaims that Calvin's view of union is *theosis*.[129]

Perhaps even more surprising than his *theosis* language, Calvin uses language resembling that of *perichoresis* to describe the union of Christ and the believer. The quotation from Calvin's comment on John 17:21 above shows that he believes the divine perichoretic life is shared with all who believe.[130] Phil Butin notes that the christological *perichoresis* of the divine and human natures in the hypostatic union forms the basis for the complete restoration of the image of God in humanity.[131]

---

124. Billings, *Calvin, Participation, and the Gift*, 55.

125. Ibid. See also ibid., 60–61n162 for more clarification. Billings believes Calvin uses hyperbolic language for *theosis* in the same way that Irenaeus and Athanasius do. It may even be akin to the "asymptotic" language this study uses in chapter 1. For more on Calvin's rejection of the absorption of the human into the divine, see Van Buren, *Christ in Our Place*, 97–100.

126. Ibid. See also Hallonsten, "*Theosis* in Recent Research," 283, for the need to make a distinction between a full-blown *doctrine* of deification and the recognition of *themes* present within deification language.

127. Calvin, *Romans and Thessalonians*, 124.

128. Calvin, *John 17:21* (CR 75:387).

129. Canlis, "Calvin, Osiander and Participation," 181.

130. See Butin, *Revelation, Redemption, and Response*, 43.

131. Ibid., 68.

Butin continues, "The bond of Christ's relationship with God the Father is identical to the bond of the believer's relationship with God the Son, because in both cases that bond is God the Holy Spirit."[132] Calvin writes that the love with which God loves us "is none other than that which he loved his Son from the beginning. . . . It is an inestimable privilege of faith that we know that Christ was loved by the Father for our sake, that we might be made partakers of the same love and that forever."[133] Later Butin adds, "It would be difficult to overstate the importance of this interconnectedness of Christ and the church for the overall adequacy of Calvin's trinitarian understanding of the divine-human relationship. The trinitarian vision that might otherwise have been an abstract, isolated exercise in intellectual speculation reveals itself instead to be specific, corporeal, and tangible—precisely at the point of its understanding of the church."[134] Billings writes, "Relying upon interpretations of John and Paul as well as appropriations of Irenaeus and Augustine, Calvin teaches that the final end and goal for humanity is a trinitarian union of humanity with God."[135] Carl Mosser adds, "Calvin is keen to emphasize that all that Christ did was for our sake and all that he has is his only for him to give it to us. This includes the love of God the Father, the life and blessings of Christ, the Holy Spirit, and even his unity with the Father. Christ unites believers with himself in order that they may participate, as members of his body, in the inner life and love of the Trinity which he has eternally known."[136] Though Calvin never explicitly describes soteriological union as *perichoresis*, he does affirm many of the ideas that lead to and support such a description.

The Reformation through the Nineteenth Century

The three centuries following the Reformation were not as fruitful as the works of Luther and Calvin as far as union with Christ was concerned.[137] In fact, there was very little discussion of the believer's union with Christ

---

132. Ibid., 83. Butin may well need to qualify the "identical" bond, because the Spirit is connecting the creature with the Creator in the believer's union with Christ.

133. Calvin, *John 11–21*, 152. This is quoted in context in Mosser, "Greatest Possible Blessing," 47.

134. Butin, *Revelation, Redemption, and Response*, 99.

135. Billings, *Calvin, Participation, and the Gift*, 52.

136. Mosser, "Greatest Possible Blessing," 46.

137. For a few notable exceptions, see Jones, "Union with Christ"; Evans, *Imputation and Impartation*; Christensen, "John Wesley"; Gordon, *In Christ*.

in perichoretic terms from the Enlightenment through the first third of the twentieth century. Part of the reason that the doctrines of union, *theosis*, and the Trinity suffered during the period following the Reformation was the influence of Enlightenment rationalism. Deification was revived by Harnack, who thought it was proof of the Hellenization of Christianity, and his disciples.[138] The twentieth century would see a great revival of the doctrines dormant for several hundred years.

THE MODERN AND CONTEMPORARY PERIOD

Beyond his aforementioned revival of the doctrine of the Trinity, Karl Barth wrote directly on the believer's union with Christ,[139] opening the academic discussion of the soteriological union in the twentieth century.[140] This discussion has included both concepts of *theosis* and mysticism.[141] Charles Williams, an English poet and writer rather than an academic theologian, included some ideas that resemble the type of *perichoresis* for which this study argues. Although he often was speaking of "coinherence" in broader terminology than this study allows, he was one of the first English writers to use the concept outside of its trinitarian and christological contexts.[142] The remainder of this chapter will focus on the contributions pointing toward the perichoretic nature of the believer's union with Christ in the last seventy years.

---

138. Kharmalov, "*Theosis* in Patristic Thought," 158–59.

139. Barth, *Church Dogmatics* IV/3.2, 538–54. In this section, Barth states that the purpose of the Christian is to enter into union with Christ. This union begins with Christ but is reciprocally enjoyed by both Christ and the believer. He further states that Calvin's underlying principle for arranging the benefits of salvation is the believer's union with Christ on page 552.

140. This includes the monograph Smedes, *Union with Christ*, as well as academic papers such as Thieme, "Union with Christ"; and Terveen, "Union with Christ."

141. See Rakestraw, "Becoming Like God." Martin ("Mysticism," 806) writes, "Christian mysticism seeks to describe an experiential, direct, non-abstract, unmediated, loving knowing of God, a knowing or seeing so direct as to be called union with God." On mysticism in evangelical circles, see Corduan, *Mysticism*.

142. For more on Williams, see his writings, *He Came Down from Heaven*; *Descent of the Dove*; and *Image of the City*. See also the article by Hadfield, "Coinherence, Substitution, and Exchange."

Perichoretic Union—E. L. Mascall and G. B. Verity

Eric Lionel (E. L.) Mascall (1905–1993) was an Anglo-Catholic priest and historical theologian at King's College, London. As a historical theologian, he stands in line with patristic thinking on the subject of the soteriological union. In *The Importance of Being Human*, the book derived from his 1958 Bampton Lectures at Columbia, Mascall quotes Athanasius's famous quotation about humans becoming God. Mascall explains, "And in saying this, the great African doctor does not of course mean that we lose our creaturely status, but that, remaining creatures, we are, as a consequence of the incarnation, made sharers in the life of God."[143]

Building upon the thought of Paul and Irenaeus, Mascall shows that the identity between humans and their descendants is one of inclusion. Therefore, all humans are "in" Adam, and all the redeemed are "in" Christ.[144] Mascall stresses the importance of the incarnation for redeeming humanity. Commenting on the exaltation of human nature in Christ, he writes,

> In Christ human nature has been raised to a share in that eternal and divine filiality which the Son exercises in the life of the Holy Trinity. In Jesus of Nazareth, then, manhood is restored to sonship by being raised to a sonship it never had before; nature is perfected by being supernaturalized. This is itself an event of supreme significance for the whole human race which is, as it were, bathed in and infused with radiance that streams from the human nature of the incarnate Lord.[145]

Mascall continues,

> The sonship which was imparted to his own individual human nature by the incarnation is imparted to us by our incorporation into him. Thus the grace which the Christian receives, while it elevates him into the life of God and, in the scriptural phrase, makes him "a partaker of the divine nature," does this by the specific means of communicating to him, by his incorporation into Christ, the sonship which the Son of God enjoys in the Holy Trinity. We become sons in the Son.[146]

---

143. Mascall, *Importance of Being Human*, 95.
144. Ibid., 97.
145. Ibid., 98.
146. Ibid., 98–99.

Mascall also notes, "Since the Christian, through his union with Christ, is lifted up into the life of the Trinity, he himself enjoys the gift of the Spirit which the Father eternally bestows upon the Son."[147] And speaking of the unities between Christ and the believer and between the members of the church, he writes, "It is nothing less than a participation in the unity which binds together the persons of the Holy Trinity, the unity for which the Lord Jesus prayed on the night before his passion: 'That they may all be one, even as thou, Father, art in me, and I in thee, that they also may be in us.'"[148] Here Mascall seems to be speaking of the type of perichoretic union for which this study argues.

In an earlier book, *Christ, the Christian and the Church*, Mascall describes how three unities connect the Christian and the Father. The first unity is the trinitarian *perichoresis*, where the person of the Father coinheres with the person of the Son. The second unity is the hypostatic union, where the divine nature of the Son is joined to human nature. The third unity he calls "adoptive," where individual believers are joined to the human nature of Christ.[149] The latter, adoptive unity, allows incorporation into Christ "and participation in his glorified human nature, so that all he possesses in it becomes ours."[150] Incorporation and participation are present in both the trinitarian and christological perichoretic relationships, and in Mascall's description of the believer's union with Christ as well.

Mascall teaches that deification is "a result of the threefold bridge of union which, we have seen, spans the gulf between us and the Father. It is through our adoptive union with Christ and the hypostatic union of his human nature with his divine person that we are caught up into the life of union which he essentially shares with God the Father."[151] He continues,

> Two important consequences follow. One is that God dwells in the soul of the Christian in a way far more intimate than that which he is present to every finite being at its ontological root as its creator and preserver. What ascetic theology calls "the in-

---

147. Ibid., 99.

148. Ibid., 100.

149. Mascall, *Christ, the Christian, and the Church*, 92–93. Mascall does not confine the union to only the human nature of Christ. He is emphasizing that there is a union between human believers and Christ's human nature. Christ's humanity is the connecting point to the rest of humanity.

150. Ibid., 94.

151. Ibid., 97.

dwelling of the Trinity in the souls of the just" is of an altogether different order from God's "presence of immensity" in all things "by essence, presence, and power;" it is on the level of grace, not of nature; it derives from redemption, not just from creation. Its basis is our incorporation into Christ.... In Christ the Christian enjoys an intimacy with God that exceeds all that a creature could dream of. He is admitted into the very life of the triune God.[152]

Finally, as if to prove his point, Mascall notes that "the life of the church is the life of the Trinity imparted to men."[153] This language is fully in keeping with the understanding of *perichoresis* in this study.

In 1954, an Englishman named George Beresford (G. B.) Verity wrote a little book called *Life in Christ: A Study in Coinherence*. It is his only claim to fame, but this book is important in this study for no other reason than the key word in the subtitle: coinherence. It is a synonym for *perichoresis*.[154] Verity claims to follow the work of Charles Williams in applying the ideas of coinherence to the relationships found in the church.[155] He later writes concerning coinherence (*perichoresis*),

> It is the eternal relation between the persons of the Trinity: [sic] it is the eternal relation between men in Christ: [sic] we can now see the eternal relation between men in Christ and God—we "*abide*" in God and God "*abides*" in us. We shall never be God, we shall never be the same as God, the creature is eternally distinct from the Creator: and yet, when we come into the fullness of our inheritance, we and God, Father, Son, Holy Spirit will be eternally one. That is the nature of the coinherence.[156]

He summarizes,

> The term that was accepted twelve hundred years ago to express the relationship of the persons of the Godhead, the eternal Trinity in unity, is coinherence. Father, Son, and Holy Spirit are one; in that oneness each preserves his own identity. When a man is baptized into Christ he enters just such a oneness; he coinheres with the eternal Son of God as the Son coinheres with the Father.

152. Ibid., 98–99.

153. Ibid., 115.

154. As noted in chapter 1 above, Turner ("Coinherence," 112) equates *perichoresis*, *circumincessio* and *circuminsessio*, and coinherence as synonyms in Greek, Latin, and English, respectively.

155. Verity, *Life in Christ*, 190.

156. Ibid., 192.

He together with all others in the coinherence are the church, the brethren, the fellowship, the body of Christ.[157]

Like Moltmann coming after him, Verity sees coinherence as a ruling principle of created existence, though he does qualify it in a biblical way. His insights on anthropology are useful and deserve further study as well.[158]

Perichoretic Union—Jürgen Moltmann

Jürgen Moltmann (1926–) is Emeritus Professor of Systematic Theology on the Evangelical Faculty, University of Tübingen, Germany.[159] Though perhaps best known for his first work, *The Theology of Hope*, he is also one of the leading contemporary thinkers concerning the doctrine of *perichoresis*.

Moltmann begins his understanding of the Trinity and *perichoresis* from the descriptions of the divine persons in John's Gospel, and not from the one essence of God.[160] He writes, "The perichoretic concept of unity surmounts the 'dangers' of both 'tritheism' and 'modalism,' since it combines threeness and oneness without reducing the threeness to oneness or the oneness to threeness. The concept of mutuality is an ingredient in this perichoretic concept of the Trinity and its content is governed by that."[161] He continues, "The approach in terms of a perichoretic doctrine of the Trinity entails that the levels of relationship in *perichoresis* and mutuality within the Trinity, rather than the levels of constitution within the Trinity, are normative for the relationship of

---

157. Ibid., 196.

158. Ibid., 200. Verity claims that as a man and wife coinhere in marriage over time, it is a way to look into the human constitution. The "complex unity" of body, soul, and spirit may be understood, Verity states, as coinhering with one another. That would be a good starting point of a theological anthropology in a fully trinitarian context.

159. "Gifford Lecture Series, 'Biography—Jürgen Moltmann,'" *Gifford Lecture Series*, August 17, 2009, http://www.giffordlectures.org/Author.asp?AuthorID=217.

160. See Moltmann, *Experiences in Theology*, 317. Moltmann does not necessarily affirm an Eastern orientation to the Trinity either, where the Father is the *monarchia*, or origin of the Godhead. Instead, Moltmann sees an absolute equality among the three persons, thereby allowing him to reject all forms of hierarchy, from the subjugation of women to oppressive political regimes. On *perichoresis*, see Moltmann, *History and the Triune God*, 131.

161. Moltmann, *History and the Triune God*, 132.

God to creation and all the corresponding relationships in creation."[162] This quotation shows that Moltmann is willing to extend the doctrine of *perichoresis* beyond re-created humanity into all of creation, a topic beyond the scope of this study.

He charges that maintaining a transcendent distinction between God and creation creates a "theology of secularization."[163] Instead, he adopts a form of panentheism.[164] While Moltmann does nuance his understanding of levels of *perichoresis*, as shall be shown shortly, it seems as though he does not draw his distinctions quite sharply enough. Although Moltmann is correct that *perichoresis* is a fundamental aspect of how God relates, the level of intensity of perichoretic activity within the Trinity will be greater—perhaps infinitely greater—than when the Triune God interacts with his creation or when the creation interacts with itself. It does seem plausible that the world God created would reflect those perichoretic relationships in some fashion, but they remain a created reflection.

In explaining the re-creation of humanity, Moltmann first notes that Jesus the only begotten Son is Jesus's divinity, while Jesus the first born of many is Jesus's humanity. The first born is the prototype of the re-created man.[165] Moltmann believes that the sending of the Spirit opens all creation to the life of God. He writes, "All things are assembled under the head, Christ, and all tongues will confess him Lord—to the glory of the Father. All people and things then partake of the 'inner-trinitarian life' of God. They join in the responding love of the Son and will thereby become the joy of the Father's blissful love. Then the triune God is at home *in* his world, and his world exists *out of* his inexhaustible glory."[166] Moltmann summarizes his perichoretic views here: "To throw open the circulatory movement of the divine light and the divine relationships, and to take men and women, with the whole of creation, into the life-stream of the triune God: that is the meaning of creation, reconciliation and glorification."[167]

162. Ibid.
163. Ibid., 133.
164. See the criticism of Moltmann's panentheism in chapter 1 above, as well as Otto, "Use and Abuse of *Perichoresis*," and Cooper, *Panentheism*.
165. Moltmann, *Trinity and the Kingdom*, 120.
166. Ibid., 127–28. Italics in original.
167. Ibid., 178.

Moltmann links the *Shekinah* of God's presence in the Old Testament with the *perichoresis* of the New.[168] As God dwelled among Israel, the persons of the Trinity dwell among each other. *Perichoresis* is equally at home with persons of the same kind (such as the persons of the Trinity) as it is with those of a different kind (such as God and humans). This is why Moltmann has coined the phrase the "open Trinity": God wants to replicate the trinitarian perichoretic relationship with his own creation, thus Moltmann calls God "inhabitable."[169] He sees the church corresponding to the trinitarian *perichoresis*.[170] Moltmann argues that the church exists in the Trinity—more than only correspondence—showing the relationships involving members of the church with Christ and each other as perichoretic.[171]

In his 2008 article "God in the World—the World in God: *Perichoresis* in Trinity and Eschatology," Moltmann explicitly calls the relationship Christians enjoy with the Godhead perichoretic.[172] He writes,

> This is not the inner-trinitarian *perichoresis* of different persons of the same nature, but the *perichoresis* of persons of a different nature from each other. It is christological and pneumatological *perichoresis*, mediating between the inner-trinitarian *perichoresis* and the perichoretic community of human beings. In this perichoretic community between the Trinity and the human community there is also simultaneous unity and difference. We are not swallowed up in a divine ocean of finite beings in the infinite being, as some mystics tell us. Nor do we stand as aliens and foreigners forever outside the door. Instead, we find in the "wide space where there is no oppression anymore" a "room of one's own."[173]

Moltmann concludes that the relationship between the members of the church does not only constitute an analogy of the Trinity but also the church is an inclusion in the Trinity as well.[174] Moltmann describes

---

168. Moltmann, *Experiences in Theology*, 316.

169. Ibid., 323.

170. Ibid., 329.

171. Ibid., 330. This idea is at the foundation of Moltmann's theology of liberation, because the Trinity is his "social programme" (ibid., 332). See also Bauckham, *Theology of Jürgen Moltmann*, 161–66.

172. Moltmann, "God in the World," 373.

173. Ibid., 376. The quotes are from McDougall, "Room of One's Own?"

174. Ibid., 377.

the relationship between believers and Christ as a kind of *perichoresis*, which is why his views are included in this study. But his views are divergent from this study in a number of ways, including the surrender of the transcendence of God, the denial of lost humanity, and his recurrent panentheism. Despite these differences, he is included here due to his insights on *perichoresis*, although his "third type" of *perichoresis* is not exactly the same as that for which this investigation argues.

Perichoretic Union—Colin Gunton

Colin E. Gunton (1940–2003) was a British United Reformed systematic theologian at King's College, London. Among his other notable achievements, he helped found the *International Journal of Systematic Theology* in 1999.[175] He is an important contributor to the discussion of the perichoretic union of Christ and the believer.

Colin Gunton addresses *perichoresis* in the book produced from his Bampton Lectures, *The One, the Three, and the Many*. He begins by discussing the trinitarian *perichoresis* but quickly moves on to ideas found in creation. He notes that *perichoresis* is "a concept heavy with spatial and temporal conceptuality."[176] He continues, "Because the one God is economically involved in the world in these various ways, it cannot be supposed other than the action of Father, Son, and Spirit is a mutually involved personal dynamic. It would appear to follow that in eternity Father, Son, and Spirit share a dynamic mutual reciprocity, interpenetration, and interanimation."[177]

Gunton quickly moves on to show how *perichoresis* can be used to describe the inter-relatedness of creation. He writes, "Let me begin with a proposal. It is that we consider the world as an order of things, dynamically related to each other in time and space. It is perichoretic in that everything in it contributes to the being of everything else, enabling

---

175. Barrett, "Biography of Colin E. Gunton," *Theopedia*, http://www.theopedia.com/Colin_E._Gunton.

176. Gunton, *One, the Three, and the Many*, 163.

177. Ibid. On page 164, he writes that the trinitarian *perichoresis* "implies that the three persons of the Trinity exist only in reciprocal, eternal relatedness. God is not God apart from the way in which Father, Son, and Spirit in eternity give to and receive from each other what they essentially are," and, "The three do not merely coinhere, but dynamically constitute one another's being."

everything to be what it distinctively is."[178] Because God is perichoretic, it stands to reason that creation should bear some perichoretic tendencies since God created it. Gunton asserts that there is a "created *perichoresis*" where "everything in the universe is what it is by virtue of its relatedness to everything else."[179] Gunton shares with Moltmann the idea that the creation reflects the relationships inherent in the creator.[180]

Gunton affirms a perichoretic existence in humans as well. He writes, "As made in the image of God we are closely bound up, for good or ill, with other human beings. It is not simply that we enter into a relationship with them."[181] That is, a perichoretic relationship is already in existence at the level of created humanity. He continues,

> A doctrine of human *perichoresis* affirms, after philosophies like that of John Macmurray, that persons mutually constitute each other, make each other what they are. That is why Christian theology affirms that in marriage the man and the woman become one flesh—bound up in each other's being—and why the relations of parents and children are of such crucial importance for the shape that human community takes. Our particularity in community is the fruit of our mutual constitutiveness: of a perichoretic being bound up with each other in the bundle of life.[182]

Gunton qualifies his use of *perichoresis* as an analogy because the Godhead is infinite while created, finite beings have limitations.[183] However, he notes that Christ is the one who reconciles the personal and the impersonal perichoretically.[184]

Moving toward his views on the church, Gunton sees a perichoretic relationship there also.[185] One of the main influences on Gunton's

---

178. Ibid., 166.

179. Ibid., 172.

180. See Buxton, *Trinity, Creation, and Pastoral Ministry*, 128.

181. Gunton, *One, the Three, and the Many*, 169.

182. Ibid., 169–70. The human *perichoresis* is not what this study argues. Gunton seems to begin here and move toward the church (at least in terms of the chronology of his writing), while this study begins with the trinitarian *perichoresis*, moving through the christological to the soteriological.

183. Ibid., 170.

184. Ibid., 178–79.

185. Gunton seldom addresses the relationship of the individual believer and Christ. His context is almost always the church as a whole. Consequently, one can see how he would think about individual believers' union with Christ by observing how he treats

thinking is John Zizioulas. Gunton accepts his ontology of relationality to form his own ideas concerning the relationships within the church.[186] He writes, "We are persons insofar as we are in right relationship to God."[187] Right relationship implies redemption.

The person responsible for the redemption is Christ. Commenting on *enhypostasia* as the basis for the universality of Christ's atoning work, Gunton writes, "Because it is the Word's humanity, it is real and particular humanity, and yet carries with it significance for the rest of humankind. If the mediator of creation takes flesh, then Jesus is related, as a matter of fact, to all flesh, and, indeed, to the whole order of creation."[188] He continues, "To be part of the creation means to be related to the Father through the Son and in the Spirit. But the creation, and particularly the human creation, has lived as if this relation were not real, and so has become subject to the slavery to sin and corruption. The fact that the Son takes flesh in the midst of time means that the relationship is reordered and renewed: [sic] redirected to its original and eschatological destiny."[189] The church functions as the community where this reconciliation takes place.[190]

Gunton begins with "the hypothesis that the sole proper ontological basis for the Church is the being of God, who is what he is as the communion of Father, Son, and Spirit. Where does it lead us?"[191] His answer is that "the church is seen as called to be a, so to speak, finite echo

---

the church's union with Christ.

186. See Zizioulas, *Being as Communion*; Zizioulas, "On Being a Person"; and Schwöbel, "Introduction." Schwöbel says Zizioulas moves from an ontology of substance to an ontology of love to preserve particular personhood. To explain the totality of human nature as being derived from Adam is not possible, because it would "require a constant relationship between Adam and the totality of humanity—a constancy of being which is impossible for a finite being." Zizoulas argues that in the hypostatic union, the being of the person is primary above the natures, because "the natures only have being insofar as they are particularized in his person." So person is superior to nature. Consequently, when one is included in Christ, the "ontological foundation of personhood [is] rooted in the personal communion of the Father, Son, and Spirit, christologically established for humanity in the hypostatic union and sacramentally mediated as inclusion in the uncreated Father-Son-relationship."

187. Gunton, "Trinity, Ontology and Anthropology," 58.
188. Gunton, *Actuality of Atonement*, 169.
189. Ibid.
190. Ibid., 173–203.
191. Gunton, "Church on Earth," 66.

or bodying forth of the divine personal dynamics."[192] In Gunton's view, the church needs to be grounded in the perichoretic interrelations of the Trinity and become a perichoretic community where all is shared and none are ultimately subordinate.[193] Gunton's contributions are important in that he sees the perichoretic reflections through all creation and in the church. Gunton never explicitly affirms that the union of Christ and the believer is perichoretic, as he does with relationships within the church, but his language seems to strongly point in that direction.

Perichoretic Union—Thomas F. Torrance and Family

Thomas Forsyth Torrance (1913–2007) was one of the most important English-speaking theologians of the twentieth century.[194] After studying under Barth, he was Professor of Dogmatics at New College, Edinburgh, for over twenty-five years.[195] To summarize Torrance's teaching on union with Christ in this short section is particularly daunting, as the volume of Torrance's work is surpassed only by the critical interaction with it.

Kye Won Lee, in his excellent summary of Torrance's theology, states that union and communion with Christ is the central theme of his thought.[196] To begin an investigation of union, Torrance's trinitarian theology needs a brief discussion.[197] As a student of Barth's, Torrance was very much a trinitarian theologian. He affirmed the historical doctrine of trinitarian *perichoresis*, although he approached it with a slightly different twist.[198] Following in the same vein as Zizioulas and Gunton, T.

---

192. Ibid., 69.

193. Ibid., 76–77. For a critical interaction, see Chia, "Trinity and Ontology."

194. For a more extensive biography on Torrance, see Colyer, *How to Read T. F. Torrance*, 35–51. For a more intimate biography by his brother, see Torrance, "Thomas Forsyth Torrance."

195. Another influence on Torrance was his undergraduate mentor, H. R. Mackintosh. For Mackintosh's views on union with Christ, see Redmond, "*Participatio Christi*."

196. Lee, *Living in Union*, 2. Colyer (*How to Read T. F. Torrance*, 201–11) provides another excellent summary of his theology. Especially helpful is Colyer's understanding of Torrance's doctrine of union and what it entails.

197. For Torrance, the Trinity is the "ontological ground" and "grammar" of Christian theology. See Torrance, *Christian Doctrine of God*, 1–30.

198. For a thorough examination of *perichoresis* in Torrance's writings, see Torrance, *Christian Doctrine of God*, 168–201. On the "twist" in Torrance's doctrine of *perichoresis*, Gunton (*Father, Son, and Holy Spirit*, 44–45) writes, "Interestingly and unusually—for the concept normally performs the function of showing how three distinct persons

F. Torrance teaches that being relational is essential to being human.[199] His terminology for it is "onto-relational."[200] Gary Deddo summarizes Torrance's ideas: "If relationship is essential to who we are, then in union with Christ, we are really united, but remain distinctly ourselves without confusion with Christ. We are most truly ourselves just when we are really united to our Lord and Savior Jesus Christ. Union, then, is a continual relationship with Christ at the deepest levels of our being, not a confusion of ourselves with Christ."[201]

Torrance lays great weight on the hypostatic union of Christ as the God-man. It is the central theme in his published lectures on the incarnation.[202] It is vital for the believer's union with Christ, for that is how the believer is able to know God. In the incarnation, Torrance teaches that Christ assumed fallen human flesh in order to reach humanity where it

---

can yet constitute one God—Torrance moves from *perichoresis* to person and not the other way round, arguing that by virtue of the concept of *perichoresis* there developed a new concept of the person in which 'the relations between persons belong to what the persons are.' Because *perichoresis* characterizes the historical revelation of the one God, its meaning is derived primarily from the economy, rather than in reflection on the relation of the eternal persons. It is the reason that we can speak of God being personal in his eternal being, and here reference is made to the claim of Hilary of Poitiers that God is not solitary." The quotation is from Torrance, *Christian Doctrine of God*, 102; the reference to Hilary is from Torrance, *Trinitarian Faith*, 90. For a general introduction to Torrance on *perichoresis*, see Heltzel, "Perichoresis."

199. See here Del Colle, "'Person' and 'Being.'" While there are some general agreements about relationship as the foundation of personal ontology between Zizioulas and Torrance, there are some disagreements as well. Del Colle provides a good summary.

200. Lee (*Living in Union with Christ*, 74) writes, "The onto-relational context of person cannot but reflect *perichoresis*."

201. Deddo, "Our Participation," 143. The onto-relational citation is from Torrance, *Ground and Grammar*, 173–78.

202. See Torrance, *Incarnation*. Six of the seven chapters are devoted to the incarnation and hypostatic union. See also Torrance's discussion of the virgin birth in Torrance, "Doctrine of the Virgin Birth." To see the importance Torrance lays on the incarnation, see Torrance, "Goodness and Dignity," 321.

is.[203] He believes this began in Bethlehem and culminated in the cross.[204] Torrance's nephew Robert Walker writes,

> In the very act of assuming fallen flesh Jesus wrestles with it and sanctifies it. The whole life of Jesus is a dynamic one of wrestling, of learning obedience, of publicly identifying himself with sinners in baptism, but also of growing up in righteousness and intimate communion with the Father. In the midst of his increasing oneness with sinners, climaxed on the cross, Jesus is forging a life of perfect human righteousness and it is that positive human righteousness which lies at the heart of the doctrine of our justification and of union with him through the Spirit.[205]

Therefore, the doctrine of Christ's assumption of fallen flesh is important in another way. In his sanctification of fallen flesh, Christ is the picture of perfect humanity in every way, which makes possible a real union of Christ and the believer.

The participation of the believer in the human nature of Christ is at the heart of Torrance's doctrine of reconciliation. Describing the believer's inclusion in Christ, though he never explicitly calls it *perichoresis*,[206] Torrance writes,

---

203. Here, Torrance teaches that Christ assumed "fallen" humanity—not sinful humanity. He believes "fallen" is required to place Jesus where the rest of humanity is. He is following his teacher Karl Barth here. He is also following Gregory of Nazianzus's maxim, "What is not assumed is not healed." As long as "fallen" and "sinful" are not synonymous, Torrance may be correct, for Heb 4:15 explicitly states Jesus was without sin. But his humanity was fraught with suffering, anguish, tears, and sorrow, things that are present due to the fall. In that way, he felt the full effects of the fall, with the exception of sin. For a discussion of how Torrance balances "fallen" and "sinless," using the *an-* and *enhypostasia* to do so, see Habets, *Theosis in Torrance*, 72.

204. Torrance, *Incarnation*, xxxii. See also Torrance, *Mediation of Christ*, 50. There, he notes that the inability to grasp the idea that Jesus took on fallen humanity is the reason for so much external forensic transaction language in Western concepts of the atonement. If Christ did not assume fallen humanity, there can be no more than an external relation between him and the human race. See also Lee, *Living in Union with Christ*, 79–98; as well as Habets, *Theosis in Torrance*, 79.

205. Torrance, *Incarnation*, xxxiii.

206. Although this study did not find any specific instance of Torrance calling the soteriological union a form of *perichoresis*, Habets (*Theosis in Torrance*, 108) writes that Torrance "repeatedly speaks of ontological communion, real participation, *perichoresis*, and partaking of the divine life and love" as "cognates for *theosis* within his theology." Since Habets roughly equates *theosis* and what this study calls the perichoretic soteriological union, there may be some evidence that Torrance did indeed use *perichoresis* to describe Christian salvation.

> The fact that through the kinship which the Son of God has established with us in the incarnation, our creaturely evanescent existence is as securely anchored in the very being and life of God as Jesus Christ himself. Such is the blessed end of the atoning exchange effected in the death, resurrection, and ascension of Jesus Christ. Since he has been taken up into God, in him our humanity, in spite of its temporal changeable nature, is given a place in God, and is thus grounded in his eternal, unchangeable reality.[207]

Torrance believes Christians can only know God by participating in Christ and his knowledge of God.[208] John Morrison describes Torrance's theology as "culminating at the eternal perichoretic relations within the eternal triune Godhead at which human knowledge of God in Christ and by the Spirit finally 'arrives'—penetration and participation by grace into the ellipse of knowing and loving between the persons of the ontological Trinity."[209] Torrance describes a "cognitive union" between the believer and Christ that calls upon the Pauline doctrines of adoption and union with Christ and the Johannine idea of mutual indwelling that is the basis for the believer's knowledge of God.[210] In other words, Torrance seems to affirm that the believer knows God in a relationship with Christ that is the third type of perichoretic relationship described in this study.

There are multiple instances of perichoretic relationship language in Torrance's writings and those who interact with him. Because the relation of the Son to the Father is an internal relation inside the Godhead, the relationship of the church to the Father must likewise be internal to the Godhead because the church is the body of Christ. Torrance writes, "Since the Sonship of Christ falls within and not outside the Godhead, everything we say of the church must be consistent with the consubstantial oneness between the Son and the Father and be an expression of the union and communion between God and man effected in the incarnate life and reconciling work of the Mediator."[211] Because *per-*

---

207. Torrance, *Trinitarian Faith*, 184.

208. Purves, "Christology of Thomas F. Torrance," 69–72. See also Torrance, *Mediation of Christ*, 64–66.

209. Morrison, *Knowledge of the Self-Revealing God*, 50.

210. Torrance, *Trinitarian Faith*, 59. For more on the "cognitive union," see Torrance, *Mediation of Christ*, 35–36. See also Kruger, "Doctrine of the Knowledge of God," 368. Here Kruger states that the knowledge of God arises from a perichoretic relationship.

211. Torrance, *Trinitarian Faith*, 264.

ichoresis exists between the Son and the Father, it seems that Torrance would affirm that a perichoretic relationship must also exist between the Father and the church through Christ. Torrance, however, never uses the term *perichoresis* to describe the soteriological union, perhaps because he is unwilling to use trinitarian terminology to expressly describe it. However, Myk Habets, when describing Torrance's views on *theosis*, states that believers are "in a sort-of-perichoretic communion with the triune God—*theosis*."[212] This language seems to be that for which this study argues.

Interpreting Athanasius, Torrance continues, "This does not mean that the relation between us and Christ is precisely the same as that between the Son and the Father, although it is grounded upon it, for there is no identity in nature or equality between us and Christ as there is between him and the Father. The union between us and Christ is not one of nature but one of adoption and grace effected through the gift of the Spirit who comes to dwell in us as he dwells in God."[213] Torrance, building on the pattern set by Athanasius, sees both the trinitarian *perichoresis* and Christ indwelling the believer as a given. He notes that in the incarnation, the Son became the place (τόπος) "where the Father is to be known and believed."[214] In this analogous use of "place," Torrance describes the relationship of Christ in the believer in terms of the essential relationship between the Father and the Son. Again, this is language of a perichoretic relationship. John Morrison summarizes, "The communion of love in God has interpenetrated human existence in Christ in a way which forms a community of love and gives to human beings place of participation to share in God's own communion of love within the homoousial and interpenetrating/perichoretic relations of the Father, Son, and Spirit."[215]

Since for Torrance the union of the believer and Christ seems to be what this study calls a perichoretic relationship, one would not be surprised to find that his views on *theosis* lead in the same direction. For

---

212. Habets, *Theosis in Torrance*, 115.

213. Torrance, *Trinitarian Faith*, 265.

214. Torrance, *Space, Time, and Incarnation*, 16. This term looks back to the discussion of John 14 in chapter 2 above.

215. Morrison, *Knowledge of the Self-Revealing God*, 207. He cites Torrance, *Reality and Scientific Theology*, 182. See also the analysis of Richardson, "Trinitarian Reality," 173–97.

Torrance, *theosis* is a work of the Holy Spirit. He writes, "This is a deification, however, which more than recreates our lost humanity, for it lifts us up in Christ to enjoy a new fullness of human life in a blessed communion with divine life."[216] He continues, "To have the Spirit dwelling in us is to be made partakers of God beyond ourselves."[217] Gary Deddo, summarizing Torrance, writes, "In the Spirit God does not overwhelm us. Rather than a loss of self the Spirit provides its completion (*theosis*, *theopoiesis*, *teleiosis*). The Spirit perfects our humanity in our humanity on the basis of the humanity of Jesus Christ."[218]

To pull together the force behind Torrance's teaching on the nature of the believer's union with Christ, here is a summary in his own words:

> Men and women are savingly reconciled to God by being taken up in and through Christ to share in the inner relations of God's own life and love. It means that the eternal communion of love in God overflows through Jesus Christ into our union with Christ and gathers us up to dwell with God and in God. This is another way of saying that the incarnation, and the reconciliation that took place within it, fall within the life of God. That is what is implied in the Pauline teaching that Christ, in whom the complete being of God dwells, dwells in us, so that through a relation of mutual indwelling between Christ and us, we are enfolded within the infinite dimensions of the love of God. The Greek fathers used to speak of that experience as *theopoiesis* or *theosis*, which does not mean "divinization," as is so often supposed, but refers to the utterly staggering act of God in which he gives *himself* to us and adopts us into the communion of his divine life and love through Jesus Christ and in his one Spirit, yet in such a way that we are not made divine but are preserved in our humanity. That is what constitutes the sustaining inner cohesion of our cognitive union with Christ through faith and the very substance of our personal and corporate union with Christ through the Word and sacraments, for in Christ our human relations with God, far from being allowed to remain on a merely external basis, are embraced within the trinitarian relations of God's own being as Father, Son, and Holy Spirit.[219]

216. Torrance, *Trinitarian Faith*, 189.

217. Ibid.

218. Deddo, "Holy Spirit in T. F. Torrance's Theology," 95. Deddo cites Torrance, *Trinitarian Faith*, 198, 228; and Torrance, *Theology in Reconstruction*, 221.

219. Torrance, *Mediation of Christ*, 74–75.

This quotation summarizes many of the ideas that lead to the soteriological union being described as a perichoretic relationship, though again Torrance does not use the explicit terminology. Had he considered a third type of *perichoresis*, perhaps he would have felt free to use the term to describe the believer's union with Christ.[220]

James B. Torrance (1923–2004), brother of Thomas and father of Alan, was professor of systematic theology at the University of Aberdeen in Scotland. He stresses many of the same ideas as his brother does, especially those of the vicarious humanity in Christ and its implications for Christian worship.[221] He writes, "When the role of Christ in our humanity, in his life of worship and communion with the Father, is emphasized in New Testament fashion, then our worship is seen as the gift of participating through the Spirit in Christ's communion with the Father."[222] He continues, "By sharing Jesus's life of communion with the Father in the Spirit, we are given to participate in the eternal Son's communion with the Father in the Spirit."[223] For Torrance, the *homoousion* guarantees this perichoretic relationship because it is both internal to the Godhead (because of the presence of the Son) and external in that humanity is present, even the humanity present by participation.[224]

In the *festschrift* for James Torrance's retirement, James M. Houston expands Torrance's thinking by plainly stating that spiritual life and growth "is an introduction into the divine *perichoresis*, of intercommunion with the Father, Son, and Holy Spirit, who God is."[225] One of Torrance's students, C. Baxter Kruger, has taken up the banner of *perichoresis* as he is president and founder of *Perichoresis* Ministries in Jackson, Mississippi. He is perhaps the leading exponent of "Torrance

---

220. Torrance (*Conflict and Agreement*, 189) writes, "No union, save that of the persons of the Holy Trinity, could be closer, without passing into absolute identity, than that between Christ and his church as enacted in the Holy Eucharist." The Eucharist comment notwithstanding, it is clear how close Torrance saw the union between Christ and the believer. Since he likens it to the trinitarian *perichoresis*, there is reason to believe he may have used perichoretic language to describe the soteriological union.

221. See Torrance, *Worship, Community, and the Triune God*.

222. Torrance, "Vicarious Humanity of Christ," 130.

223. Ibid.

224. Ibid., 135.

225. Houston, "Spirituality and the Doctrine of the Trinity," 69.

theology" through his website, writings, and speaking engagements.[226] He summarizes his views of *perichoresis* thus:

> Genuine acceptance removes fear and hiding, and creates freedom to know and to be known. In this freedom arises a fellowship and sharing so honest and open and real that the persons involved dwell in one another. There is union without loss of individual identity. When one weeps, the other tastes salt. It is only in the triune relationship of Father, Son and Spirit that personal relationship of this order exists, and the early Church used the word *perichoresis* to describe it. The good news is that Jesus Christ has drawn us within this relationship, and its fullness and life are to be played out in each of us and in all creation.[227]

The part of the quotation speaking of the relationship between Christ and the believer is very close to what this study argues. Kruger is an example of how the Torrance brothers have influenced dozens of theologians.

The Torrance theological legacy has passed to the next generation. Alan, son of James, has engaged Karl Barth on his interpretation of persons in communion.[228] He has also applied the family's theological position to Christian ethics.[229] Lee summarizes Thomas Torrance's theology, which rightly applies to the whole family. He sees it as a three-wheeled chariot, each wheel representing (trinitarian) *perichoresis*, the hypostatic union, and *koinonia*, respectively. They all revolve around the axis of union and communion.[230] This shows that the whole family has ideas that imply and support soteriological union as a perichoretic relationship.

---

226. Two of his more theological books are *Jesus and the Undoing of Adam*; and *Parable of the Dancing God*. In both of these works, Kruger affirms the opening of the divine perichoretic relationship to created humanity through the incarnation and the believer's participation in Christ's vicarious humanity. Another important writing is "Bearing Our Scorn," November 25, 2008, http://www.perichoresis.org/x2/file/9fc3d7152ba9336a670e36d0ed79bc43.pdf.

227. Kruger, "Interview," November 20, 2009, http://www.perichoresis.org/content/1/3/22.html.

228. See Torrance, *Persons in Communion*. His last chapter has the most evidence of the Torrance family theology in it, including participation in the faithfulness of Jesus Christ (ibid., 321) and a stress on the vicarious humanity of Christ (ibid., 355). In the same chapter, he offers critiques of both Moltmann's and LaCugna's trinitarian models.

229. See Torrance and Banner, *Doctrine of God*.

230. Lee, *Living in Union with Christ*, 317. See almost the same description in Kruger,

Perichoretic Union—Catherine Mowry LaCugna

Catherine Mowry LaCugna (1952–1997) was a Roman Catholic feminist theologian who taught at Notre Dame. She died of cancer at only forty-four years of age but left behind some impressive work on the Trinity and salvation. Most of her thought is in her important book *God for Us: The Trinity and the Christian Life*, published in 1991.[231]

Many themes in *God for Us* are similar to those of the authors discussed above. LaCugna strongly affirms the doctrine of *perichoresis* in its historical expression. She even thinks the metaphor of a dance is useful, though she acknowledges its etymological shortcomings.[232] LaCugna believes divinization (*theosis*) is "the true communion of divine and human within the specific existence, psychology, circumstances, and limits of a human being."[233] Therefore Jesus is the divinized human being who unites the divine and human within himself. He is the embodiment of *theosis* who allows those in him to be deified as well. LaCugna sees the processes of transformation and *theosis* as evidence of what this study has called a third type of perichoretic relationship. She writes, "Conformity to Christ means participating in the very life of God, the life of communion among persons, divine and human, and among all creatures."[234]

Her contribution to the discussion of the perichoretic relationship between Christ and the believer is to bring the perichoretic relationships together into one. She writes, "'The divine dance' is indeed an apt image of persons in communion: not for an intradivine communion but for divine life as all creatures partake and literally exist in it."[235] She continues, "There are not two sets of communion—one among divine persons, the other among human persons, with the latter supposed to replicate the former. The one *perichoresis*, the one mystery of communion, includes God and humanity as beloved partners in the dance.

"God in Torrance," 373. See also the discussion of Mascall earlier in this chapter.

231. A nice summary of LaCugna's personal approach may be found in Hilkert, "Catherine Mowry LaCugna's Trinitarian Theology." Torrance ("Ecumenical Implications") describes the far-reaching possibilities of her discoveries. One of her earlier works where she begins to develop her theology in conversation with Karl Rahner is LaCugna, "Reconceiving the Trinity."

232. LaCugna, *God for Us*, 271.

233. Ibid., 296. She calls Jesus the true *perichoresis* of *theologia* and *oikonomia*.

234. Ibid., 346.

235. Ibid., 274.

This is what Jesus prayed for in the high-priestly prayer in John's Gospel (John 17:20–21)."[236] Therefore, in LaCugna's thinking, the union of the believer and Christ is not a type of perichoretic relationship; it is part of the one *perichoresis*, that existing already in the Godhead and shared with his creation, especially the Christian.[237]

To further develop her ideas, she writes, "The life of God is not something that belongs to God alone. *The divine life is also our life.*"[238] The divine life is perichoretic, so in her view the Christian relationship with God (and Christ) would seem to be also. She directly addresses the idea of *perichoresis* in humans thus: "The *telos* of human nature is to be conformed to the person of Christ who *hypostatically* unites human and divine natures. *Theosis* takes place in the economy, in the communion of persons with each other, and with all of creation. The Holy Spirit incorporates us into the very life of God, into the mystery of *perichoresis*, the 'to and fro' of being itself which exists in personhood."[239] Although LaCugna is known for equating the economic and ontological Trinity, her views on perichoretic union do not necessarily hinge on it.[240] Her insights on soteriological union seem to be valid regardless of her starting point, though her universalistic tendencies are problematic.

Perichoretic Union—Two More Voices

David. G. Attfield, a retired Anglican priest, proposes *perichoresis* as a model for understanding salvation.[241] First, he differentiates between the trinitarian *perichoresis*, "where active and continuous mutual indwelling

---

236. Ibid.

237. One criticism that may be brought against LaCugna here is that she fails to see the three distinct levels at which *perichoresis* operates, as discussed in chapter 1. That is why this study argues for a third type of *perichoresis* instead of calling it "one *perichoresis*," as LaCugna does. Her identification of the Trinity *ad intra* and *ad extra* would shape her theological choice here.

238. LaCugna, *God for Us*, 228. Italics in original.

239. Ibid., 297–98.

240. For critiques of her work, see Peters, *God as Trinity*, 122–28, and Grenz, *Rediscovering the Triune God*, 147–62.

241. Attfield, "'I in You,'" 422–23. Attfield argues that both the Roman Catholic and traditional Protestant views of salvation are inadequate. The former falls short because it is rooted in the belief in real universals, and does not hold in an era where universals are rejected. The latter fails, in his opinion, because double imputation offends the intuitive notion of ethical justice and therefore cannot completely represent the salvation process.

is maintained by love and choice," and the divine-human *perichoresis*, where the Christian must depend on God's grace to guide his will "from moment to moment."[242] By understanding salvation as a perichoretic system, Attfield argues, divine participation in sinful humanity and humanity's participation in the sinless divine is the key to understanding salvation rather than imputation. He writes, "The trinitarian notion of *perichoresis* can be adapted to the needs of soteriology, the theory of salvation. Other views of the identity of Christ and the Christian fail to analyze adequately this union that is required by most of the atonement theories formulated in Christian history and by the language of the New Testament and its doctrines of justification and sanctification."[243] Attfield concludes, "If Christian theology can accept [*perichoresis*] as a satisfying positive account of the mystery of love of three persons in one God, maybe the mystery of salvation can be accepted as a similar mystery. Thus this attempt to conceptualize the union of Christ with Christians can be conceived as an exercise in faith seeking understanding."[244]

Though this subsection does not interact with Attfield's ideas on imputation, his argument does have merit. His understanding of salvation as a perichoretic system has explanatory power. It helps to avoid some of the "legal fiction" language that has accompanied the Protestant doctrine of justification since Luther's day. If both sides participate in one another, as Attfield suggests, there is no longer any fiction present.

British ethicist Justin Thacker uses the concept of *perichoresis* in answering postmodern critiques against Christianity. He is willing to entertain the idea that perichoresis exists on a number of levels; it does not remain confined to its trinitarian context.[245] He argues that "theological knowing consists in a perichoretic participation in God which operates tacitly to enable a pneumatological interpretation of the revelation of Jesus Christ."[246] Therefore, Christians are able to know God because they participate in a perichoretic relationship with God. Thacker argues that the *perichoresis* between the believer and Christ is one where Christ

---

242. Ibid., 426.

243. Ibid., 428.

244. Ibid.

245. Thacker, *Postmodernism*, 41–45. Here recall his discussion of three levels of *perichoresis* reviewed in chapter 1 above.

246. Ibid., 37.

enters into humanity to transform it, while the believer enters into what Christ has become, that is, "redeemed and reconciled humanity."[247]

Describing his view of the perichoretic relationship in the soteriological union in detail, Thacker writes,

> The interpenetration is seen in that Christ, though in himself entirely without sin, entered so fully into our humanity that he became sin. Without ceasing to be God, he became also sinful man. He penetrated fully the state that we're in. As has been noted, in his own life he then redeemed and transformed that humanity by the obedience that he demonstrated, a transformation that was vindicated at the resurrection, so that the *perichoresis* from our side is seen in our participating and sharing fully in that redeemed humanity that Christ has made available. We enjoy a relationship with God only and precisely to the extent that we are "in Christ," joined with him and participating in the redemption that he has made available.[248]

Thacker's main contributions are to differentiate the types of *perichoresis* into three, as this study has done, as well as to build in safeguards that show that the term *perichoresis* means different relationships depending on usage.[249] If *perichoresis* is only confined to its trinitarian usage, then no other perichoretic relationship exists. Because the term applies to Christology as well, then the type of relationship the persons of the Trinity share, though not corresponding in every detail, has been opened to the created world in a way that allows it to be called *perichoresis*, though of a third type. Both he and D. G. Attfield speak of the soteriological union in overtly perichoretic language.

CHAPTER SUMMARY

This chapter has attempted to demonstrate that the Christian doctrine of salvation has often included ideas related to a third type of perichoretic relationship between Christ and the believer. As chapter 2 provided the biblical foundation for the idea, this chapter has traced it through the history of the church. This chapter started with an examination of the close relationship between perichoretic union and *theosis*. Dumitru Staniloae writes, "As a work of raising up believers to intimate com-

---

247. Ibid., 51. Thacker cites the argument of Hooker, *From Adam to Christ*, 42.
248. Ibid., 53–54.
249. Again, see ibid., 44.

munion with God, salvation and deification are nothing other than the extension to conscious creatures of the relations that obtain between the divine persons. That is why the Trinity reveals itself essentially in the work of salvation and that is why the Trinity is the basis on which salvation stands."[250] Thus the teachings of the fathers and Reformers pointed toward soteriological union as a perichoretic relationship, and that much more clearly in fathers than Reformers. As the church moved into the middle of the twentieth century, *perichoresis* language became more common to describe the believer's union with Christ. The next chapter will also explore some theological metaphors of the soteriological union that contain reflections of perichoretic ideas: covenant, marriage, and adoption.

---

250. Staniloae, *Experience of God*, 248.

4

Theological Issues

THIS CHAPTER FOCUSES ON the theological issues concerning the soteriological union as a third type of perichoretic relationship. It examines three key biblical pictures of the believer's union with Christ: the New Covenant, the metaphor of marriage, and the adoption of the believer into the family of God. It shows how the idea of a third type of *perichoresis* in the soteriological union sheds light on the biblical pictures, while in turn the understanding of the soteriological union deepens. It illustrates how these biblical pictures enhance Christian understanding of the union between Christ and the believer. This chapter also includes two theological benefits of seeing the soteriological union as a third type of perichoretic relationship: the explanatory power of *perichoresis* and the ability of *perichoresis* to uphold both unity and diversity simultaneously.

The three pictures of the believer's union with Christ this chapter describes share two common characteristics. First, all have their origins in the Old Testament, in the lives of God's chosen people of long ago. Second, these are not mutually exclusive ideas, as there will often be overlap among marriage, adoption, and covenant. The three ideas are metaphors to help the believer understand his or her union with Christ.

THE BLOOD OF THE COVENANT: A PICTURE OF A PERICHORETIC RELATIONSHIP

This section argues that the concept of a covenant helps reveal the perichoretic nature of the soteriological union.[1] To build the argument, this

---

1. This investigation only surveys the covenants between God and humans in the Old Testament. Unilateral covenants would not exhibit perichoretic traits.

section will examine the Old Testament basis for covenant, noting how it contains the seeds of perichoretic thinking. Key topics will include the idea of covenant itself and the offerings of Israel's sacrificial system.[2] The section then shifts to the prophecy of the new covenant and how Jesus's death is a covenant act by the God-man. This section attempts to show that a covenant is a physical representation of the perichoretic relationship existing between Christ and the believer.

Covenant in the Old Testament

The concept of covenant is very important in the Old Testament.[3] It is so important that Steven McKenzie believes that "covenant is the principal image used in the Bible to express the relationship between God and humans."[4] Paul Kalluveettil writes that "the idea, 'I am yours, you are mine' underlies every covenant declaration."[5] Gleason Archer defines a covenant as "a compact or agreement between two parties binding them mutually to undertakings on each other's behalf."[6] O. Palmer Robertson, showing the terms "make a covenant" and "cut a covenant" to be synonymous due to the shedding of blood, defines a covenant as "a bond in blood, sovereignly administered."[7]

---

2. Just to note, the selection of the offerings is not a full treatment of the Mosaic covenantal rituals by any means. Perhaps they are not even the clearest examples. Space requires selectivity here, and a fuller treatment of this idea would possibly be book-length in its own right.

3. The treatment of the idea of "covenant" in this study is very narrow, using it as background information for discussing the work of Christ in light of the new covenant in his blood. Therefore, much of the study of how ancient covenants operated is not discussed. For a more thorough study on the ancient use of covenant, see the following: McCarthy, *Treaty and Covenant*; McCarthy, *Old Testament Covenants*; Baltzer, *Covenant Formulary*; and Mendenhall, *Law and Covenant*. For the importance of the idea of covenant in the life of Israel, see Wright, *New Testament and the People of God*, 261: "The compilers of the Pentateuch saw the initial fulfillment of the covenant in the events of the exodus, and thus understood the Torah as the covenant document which, grounded upon the faithfulness of Israel's God, provided for his people the way of life by which they should express their answering fidelity to him."

4. McKenzie, *Covenant*, 8.

5. Kalluveettil, *Declaration and Covenant*, 212.

6. Archer, "Covenant," 299.

7. Robertson, *Christ of the Covenants*, 8, 15. The work of Trumbull, *Blood Covenant*, is helpful here, as he has meticulously researched the existence of blood covenants throughout practically all the ancient world.

In the Old Testament, blood symbolized life (Gen 9:4; Lev 17:11; Deut 12:23).[8] Therefore, two parties entering into a covenant in blood pledged their lives to one another by pledging the perceived source of that life—their own blood—to one another.[9] In the divine covenants, God pledged his own fidelity to his covenant partner (Noah, Abraham, and Israel, as the case may be) in blood.[10] Of course God has no blood, and the shedding of human blood would bring forth death. So an animal was chosen as a stand-in for both parties.[11] This section will argue that the foundational idea behind a covenant is a shared, or common, life.

---

8. There are numerous scholars who claim that blood symbolizes life. Shelton (*Cross and Covenant*, 65) explains how the term "blood" functions as a synecdoche in the Old Testament: "In a sacrificial or atonement context, blood represents the giving of life as the offerer of the sacrifice of atonement presents the offering in obedience to the commands of covenant Law." He then quotes Lev 17:11. For more on the synecdoche of blood, see Sheeley, "Nothing (a)B(o)ut the Blood." See also Vervenne, "Blood Is the Life"; Walvoord and Zuck, *Bible Knowledge Commentary*, 285; Callaway, *Faces of the Old Testament*, 17; Dyrness, *Themes in Old Testament Theology*, 92; Hanson, "Blood and Purity," http://www.kchanson.com/ARTICLES/blood.html; and Brand and Yancey, "Blood, Part 2," *Christianity Today*, July 2003, http://www.christianitytoday.com/ct/2003/julyweb-only/7-7-45.0.html?start=6. On the uniqueness of this view of blood to Israel, see McCarthy, "Symbolism of Blood and Sacrifice," and McCarthy, "Further Notes." This contrasts with pagan notions of blood where the blood held some kind of divine, mystical power to ratify a covenant agreement. See also McCarthy, *Treaty and Covenant*, 56. For the opposing view that blood means "death," see Morris, *Apostolic Preaching*, 126–28; and Stibbs, "Meaning of the Word 'Blood,'" *Theological Studies*, http://www.theologicalstudies.org.uk/pdf/blood_stibbs.pdf. Morris later admits to allowing blood to mean "life given up in death," which this study allows, in Morris, *Atonement*, 55.

9. As Trumbull (*Blood Covenant*, 3–6) notes, this was often done by each party drinking or co-mingling the other's blood, symbolizing ingesting the life of the other into his own. The two separate lives symbolically became one. Another variation of the blood covenant in ancient times was the eating flesh and/or drinking blood of a sacrificial animal, that stood in for both parties. See Trumbull for numerous examples from the ancient world.

10. McConville, "*Berit*." For a thorough exposition of the various covenants and how they relate to Christian doctrine, see Pink, *Divine Covenants*. For a detailed explanation of the various types of covenants existing in the ancient Near East, see Hahn, *Kinship by Covenant*, 26–369.

11. In his covenant with Noah, God forbade the eating of blood because life is in the blood (Gen 9:3–6). God prohibited Noah and his offspring from having control over life and blood, since God was the author of life. In the offerings of Israel, blood was always important and holy, because it symbolized life. Trumbull, *Blood Covenant*, 214, notes that because man is made in the image of God, only God—or his appointed minister of justice—could rightly take life from man.

If life is shared in such an intimate way as a blood covenant symbolizes, then two persons, insofar as possible, "indwell" one another and mutually participate in one another.[12] These are the key components of the trinitarian and christological varieties of perichoretic relationships as shown in chapter 2 above. It is the "shared" or "common" life aspect between two parties that gives a covenant its perichoretic overtones and simultaneously makes it a working metaphor for the union of God and his people.

Though individuals could enact covenants with others, this section focuses on covenants between God and his people. In the Old Testament, God made covenants with Noah, Abraham, Israel (through Moses), and David. All of these covenants are connected, pointing ahead to a new covenant God will enact in his Messiah.[13] In each of these covenants, God is the prime actor who takes upon himself the burden to bring the end result he desires.[14]

The Mosaic Covenant shaped the religious thought of ancient Israel. This covenant is a renewal and partial fulfillment of the covenant God made with Abraham.[15] The Mosaic covenant was enacted with blood. Exodus 24:6–8 says,

> And Moses took half of the blood and put it in basins, and the other half of the blood he sprinkled on the altar. Then he took the book of the covenant and read it in the hearing of the people, and they said, "All that the LORD has spoken we will do, and we will be obedient!" So Moses took the blood and sprinkled it on the people, and said, "Behold the blood of the covenant, which the LORD has made with you in accordance with all these words."

Moses divided the blood that inaugurated the covenant with Israel, with half going to God (the altar) and the other half sprinkled onto the people. Keil and Delitzsch explain why the blood was symbolically divided as it was:

---

12. Trumbull (*Blood Covenant*, 7) notes that the blood covenant union is closer than even the birth union, and he points to Prov 18:24 for support. He writes, "As it is the inter-commingling of very lives, nothing can transcend it" (6–7).

13. On how each successive covenant builds upon the previous one, see Robertson, *Christ of the Covenants*, 28–52.

14. Horton, *Covenant and Salvation*, 16–17.

15. Williamson, *Sealed with an Oath*, 94–95. See also Exodus 2:23–25.

> As the only reason for dividing the sacrificial blood into two parts was, that the blood sprinkled upon the altar could not be taken off again and sprinkled upon the people; the two halves of the blood are to be regarded as one blood, which was first of all sprinkled upon the altar, and then upon the people. In the blood sprinkled upon the altar, the natural life of the people was given up to God, as a life that had passed through death, to be pervaded by his grace; and then through the sprinkling upon the people it was restored to them again, as a life renewed by the grace of God. In this way the blood not only became a bond of union between Jehovah and his people, but as the blood of the covenant it became a vital power, holy and divine, uniting Israel with its God.[16]

Perhaps the symbolism here is that in the one sacrifice is the joining of God and man, in one being and one act—a shared life.

The "covenant formula" of Israel is found several places in the Old Testament. It states that God will dwell in the midst of his people, they will be his people, and he will be their God.[17] Robertson calls this formula the "Immanuel Principle," since the heart of the covenant is "God is with us."[18] This is not the explicit "mutual indwelling" language of Paul and John, but there is a sense that God is in the midst of his people and they dwell securely in his presence. There is also an imperfect mutual participation in keeping the covenant requirements. Thus there is a faint echo of the elements of a perichoretic relationship present in the Old Testament covenant. Robertson, as a covenant theologian, uses the "Immanuel Principle" throughout the differing expressions of the covenant to show they are a single, oft-renewed covenant between God and his people.[19]

Covenant theologian J. Ligon Duncan III explicitly connects the covenant and *perichoresis*: "God's covenant communion with us is modeled on and a reflection of the intra-trinitarian relationships. The shared life, the fellowship of the persons of the Holy Trinity, what theologians

---

16. Keil and Delitzsch, *Pentateuch*, 2:158.

17. See Scott, *Adoption as Sons of God*, 197–201. Scott lists two main examples of the "covenant formula" in Lev 26:12 and Ezek 37:27.

18. Robertson, *Christ of the Covenants*, 46. Robertson develops the theme of God dwelling with his people, beginning with the tabernacle of Israel, through the incarnation, the indwelling, and ending with the City of God.

19. Ibid. See also Vlach, "New Covenant Theology." Robertson and other covenant theologians would see the unity of the Old Testament and New Covenants due to all of them being part of the covenant of grace.

call *perichoresis* or *circumincessio*, is the archetype of the relationship the gracious covenant God shares with his elect and redeemed people."[20] By linking the idea of covenant to inner-trinitarian life, covenant theologian Ralph A. Smith believes it is the key to all theological understanding.[21] This study does not seek to enter into the debates on covenant theology. What is important here is to note the perichoretic overtones within the idea of the covenant.

Old Testament Sacrifice as Covenant Ritual

All of the sacrifices God commanded Israel to perform were part of his covenant with them.[22] The first seven chapters of Leviticus proscribe the offerings of the Israelites. The first, in order of execution, was the sin offering and/or the guilt or trespass offering.[23] Next came the three "free will" offerings—the burnt offering, the meal offering, and the peace offering.[24]

The sin offering was the first sacrifice an Israelite made. It was a mandatory offering due to personal sin or, as Philip Jenson notes, for ritual purification.[25] In laying one hand upon the head of the animal as a sign of his union with it while he cut its throat with the other, the Israelite acknowledged that the animal was taking his place in death.[26] Larry Shelton notes how the atonement is made by the animal's life,

---

20. Duncan, "What Is Covenant Theology?" http://www.fpcjackson.org/resources/apologetics/Covenant%20Theology%20&%20Justification/ligoncovt.htm. See also Shelton, *Cross and Covenant*, 22.

21. Smith, "Trinitarian Covenant in John 17," http://www.berith.org/essays/j17/10.html.

22. Like the previous subsection on covenants, this one concerning sacrifice is sparse in its introductory nature. For more information concerning Old Testament sacrifice, see Anderson, *Sacrifices and Offerings*.

23. Concerning the difference between the sin and trespass offering, Edersheim (*Temple*, 94) writes, "[The sin offering] made atonement for the person of the offender, whereas the trespass offering atoned for only one special offense."

24. All but the meal offering involve the bloody sacrifice of an animal. The sin, burnt, and peace offerings are important to this discussion.

25. Jenson, "Levitical Sacrificial System," 29–30. This is a very short synopsis of the sin offering. For a detailed account of the different types of sin as well as offerings for them, see Anderson and Culbertson, "Inadequacy of the Christian Doctrine of Atonement."

26. Wenham, "Theology of Old Testament Sacrifice," 79–80. McKenzie (*Covenant*, 106) notes that there was no transference of 'sinful material' in the laying on of hands. In his words, laying on of hands "expresses an identification in the sense of a delegated succession, a serving in the place of."

"representing the sacred life of the offerer": "the collective lives of the nation are symbolically offered up and incorporated into the holy so that they now have community with God."[27] He notes how "in an identification symbolized by the laying on of hands, the *nephesh* [life] is dedicated to the sanctuary and consecrated to the holy."[28] The identification unites the lives of the offerer and offering, much like the participation of the believer and Christ described in chapter 2 above does.

Shelton continues, "Because of the commitment of the offerer's life to what is holy, God did not simply consider the offering *as if* it were the offerer; it *really was* the offerer. The reality of ritual identification is not simply a fictional 'let's pretend' action, but a genuinely realistic portrayal of the relational reality that was represented by the identification between the subject (offerer) and the object (offering)."[29] There was a real participation in the life of the offerer in the offering, which foreshadows the real participation of the believer in the death, burial, and resurrection of Jesus that may, from chapter 2, be rightly called perichoretic.[30] The covenant participation in the Israelite sin offering is a shadow of the perichoretic soteriological union that it typifies.

The burnt offering was the main sacrifice of ancient Israel, both individually and collectively. Many commentators believe the chief function of the burnt offering is to atone for sin, but perhaps there is a different explanation.[31] The sin offering dealt with sinfulness, so for the burnt offering to do the same would seem redundant. A second opinion is that the burnt offering is the total surrender to God, or at

---

27. Shelton, *Cross and Covenant*, 56.

28. Ibid. The idea of being dedicated to the sanctuary should be a reminder of how Jesus is presented as a replacement of the temple in chapter 2 above. The joining of the lives of the offering and offerer and dedication of both to the place where God dwells helps unveil the relational nature of the work of Christ even more.

29. Ibid., 56–57. Italics in original.

30. The real participation is represented physically in the offerer's symbolic laying of his (it was always a man who sacrificed) hand on the animal and committing the act of slaying it. The author had to be keenly aware of his own death at the death of the sacrifice.

31. Among those surveyed that believe the burnt offering is for sin include Rooker, *Leviticus*, 85, and Wenham, *Book of Leviticus*, 63. Wenham makes the better argument, suggesting the burning of the animal on the altar symbolizes God's wrath burning against sinful man, if the fire does indeed symbolize God's judgment. Hartley (*Leviticus*, 18) offers a mediating position, stating that the burnt offering is an atoning sacrifice while maintaining that it allowed man to maintain fellowship with God.

least the willingness to do so, of the person making the sacrifice. H. Clay Trumbull, as a representative of the alternative view, describes the burnt offering symbolizing "the entire surrender to God, of the individual or of the congregation, in covenant faithfulness; the giving of one's self in unreserved trust to him with whom the offerer desired to be in loving oneness. It was an indication of a readiness to enter fully into that inter-union which the blood covenant brought about between two who had been separated, but who were henceforth to be as one."[32] The "inter-union" between two who "were henceforth to be one" strongly resembles some of the perichoretic language already discussed above.

The peace offering, or "offering of completion," was the final offering an Israelite gave.[33] Some of the animal would be offered to God by fire, some the priest would keep to consume himself, and the rest was for the Israelite and his family to eat in a type of covenant meal. Edersheim describes the peace offering as the "most joyous" of all in which God was both the guest and the host of the meal.[34] Commenting on the tie between the animal's blood and the meal, McCarthy notes that the sacrificial rites possess the idea of creating kinship between God and the Israelite. He continues, "The covenant meal means admission into the family circle of another, but the blood rite is especially vivid. Yahweh and the people are considered to be related by blood, for they have somehow shared the same blood in the rite."[35] Here God and the Israelite were symbolically portrayed as blood relatives as the covenant

---

32. Trumbull, *Blood Covenant*, 249. He adds later on the page, "The offering was not, indeed, understood as in itself compassing inter-union; it indicated rather a desire and a readiness for inter-union—anew or renewed; so both the substitute-body and the substitute-blood were offered at the altar of typical surrender and consecration." Edersheim (*The Temple*, 93) agrees: "It symbolized the entire surrender unto God, whether of the individual or of the congregation, and His acceptance thereof. Hence, also, it could not be offered 'without the shedding of blood.'" Beckwith ("Death of Christ as a Sacrifice," 130–35) substantially agrees, as he sees the burnt offering as consecrating oneself to God. Shelton, *Cross and Covenant*, 59, takes a similar view to that of Trumbull.

33. Edersheim (*Temple*, 99) states that "offering of completion" is an acceptable Hebrew rendering for "peace offering." It is described in Lev 3.

34. Ibid.

35. McCarthy, *Treaty and Covenant*, 173. Here, of course, both God and the Israelite both "partake" of the same animal flesh (God's portion is burned on the altar, while the offerer's portion is eaten). The partaking of flesh has the same effect as partaking of blood, as it is the seal of the covenant. See Ricker, "Covenant in the Old Testament," *International Standard Bible Encyclopedia Online*, http://www.searchgodsword.org/enc/isb/view.cgi?number=T2377.

is renewed.³⁶ This renewal, symbolizing the sharing of life in such an intimate way, means both mutual indwelling and participation are taking place.³⁷ Again, these are the key elements of a perichoretic relationship as discussed in this study.

Walther Eichrodt affirms God's desire to give Israel "a share in his own life."³⁸ A "share in his own life" has been discussed as explicitly perichoretic language in chapters 2 and 3 above. The covenant was a tangible way of portraying such a sharing. The Old Testament covenants were imperfect however, as Hebrews 7:19–28 shows.³⁹ For example, Trumbull also notes that of the blood of every personal Israelite sacrifice, none ever made it into the Holy of Holies, the dwelling place of God. Thus none of his offerings ever secured a complete union in God's presence.⁴⁰

If the above interpretations of the offerings are correct, then in the new covenant Christ embodies all of these offerings. He is the sin offering, taking both the depth of human alienation due to sin and the result thereof (death) upon himself.⁴¹ As the incarnate Son, he is the burnt offering symbolizing the desire for human union with God. As the fully deified man, he is likewise the peace offering of completed fellowship in communion. As Homer Kent describes the new covenant, "[It] would be a different sort than the Mosaic one he had given. It would bring a

36. See Chennattu, *Johannine Discipleship*, 58.

37. Again, this type of intimate sharing represented here goes far deeper than blood relatives or even members of the same household. As has been noted above by Trumbull (*Blood Covenant*, 7), it is the closest possible relationship between humans.

38. Eichrodt, *Theology of the Old Testament*, 1:157.

39. These sacrifices, though they show glimpses of perichoretic ideas, could not fully consummate the true union of man and God. As Whitcomb states in "Christ's Atonement and Animal Sacrifices," what happened to the worshipper was, "temporal, finite, external, and legal—not eternal, infinite, internal, and soteriological" (209). Whitcomb cites Bruce (*Epistle to the Hebrews*, 201), who writes, "The blood of slaughtered animals under the old order did possess a certain efficacy, but it was an outward efficacy for the removal of ceremonial pollution." Shelton (*Cross and Covenant*, 57–58) argues that the penitent heart of the Israelite making the sacrifice (and therefore acknowledging his lack before God) was the real cleansing in the ritual. While this may be debated especially in light of Psalm 51, the Old Testament is clear that sacrifice without a penitent heart is empty (see Prov 15:8; Isa 1:10–13; and Jer 6:20 for a few examples).

40. Trumbull, *Blood Covenant*, 252.

41. Paul writes in 2 Cor 5:21 that God made Christ who knew no sin to be sin on our behalf. That means he was a sin offering. Hebrews 9:28 echoes, "So Christ also, having been offered once to bear the sins of many." See also Rom 8:3. Thus Christ embodies the sin offering.

spiritual transformation by an inward change, not just by imposition of external code (Jer 31:33). Forgiveness of sins would be complete, and the knowledge of God would be universal among participants (Jer 31:34). God also called it an everlasting covenant."[42] The New Covenant is fulfilled in Christ, admitting both Jews and gentiles.[43]

The Life and Death of Jesus as a Covenant Act

In John 6:51, Jesus says that the bread he will give for the life of the world is his flesh, saying, "Truly, truly, I say to you, unless you eat the flesh of the Son of Man and drink His blood, you have no life in yourselves. He who eats My flesh and drinks My blood has eternal life, and I will raise him up on the last day. For My flesh is true food, and My blood is true drink. He who eats My flesh and drinks My blood abides in Me, and I in Him" (John 6:53–56).[44] At these words, many stopped following him.

Why was Jesus's statement so difficult for the Jews to believe? The Jews drank no blood, yet they did not grasp the intended, symbolic meaning of Jesus's words. In a survey of the major commentaries on John, there are several different opinions, ranging from symbolism to the Eucharist, to explain what Jesus means.[45] The "mutual abiding" language in John 6 is similar to the "reciprocal immanence" of the vine and branches in John 15. When surveying Jesus's words in John 15 in chapter 2 above, this study concluded that the vine and branches text represented

---

42. Kent, "New Covenant and the Church," 291. Isaiah and Ezekiel mention the new covenant as well. Also, Kaiser ("Old Promise," 14) states that the new covenant exists in sixteen or seventeen passages in the Old Testament, under different names.

43. Ware, "New Covenant," 70–73. Williamson (*Sealed with an Oath*, 179–81) says much the same. Hillers (*Covenant*, 180) notes how the author of Hebrews keeps much of the terminology of the Mosaic covenant, reinterpreting the terminology so that it describes what Christ did, with Jesus as the new Moses.

44. Again, the NASB capitalizations are retained.

45. For example, Köstenberger (*John*, 216–17) believes that the "flesh and blood" is symbolic of the entirety of one's being, which will be delivered to death for the sake of the world. Köstenberger also notes in his explanation of the disciples' reply, "This is a difficult statement; who can listen to it?" (John 6:60), the word "difficult" means "offensive." And the phrase "listen to" is in the context of obeying. Schnackenburg (*Gospel according to St. John*, 2:63) connects Jesus's words directly to the sacrament of Eucharist, writing, "In the earthly and human sphere there is no counterpart to such mutual permeation without a surrender of personality." Borchert (*John 1–11*, 272–73) suggests the Christian must "inwardly ingest" Christ rather than depend upon the elements of the Eucharist. Carson (*Gospel according to John*, 296–97) thinks eating and drinking of the flesh and blood is a metaphor for beholding and believing.

perichoretic language. It would seem that John 6 possesses perichoretic language as well. William Robertson Smith writes, "The notion that, by eating the flesh, or particularly by drinking the blood, of another living being, a man absorbs its nature or life into his own, is one which appears among primitive peoples in many forms."[46] Again, ingesting the blood of another symbolizes absorbing his life. As Clay Trumbull writes concerning Jesus's words,

> The fact that he did speak thus, so long before he had instituted the memorial supper, has been a puzzle to many commentators who were unfamiliar with the primitive rite of blood-covenanting, and with the world-wide series of substitute sacrifices and substitute forms of communion which had grown out of the suggestions, and out of the perversions, of the root symbolisms of that rite. But, in light of all these customs, the words of Jesus have a clearer meaning. It was as though he had said: "Men everywhere long for life. They seek a share in the life of God. They give of their own blood, or of substitute blood, and they taste of substitute blood, or they receive its touch, in evidence of their desire for oneness of nature with God. They crave communion with God, and they eat of the flesh of their sacrifices accordingly. All that they thus reach out after, I supply. In me is life. If they will become partakers of my life, of my nature, they shall be sharers of the life of God."[47]

This language strongly resembles that which this study has described as a third type of *perichoresis*, albeit asymmetric, in the soteriological union.[48] The believer partakes of Jesus's blood (life) in his union with Christ. Two parties partaking of common blood, either physically or symbolically, represents the two parties sharing the same life. In this way, a covenant becomes a tangible symbol of the kind of close, intimate

---

46. Smith, *Lectures*, 313.

47. Trumbull, *Blood Covenant*, 276–77. Whether oneness of nature is possible or not, immortality and sharing life with the divine has been a goal of people throughout recorded human history.

48. The asymmetry becomes clear here. The believer is freely able to partake of the life Jesus has to offer, by sharing in his death, burial, and resurrection. There is also a sense in which Jesus partakes of the believer's life in the incarnation, and taking upon himself the sum total of human estrangement on the cross, but these events are not parallel. That is evidence of the asymmetry of the soteriological *perichoresis*. Just as Christ's human nature could not become infinite (temporally at the very least) in the hypostatic union (thus showing the asymmetry of the christological *perichoresis*), likewise the sharing of life in the soteriological *perichoresis* largely flows (with the exception of the incarnation—and that is another category) in one direction.

union that is finally realized in the union of Christ and the believer. It may be said here that a blood covenant, at least those in the Old Testament that point toward the work of Christ in the New, is a physical representation of a third type of perichoretic relationship this study has discussed. Trumbull's language above also demonstrates *theosis*. Those who heard Jesus's words, though they understood the prohibitions against drinking blood, missed their full, perichoretic, covenantal significance.[49]

Invoking thoughts of Passover, John the Baptist called Jesus "the Lamb of God who takes away the sin of the world" (John 1:29).[50] Jesus, the saving Lamb of God, was crucified on Passover. The Last Supper was a Passover meal.[51] Robert Sherman notes that John records him dying at the moment the Passover lambs were killed.[52] In 1 Corinthians 5:7, Paul calls Jesus the Passover lamb. Jesus, in Luke 22:20, uses the words "new covenant in my blood" in describing the Passover meal at the Last Supper.[53]

Bernard Cooke identifies common flesh as one of the main themes in a covenant. He writes, "This common flesh provides biologically what a covenant agreement does in a legal fashion: a brotherhood. . . . So, at the Supper, when Jesus gave his body to eat, he was performing what was essentially a covenant action."[54] Partaking of a common meal often has the same covenantal significance as does ingesting, physically or symbolically, common blood.[55] The familiar perichoretic themes of mutual indwelling and participation become more apparent in the sharing of the covenant meal.

This readiness to enter or renew such a covenant is the fulfillment of the burnt offering from the days of Abel onward. It is the sacrifice of

---

49. Trumbull, *Blood Covenant*, 278.

50. The Passover was one of the highest days in Jewish life, as it was a solemn memorial of God's covenant faithfulness to Abraham to lead his descendants out of slavery in Egypt.

51. There is debate about whether the meal Jesus shared with his disciples was the Passover meal or simply another meal during the week. For a summary of the debate, see McKnight, *Jesus and His Death*, 264–73.

52. Sherman, *King, Priest, and Prophet*, 176.

53. Kent, "New Covenant," 292–93. McConville ("*Berit*," 753) notes how the "Old Testament covenant is evidently seen as having its fulfillment in the life, and especially the death, of Christ." Kent (ibid., 293) also notes Paul's "new covenant" language, as well as the same language in Hebrews (ibid., 294–95). Cooke ("Synoptic Presentation") sees the connection of the new covenant in the Last Supper and that foretold in the Old Testament prophets.

54. Cooke, "Synoptic Presentation," 26–27.

55. Chennattu, *Johannine Discipleship*, 58.

self-surrender.[56] Romans 12:1, the command to present one's own body as a living sacrifice, is the picture of New Testament self-surrender. Now it remains to see how the believer participates perichoretically in Christ's covenant action.

The Covenant as a Basis for the Believer's Union with Christ

The main idea of this section is that a covenant is a physical representation of the perichoretic relationship existing between Christ and the believer. A covenant is a tangible way of approximating the closeness and intimacy that the soteriological union possesses—so much so that there is often an identity between the soteriological union and the New Covenant. That is why the Bible and Christian history have said that salvation in Christ *is* the New Covenant. Once the Christian, in faith and repentance, has turned from sin to Christ, she has taken the obligations of the New Covenant in Christ upon herself. Therefore the life Christ has given becomes hers, and she has entered into covenant with Christ. This New Covenant is the believer's union with Christ—the soteriological union.

The covenant God made with Noah forbade the ingesting of blood. This prohibition of blood was one of the few Jewish rituals specifically passed down to Christians for both Jewish and gentile believers to follow (Acts 15:20, 29). While the blood covenants of the pagan nations ritually included the ingesting of blood, the God of Israel would not allow it, neither in civil covenants nor the ones he made.[57] The blood in a pagan religious rites was a symbol of the life of the god. Thus whenever a pagan drank the blood of a sacrificed animal, he was symbolically ingesting the life of the god. Trumbull writes,

> In the Mosaic ritual, however, all drink offerings of blood were forbidden to him who would enter into covenant with God; he might not taste of the blood. He might, it is true, look forward, by faith, to an ultimate sharing of the divine nature; and in anticipation of that inter-union, he could enjoy a symbolic intercommunion with God, by partaking of the peace offerings at the table of his Lord; but as yet the sacrificial offering which could supply to his death-smitten nature the vivifying blood of an everlasting covenant was not disclosed to him.[58]

---

56. Trumbull, *Blood Covenant*, 249–51.
57. Ibid., 251.
58. Ibid., 251–52.

The analogy of the sacrifice ends here. Drinking the blood of the sacrifice would share the life of the victim. God wants more. He wants to share his own life.

Therefore, no one less than God could give the life that was to be the source of a true divine inter-union. God would not allow any animal to stand in for the qualitatively real life he offered. Also, since human life resided in blood (Lev 17:11), no one greater than a man who possessed life in blood could offer it. Therefore, the one who enacted the new covenant that would bring life—God's life—to dead men and women would have to be not less than God and not greater than human at the same time. In short, he must be the God-man.

When Jesus lifted up the cup at the Last Supper, he said it was the cup of the new covenant in his blood. It contained not blood but wine. Neither the Jew nor Christian may drink real blood.[59] The wine was a symbol of his blood—the blood that makes believers share in his life.[60] Thus when people drink of the cup in faith, they are testifying to their perichoretic union with Christ in his death and resurrection, the sharing of his life, and the everlasting covenant that holds it all together.

This is the fulfillment of the peace offering. Everyone—God, priest, and family— participated in the peace offering. It was the joyous communion meal. For the Christian, the peace offering allows the Last Supper to become the Lord's Supper. Believers participate in the symbolic meal showing that they have entered into a covenantal union with God through the blood of Christ. For this communion to be as close as possible, the life he poured out was both fully human and fully divine. The salvation of a Christian, the believer's union with Christ, is enacted through a blood covenant where the believer is a participant through faith in the death, burial, and resurrection of Jesus, the Godman. Believers drink the peace-offering cup to show their participation in that covenant, symbolizing the infusion of divine life they now possess. They participate in Christ; Christ participates in them. Christ and the believer indwell one another with common life, as illustrated by symbolically partaking of common blood.[61] Thus the New Covenant

---

59. See Acts 15 as well as the Old Testament texts mentioned above.

60. Though Roman Catholics and Lutherans would disagree, this study does not hold the "real presence" view of communion. The point of the paragraph can be made either way, however.

61. While Jesus did not drink the cup at the Last Supper, the blood/life was already

pictures a third type of perichoretic relationship possessing the essential elements of the trinitarian and christological *perichoresis*.

When Jesus drank from the cup, he said, "But I say to you, I will not drink of this fruit of the vine from now on until that day when I drink it new with you in My Father's kingdom" (Matt 26:29 and Mark 14:25). If the cup of the Lord's Supper is the rite of union with Christ in his shed blood (life), the next time he drinks it will be "new" in the Father's kingdom.[62] Union with Christ as a perichoretic relationship in the new covenant exists already, but full consummation will come in the eschaton.[63]

In much of the Protestant Christian world, there are two "sacraments" or "ordinances"—baptism and the Lord's Supper. Martha Ellen Stortz sees these as being the tangible symbols of the believer in Christ and Christ in the believer, respectively.[64] The once-for-all symbol of entry into the covenant (and thereby the perichoretic soteriological union) is one's baptism.[65] Tee Gatewood writes, "Baptism, according to Paul, is a sacrament of mysterious union that incorporates the people of God into the person of the Son. Through baptism we participate in his death, resurrection, and new life."[66] The repeated practice of covenant renewal is the Lord's Supper.[67] These two ordinances are the symbols of the perichoretic covenantal relationship between Christ and the believer.

---

his. The blood/life is common, because Jesus possesses it already, and is giving it to the Christian. He need not drink to "partake." The asymmetry is still in view, because Christ is sharing something with the believer for which there is no real counterpart. The believer cannot give "life" back to Christ in the sense in which he gives it.

62. Both Morris (*Gospel according to Matthew*, 661–62) and France (*Gospel of Matthew*, 995) see the eschatological ramifications in Jesus's words.

63. See also the comments of Lane, *Gospel according to Mark*, 508–9.

64. Stortz, "Indwelling Christ."

65. See Hunsinger, "Dimension of Depth." Hunsinger writes that Calvin believed that the Christian "enters into inseparable union with" Christ at baptism (156). Similarly, Hunsinger quotes Torrance as saying that in baptism Christ's finished work "takes effect in us as our ingrafting into Christ and as our adoption into the family of the heavenly father" (163). The Torrance quotation is from *Theology in Reconciliation*, 88.

66. Gatewood, "Alive to God in Christ," 11. He also notes that T. F. Torrance teaches that the baptism of the Christian is "partaking through the Spirit in the one unrepeatable baptism of Christ" (12).

67. Smith, *Holy Meal*, 67–80. Smith outlines several other meanings in the communion meal as well.

Summary of the Perichoretic Nature of Covenant

Jesus was a Jew and thus was born into a people who already enjoyed a covenant with God. The Mosaic covenant of Israel, the basis of their national faith, is a covenant in blood, highlighted by its sacrificial system. The sacrifices portray an animal shedding its blood to reconcile the nation to God. It also foretells a new covenant where God will dwell in the hearts of people—language foreshadowing the perichoretic relationship the New Testament makes explicit. Jesus is the God-man who gives his life—life that is both fully human and fully divine—so that others may share in it in a depth and quality that allows the union between him and the believer to be rightly described as a perichoretic relationship. The idea of a covenant is a tangible way of understanding such a perichoretic relationship—one that could be understood by the ancient peoples as well as those of today. In the next section, the institution of marriage will be considered, and its perichoretic characteristics will be examined.

THE BRIDE OF CHRIST: THE PICTURE OF A PERICHORETIC RELATIONSHIP

Marriage is a concept with both physical and spiritual ramifications. Marriage between a man and a woman has the potential to be the closest of all human relationships.[68] Spouses can be so close that they become part of each other (Eph 5:28).[69] Unlike the relationship between parents and children (and similar to a covenant), there are no blood ties in marriage.[70] In addition to its physical aspects, marriage is often portrayed in the Bible as a metaphor for the relationship between God and his people. This section will argue that marriage is a relationship where a man and a woman become one flesh yet remain distinct individuals. It is reflective of the perichoretic relationship existing between Christ and the Christians, who comprise the church. Since this study examines the relationship between Christ and the individual believer, the discussion here will focus only on the individual aspects of what is more often a corporate reality.

---

68. Ortlund, *God's Unfaithful Wife*, 23.
69. Engelsma, *Marriage*, 15.
70. Ibid., 17.

Marriage as a Covenant

In the previous section, it was argued that the blood covenants of the Old Testament as well as the New Covenant are tangible ways of understanding the depth and intimacy of God's relationship with his people, expressed most fully in the soteriological union between Christ and the believer. Several authors have argued that marriage is a type of covenant relationship also, although not one in blood.[71] They present solid cases, which may indicate that marriage likewise could be a picture of the soteriological perichoresis because of its covenantal implications. While that may be true, this study will show that marriage sheds additional light directly on the believer's union with Christ as the perichoretic relationship they share.

Marriage in the Old Testament

The biblical foundation for marriage goes all the way back to the creation of humankind. God made humanity as male and female. Their mandate was to procreate, fill the earth, and have dominion over it. Because Eve was created from the flesh of Adam, there is a real sense of mutual indwelling between the first couple. Their life was shared from a common source, since Eve derived her life directly from Adam.[72] Their active participation in each other's lives in Eden points to a relationship with perichoretic qualities before the fall, though this relationship is not on the same level as the soteriological union.[73]

The unique promise of oneness in marriage is given in Genesis 2:24: "For this cause shall a man leave his father and mother and be joined to his wife; and the two shall become one flesh." Raymond Ortlund writes, "The new life created by a marriage fuses a man and wife together into

---

71. See Engelsma, *Marriage*; Tarwater, *Marriage as Covenant*; and Hugenberger, *Marriage as a Covenant* as examples of works that argue explicitly that human marriage is a covenantal relationship modeled after God's covenants with his people.

72. Ortlund (*God's Unfaithful Wife*, 23) states that "human marriage is premised in the making of the woman out of the very flesh of the man, so that the bond of marriage reunites what was originally and literally one flesh." This subsection only intends that Adam and Eve were once one flesh, so Adam and Eve, at least, physically indwelt one another.

73. The degree of intimacy of mutual indwelling and participation between Adam and Eve in their innocence was not as deep as that in the soteriological union. It is only meant here to be a reflective picture of a created relationship with discernable, yet faint perichoretic qualities.

one, fully shared human experience, prompting mutual care, tenderness, and love."[74] David Engelsma concurs, "'One flesh' refers to the becoming one of the entire nature of the man and the woman. There is a oneness of bodies and souls, of thinking and desiring, of hopes and disappointments, of labors and goals. There is a oneness of the whole of earthly life; the husband and wife share one life."[75] The two people do not merge into one person, but neither are they completely separate. Here is the perichoretic property of preserving unity in diversity—the ideal of one life with mutual participation—that is reflective of a perichoretic relationship.

The fall changed everything. Sin and its resulting curse shattered the reciprocal unity of Adam and Eve. The perfect institution of human union eventually became one of domination, deceit, and adultery. God chose Abraham for himself, and the nation of Israel became his people. God would utilize human marriage as a metaphor for his relationship with idolatrous Israel, beginning overtly in the Old Testament prophets.[76]

The Old Testament language depicting God and Israel in a marriage relationship abounds. God is jealous—it is even part of his name (Exod 20:4–6).[77] The pagan neighbors practice religions described as "whoredom."[78] The prophets portray idolatry (spiritual unfaithfulness) as adultery (marital unfaithfulness) in sometimes graphic detail. The book of Hosea is a living re-enactment where Hosea portrays God as a jilted lover married to the unfaithful woman Gomer (representing Israel).[79] Ezekiel 23 utilizes explicit language to show the depths of Israel's adulterous idolatry. There are many other examples of such language in the prophets,[80] which set the stage for the coming lasting marriage between God and his people.[81]

74. Ortlund, *God's Unfaithful Wife*, 22.

75. Engelsma, *Marriage*, 18.

76. Ortlund, *God's Unfaithful Wife*, 25. Ortlund argues that the implied metaphor of Israel as God's unfaithful wife goes all the way back to the founding of the Mosaic covenant, although it is not explicitly stated.

77. Ibid., 31–33.

78. Ibid.

79. Chavasse (*Bride of Christ*, 29) notes that Hosea was one of the earliest writing prophets, putting the marriage analogy of Israel and God into the eighth century BC.

80. Ortlund, *God's Unfaithful Wife*, 25–136. Ortlund's examination of Old Testament prophetic language is extensive. He also (137) notes that Jesus uses the same language of an "adulterous generation" when chastising the Jews' demand for a sign (137).

81. Englesma (*Marriage*, 21) states, "The Old Testament foretold the mystery of the

Marriage in the New Testament

Often, the New Testament describes Jesus as a bridegroom.[82] In John 3:29, he is called the bridegroom by John the Baptist. He describes himself as a delayed bridegroom (Matt 25:1–13). The kingdom of heaven is a marriage feast for the son of the king (Matt 22:2–14). There is a marriage supper of the lamb where the bride is the church (Rev 19:6–10). Perhaps even John 14:2–3 speaks of Jesus as the bridegroom.[83]

There are two passages in Paul's letters comparing the believer's union with Christ to human marriage—1 Corinthians 6:12–20 and Ephesians 5:22–33. In both passages, the idea of two becoming one is stressed. The former speaks more clearly concerning the individual believer, while the latter discusses the church as a whole.[84]

In a passage condemning sexual immorality, Paul makes the case that since the believer is part of Christ and the temple of the Spirit, lying with a prostitute joins a man to her as he is joined to Christ.[85] He who does so becomes "one body" with her (1 Cor 6:16). Aaron Son states that although the believer's union with Christ is not physical, "The analogy does suggest, however, that Paul conceives the union with Christ to be as

---

union of Christ and the church, and it described that union as a marriage."

82. Chavasse, *Bride of Christ*, 49–58, states that the Messiah as bridegroom was not something that needed proven in the gospels, as he believes it was standard in Jewish thinking that it was so. On page 58, he notes that it was no accident that the first miracle Jesus performed was at a wedding. See also McWhirter, *Bridegroom Messiah*.

83. See Showers, *Maranatha Our Lord*, 164–65. He sees the language of John 14:2–3 as describing a Jewish wedding ceremony, where Jesus is the groom and the church is the bride. Jesus's choice of words ("I go to prepare a place for you" and "I will come again to receive you to myself") lend Showers and others to believe that he was utilizing the then-familiar language of engagement for marriage to describe his death/resurrection/ascension and second coming. His position, though not mentioned in the commentaries, has support from Jewish sources such as Mielziner (*Jewish Law*, 77–89) which describes the common marital practices of the Jews in the Second Temple period. He emphasizes much of what Showers describes, showing that Jesus's words in John 14:2–3 conform to the actions of a Jewish wedding. See also Cohn, "Marriage," 7:370–76. For Old Testament examples of marriage, see De Vaux, *Ancient Israel*, 22–38. While this is not a major point of this study and is hence footnoted, it is an area that deserves further scholarly exploration.

84. Chavasse (*Bride of Christ*, 83) states, "While primarily the bride of Christ is the church, in a secondary sense each individual member is *consequently* wedded to Christ. Christ has one bride; but each of the several members, individually as well as corporately, partakes of the bridal status and privileges." Italics in original.

85. Son, *Corporate Elements*, 148.

real as the physical union created by sexual intercourse."[86] Concerning 1 Corinthians 6, Ortlund writes,

> But the striking feature of this theological paradigm is that the believer is even more intimate with the Lord than with his or her spouse, for this is a union of spirit, and spirit always leads one more deeply into reality than does flesh. The "cleaving of the LORD" of Deuteronomy 10:20 is now seen to be actualized through a joining of the believer's spirit with Christ. No more profound communion exists than that between the believer and the Lord, and Paul's logic encourages the view that this communion is, as it were, super-marital in nature and already joined.[87]

The husband and wife, typified by Adam and Eve, are one flesh, while Christ and the Christian are one spirit.[88]

Ephesians 5:22–33 describes the relationship of Christ and the church (and therefore by extension each individual believer) as a marriage.[89] In the middle of an instructive passage describing how Christian couples are to relate, Paul likens human marriage to the relationship of Christ and the body of believers—the church. He draws upon the original creation language of Genesis 2 and calls the words "For this cause shall a man leave his father and mother and be joined to his wife; and the two shall become one flesh" a mystery, which ultimately concerns Christ and the church.[90]

86. Ibid.

87. Ortlund, *God's Unfaithful Wife*, 146. See also a discussion of Martin Luther's views on marriage as a model for salvation in Garcia, *Life in Christ*, 56–68.

88. Son, "Implications," 114. Additionally, Englesma (*Marriage*, 20) states that God is the one who joins the man and woman together, not either spouse. Building on the "one spirit" relationship of Christ and the Christian, Fowler ("Three Divine Onenesses," http://www.christinyou.net/pages/3divineonenesses.html) notes how the three perichoretic onenesses co-exist. The trinitarian oneness is three persons, yet one God. The christological oneness is two natures, yet one Lord. The oneness of the believer and Christ is two human persons, yet one spirit. The trinitarian imagery of God, Lord, and Spirit is too obvious to ignore.

89. For a more detailed discussion of the passage, see Son, *Pauline Anthropology*, 149–56; Miletic, *"One Flesh"*; Sampley, *Two Shall Become One*; and Dawes, *Body in Question*.

90. For more on the "great mystery," see Dawes, *Body in Question*, 178–91. In an otherwise fruitful discussion, Dawes compares the all the uses of "mystery" in Ephesians. He ignores the common theme of union that Sampley (*Two Shall Become One*) sees, but instead calls the relationship of Christ and the church "vertical" while other mystery unions in Ephesians are "horizontal." The incarnation guarantees this mystery to have a "horizontal" component as well.

Raymond Ortlund notes that the idea of a man leaving parents and being joined to his wife causes a husband to put his wife above all other human relationships. If Christ is indeed to be the husband of the church, then his relationship with believers has no other relationship above it.[91] Moreover, as Eve was created out of the flesh of Adam (therefore being "bone of his bone"), Christians are also of the flesh and bones of Christ, language undoubtedly pointing to the creation of the Church out of the very life of the human Christ (Eph 5:30).[92] David Engelsma notes how Eve was created from Adam's flesh. This is why their relationship could be so strong. So it is with the church being made from Christ.[93] Jean Daniélou notes that God's presence drew Adam out of himself when he created Eve, "that mysterious foreshadowing of the creation of the church."[94]

There is one important conclusion to be drawn. Son notes that Paul's anthropology "implies that Paul understands man as a being whose existence is not limited to his individual person. He views man as extending himself beyond his individual boundaries to form a corporate unity (body) with others and with Christ, but without losing his own individuality. . . . This means in Paul's thought man exists not only individually but corporately."[95] Humans have the ability to transcend themselves so that real indwelling and participation in others is possible. Human marriage, even though it is an imperfect and vestigial picture of the soteriological union, shows that human beings are able to have real perichoretic relationships. A person can transcend the limits of her own "space" just as Adam did in his wife. This makes perichoretic relationships between humans distinctly possible.[96]

---

91. Ortlund, *God's Unfaithful Wife*, 21.

92. Though this reading is a textual variant ("of his flesh and of his bones" does not occur in many modern translations), Hoehner (*Ephesians*, 769–70) accepts it "with great hesitation." He accepts it due to "overwhelming external evidence and because it is the harder reading with regard to its internal evidence." See his discussion on 769n3, where the clause is quoted and taught as far back as Chrysostom.

93. Englesma, *Marriage*, 21.

94. Daniélou, *God and the Ways of Knowing*, 215.

95. Son, *Pauline Anthropology*, 169.

96. This line of reasoning would almost have to be employed if one were to study the perichoretic relationships among the members of the church, which this study omits. Again, "space" is meant relationally.

Marriage as a Vestige of a Perichoretic Relationship

United in marriage, a man and a woman become one flesh (Gen 2:24). The man and woman are one yet simultaneously distinct. Neither he nor she loses his or her personal identity, yet a union of both is likewise present. In this, marriage is a created vestige of the trinitarian *perichoresis*, in that the persons of the Trinity are distinct but still one God. Commenting on the preservation of identities in the relationship between Christ and the church, Wolfhart Pannenberg writes,

> If believers are thus "ecstatically" [outside themselves] lifted above themselves by the Spirit so as to be in Christ through faith, this does not mean that along the lines of mystical union, they merge into Christ or through him into God, that they are no longer even aware of their own distinction from Christ and from God. Instead, believers know very well that their own existence is different from Jesus Christ, in whom they believe, even though they are united to him by faith. An irrevocable part of their union with Christ in faith is awareness of the difference between their own existence and him as their head.[97]

Thus the believer's union with Christ, of which marriage is an analogy, preserves the distinctions of the partners while at the same time providing a union of mutual interpenetration.

David Cunningham, citing his relationship with his own family, writes, "I am 'related' to my wife and daughters, yes, but more than this: I dwell in their lives and they in mine. They are fundamentally constitutive of who 'I' am. Therefore, when you ask me how 'I' am doing, my answer will reflect on how 'they' are doing as well."[98] He shows how both marriage and family depend on close, interpersonal relationships marked by a sense of indwelling and participation. It is not as intimate or close as the soteriological *perichoresis*, but it does echo it in the created order. Colin Gunton affirms much the same:

> A doctrine of human *perichoresis* affirms, after philosophies like that of John Macmurray, that persons mutually constitute each other, make each other what they are. That is why Christian theol-

---

97. Pannenberg, *Systematic Theology*, 2:452.

98. Cunningham, *These Three Are One*, 169. Here, his use of "communion" and "participation" resembles the key components of a perichoretic relationship shown in chapters 1–2 above. Participation is a key element, and if by communion he means the idea of mutual indwelling he provides in his quote, then perichoretic overtones would surely be present.

ogy affirms that in marriage the man and the woman become one flesh—bound up in each other's being—and why the relations of parents and children are of such crucial importance for the shape that human community takes. Our particularity in community is the fruit of our mutual constitutiveness: of a perichoretic being bound up with each other in the bundle of life.[99]

Both Cunningham and Gunton see the perichoretic nature of marriage as reflective of the ability of humans to go beyond the limits of the physical body.

Michael Lawler argues for the perichoretic nature of marriage in bringing a real unity between two people.[100] He writes, "That cannot be, I suggest, except by *perichoresis*. To become one marital person, each spouse must actively make room for and interweave hand in hand with the other, physically, psychologically, religiously, in such wise that each shares as full and equal spouse in the one concrete nature of this marriage."[101] Though Lawler pursues the communal aspect of perichoretic relationships within the church as a whole, he does not hesitate to describe the relationship between spouses as a relationship reflecting the trinitarian *perichoresis*, although on a far lesser scale.

Peter Leithart, in arguing for a view of *perichoresis* that expands beyond the Trinity, writes concerning human marriage,

> Marriage, including sexual union, is perhaps the clearest created vestige of divine *perichoresis*. Quite literally, a man envelops and encompasses a woman in a loving embrace, while the woman encompasses the man. A man "enters" the woman who has entered him, and in this mutual containment they become "one flesh." Perichoretic union in marriage extends beyond the bedroom. Husbands make room for their wives in their lives, their projects, their dreams, their labors. Wives do the same, but husbands have particular trouble with this. Many wives, but few husbands, could echo Portia's pained lament to Brutus: "Dwell I but in the suburbs of your good pleasure?"[102]

---

99. Gunton, *One, the Three, and the Many*, 169–70.

100. Lawler, "*Perichoresis*," 55. Lawler, a Roman Catholic, sees marriage as a sacrament, which explains why he understands it both socially and religiously.

101. Ibid., 58.

102. Leithart, "Making Room," http://rdtwot.wordpress.com/2008/03/03/making-room-by-peter-j-leithart/.

Here, Leithart sees the explicit connection between *perichoresis* and marriage, both sexually and in all facets of life.

Contemporary monographs on marriage notice the analogy between *perichoresis* and marriage. Adrian Thatcher writes that *perichoresis* "prompts us toward affirming our own identity as a person while recognizing that other persons make us who we are and we help make other persons what they are."[103] He continues, "*Perichoresis* is an appropriate term to describe a relation to another person in whose care we place ourselves and for whom we care. *Perichoresis* may imply a continuity of presence that friendship does not. Language which has been historically reserved for reverent musings about the holy mystery of God is especially appropriate for filling the hiatus in compiling a theology and spirituality of marriage."[104] Although Thatcher does not speak of the huge divide between created vestiges of *perichoresis* and the intra-trinitarian relationships, at least he recognizes some similarities. In this way his comments are insightful, though he goes on to argue that the concept of *perichoresis* removes all ideas of order in marriage, which the final section of this chapter will show is an unwarranted move.[105]

In a perhaps more biblically balanced treatment of marriage, Jack and Judy Balswick draw comparisons between the closeness of human marriage and the trinitarian *perichoresis*. They write, "The relational nature of marriage is analogous in human form to the divine Trinity. As Father, Son, and Holy Spirit (three distinct persons) mutually indwell in a trinitarian fellowship, spouses mutually indwell in the marriage union. . . . As spouses mutually permeate one another they achieve an interdependency (emotional connection) in which neither spouse loses distinctiveness. Unity and distinction coexist."[106] Commenting on the similarity between *perichoresis* and marriage, the Balswicks write, "In marital terms, both spouses bring their distinct selves (mutual interiority) while making space for the other (mutual permeation) so they can indwell each other (interdependence) and become an entity (union) that

---

103. Thatcher, *Marriage after Modernity*, 231.

104. Ibid., 232. Thatcher's first sentence in this quote is an example of drawing the implications of *perichoresis* a bit too far. It is included here to show that contemporary scholars are understanding marriage in perichoretic language, even though they may not nuance the obvious asymmetry between the trinitarian *perichoresis* and created reality completely.

105. Ibid.

106. Balswick and Balswick, *Model for Marriage*, 32.

transcends themselves."¹⁰⁷ As two spouses become one without a loss of identity, so does the union of the believer and Christ not destroy the identity and uniqueness of the believer.¹⁰⁸ Just as in the trinitarian *perichoresis*, individuality is preserved in unity. Again, this is a created vestige of divine life (not at the trinitarian level, but the vestige is present).

It is important to note that both Thatcher and the Balswicks argue in the context of Christian marriage. The presence of the Spirit in both spouses makes a marriage that exhibits perichoretic tendencies more likely. Miletic notes that in Christian marriages, the husband must not dominate the wife because it will violate the love of Christ.¹⁰⁹ When husbands and wives are filled with Christ's love, they open themselves up to participate in the other by seeking the good of the other, and the traditional power structures of dominance are overthrown. Miletic calls this husband/wife of Ephesians 5 the new Adam/Eve, which produces eschatological unity.¹¹⁰

Summary of Marriage

This section has shown that marriage, in its fullest context apart from sin, is a clear vestige of the trinitarian *perichoresis* in the created order.¹¹¹ This section has also demonstrated how the covenantal relationship between God and his people (and therefore by extension each individual person among that people) is described as a marriage relationship in both the Old and New Testaments. The marriage language in Scripture conveys the intended closeness of the bond between God and his people. That closeness may be interrupted by idolatry and sin, but the relationship is intended to mirror and even exceed the closest possible human bond—that between husband and wife. This line of thinking is important to the thesis of this study for two reasons. First, it shows that a perichoretic relationship can include humans, not just the divine Persons. Second, human marriage is a symbol of the union, and Paul shows marriage was instituted to reflect the union. Human marriage makes one flesh. The ul-

---

107. Ibid, 33.

108. Ibid, 84.

109. Miletic, *One Flesh*, 118.

110. Ibid., 120.

111. Though Leithart ("Making Room") and others quoted above connect marriage with the Trinity, none explicitly connect marriage and soteriological *perichoresis*. That is inferred as outlined above.

timate marriage is one spirit.[112] It is direct biblical language that deepens a Christian's understanding of the believer's union with Christ.

ADOPTED INTO THE FAMILY

This section will show how the perichoretic relationship of Christ and the believer and the believer's adoption into the family of God interrelate. Adoption, like *theosis*, is closely related to the believer's union with Christ. While *theosis* is the believer's participation in the divine nature, adoption is the way in which the perichoretic life of the Trinity as a whole is shared with the believer. That perichoretic life of the triune God is made available to the believer because of a chain of perichoretic relationships spanning the Godhead and the believer: the trinitarian, christological, and the soteriological. While these three perichoretic relationships are not inherently equal, they all may rightly be called perichoretic.[113] This means that, as far as is possible, both mutual indwelling and participation in the other are present. Adoption occurs when the believer is joined in perichoretic union to the Son, so that by grace she becomes a child of the Father because of her inclusion in the Son. This inclusion, in turn, opens up the ability to have a perichoretic relationship with the triune God. In logical sequence, the soteriological union creates the way of adoption, which in turn allows the process of theosis to occur. This will hopefully become apparent as the section progresses.

The Children and Sons of God in the New Testament

Unlike the previous sections dealing with communion and marriage, the concepts of the fatherhood of God and God having human children are not common in the Old Testament.[114] There are few references to God as Father in the Old Testament, and most of those concern Israel, rather than individuals, as his child.[115]

---

112. Ortlund, *God's Unfaithful Wife*, 137.

113. See the discussion of the various levels of *perichoresis* in chapter 1 above.

114. See the discussion of Scott (*Adoption as Sons of God*, 61–117) as he discusses the idea of adoption in the Old Testament and ancient Near East. The best text he finds is the possible adoption of the Davidic king in 2 Sam 7:14.

115. Cook ("Concept of Adoption," 138) notes how Paul in Rom 9:4–5 describes Israel's sonship as an adoption. This is interesting, but is not the focus of this section. Miles ("Israel as Foundling," 16–24) notes that adoptive fatherhood of God is noticeable in Israel after the founding of the monarchy.

Theological Issues 153

The New Testament makes a dramatic shift. Jesus speaks of his Father repeatedly in the Gospels. Both John and Paul speak of other humans becoming children of God, although their language and methods vary. Below is a short summary of "child of God" language in the two New Testament authors.

John speaks of both Jesus and believers as children of God. John makes a distinction between the two in his language. He calls Jesus the υἱός (son) of God while calling other human children of God by a different word for children, τέκνα.[116] Describing the difference, Leon Morris writes, "The term John uses is τέκνα. He never uses υἱός of men's sonship to God, but keeps this term for Christ. He alone has full rights to what the term denotes. The nearest John gets to it is when he refers to men becoming υἱὸς φωτός (12:36)."[117]

Paul, on the other hand, uses both υἱός and τέκνα to describe the children of God.[118] John does not utilize the Pauline term for adoption, υἱοθεσία.[119] In his major study on Pauline adoption, James Scott concludes that Paul borrows a Hellenistic term to describe salvation in terms of a new exodus in Galatians.[120] Trumper sees the difference in approach between the sonship languages of John and Paul, respectively, as "birth and nature" in the former and "status and freedom" in the latter.[121] D. A. Carson adds, "The language [of John] is unlike that of Paul, who describes both Jesus and the believer as 'son' of God, but believers are sons only by adoption. Thus both writers presume a distinction between the 'sonship' of believers and the unique 'sonship' of Jesus."[122] The question is whether this distinction is based on the quality of sonship (as Carson

---

116. Trumper, "Metaphorical Import," 136. Trumper, following Vellanickal, *Divine Sonship*, 91–92, and Smail (*Forgotten Father*) sees this as a clear distinction in John's writings. He associates τέκνα with the new birth, since it etymologically derives from a word meaning "procreate." The idea of τέκνα does include a similarity of nature that one gains from the parent at birth.

117. Morris, *Gospel according to John*, 98n74. Commenting on the first instance of the term "children of God" in John (John 1:12), Lincoln (*Gospel according to St. John*, 102) notes other places the phrase "children of God" is mentioned in John's writings include John 8:41–7; 11:52; 13:33 (little children); and 1 John 3:1–2, 10; 5:2.

118. Ibid.

119. Trumper, "Metaphorical Import," 135. For the etymological origins of υἱοθεσία, see Cook, "Concept of Adoption," 133.

120. Scott, *Adoption as Sons of God*, 267–68.

121. Trumper, "Metaphorical Import," 137.

122. Carson, *Gospel according to John*, 126.

may be implying with "only") or the ontological distinctions (God-man vs. human-only) of the persons involved. This section will argue that the latter is the case.[123]

Adoption (υἱοθεσία) is a uniquely Pauline term that occurs five times in his letters (Gal 4:5; Rom 8:15, 23; 9:4; and Eph 1:5). All but one usage suggest adoption is a past event.[124] The other, Romans 8:23, focuses on the eschatological aspects of adoption.[125] Like John, Paul does not confuse the sonship of Christ with the adoption of believers.[126] There are differences in their approaches also, as Trumper writes, "Paul, in contrast to John, focuses on redemption *from* bondage *to* sonship *by* adoption (through union with Christ) resulting in freedom for the grown-up sons and daughters of God."[127] What is important to show now is that everything Christ possesses in his sonship (the ontological differences excepted) is available to the adopted children of God because of their participation in the sonship of the incarnate Son.

Jesus himself had no biological father, but he was the adopted son of Joseph the carpenter, as Joseph was married to Jesus's mother. Although the Bible never mentions that Jesus was adopted by Joseph, it may be inferred from the text. He is "the carpenter's son" (Matt 13:55). Mary, who knows the facts of Jesus's virgin birth, even calls Joseph the father of Jesus (Luke 2:48). Since Jesus's family and neighbors saw Joseph as his father, it is reasonable to assume that Joseph fulfilled the role of Jesus's adopted father.

Jesus's adoption is biblically meaningful because textually it is through Joseph that the messianic prophecies concerning the son of David are transmitted to Jesus. Again, Joseph was not Jesus's biological father; the evidence from Jesus's friends and family suggests he was his adoptive father. If Jesus were the son of David biologically, he would

---

123. Romans 8:29 seems to make no distinction in the sonship of Christ and believers, as Christ, the Son by nature, becomes the first-born of many brethren. The ontological distinctions (that is, Son by nature vs. children by grace) between Christ and other human children of God do not appear to posit a different quality of sonship within the text.

124. Cook, "Concept of Adoption," 139.

125. Ibid. Sanders (*Paul*, 69) states that adoption is the redemption of the body.

126. Burke, *Adopted into God's Family*, 124.

127. Trumper, "Metaphorical Import," 139. Italics in original. Trumper argues that John speaks more of regeneration, or new birth, in his "children of God" references, while Paul speaks directly to the matter of the adoption of children of God.

have to be so through his mother. But the Bible does not connect Jesus to David through Mary. It connects them through Joseph. So if Jesus is the messianic descendant of David through Joseph, as the text indicates, he is so by adoption.[128] The messianic prophecies belonged to Christ because they belonged to Joseph and his forefathers—all the way back to David. The New Testament genealogies show the Davidic line coming through Joseph, not Mary. Because the text is clear that the Davidic line comes through Joseph, the Messianic promise is conferred to Jesus through adoption rather than biology.

J. Gresham Machen, appealing to adoption, cites the Mosaic Law where if a man dies, his brother can give him children. Since no other man could dispute with Joseph over being the "father" of Jesus, he writes concerning Joseph, "The child Jesus could be regarded as Joseph's son and heir with a completeness of propriety which no ordinary adoptive relationship would involve."[129] The adoption of Christ into the Davidic line of Joseph did not make the messianic titles any less his. Jesus is still the Son of David—by adoption. If something so precious as the messianic promise can be conferred by adoption, can it be argued that the Father's adoption of human children implies anything less than the fullest possible sonship, ontological differences excepted?

Adoption as Incorporation

This study has argued that based on the biblical descriptions of both the trinitarian and christological *perichoresis*, mutual indwelling and active participation in the other are the main elements constitutive of a perichoretic relationship. Due to the mutual indwelling inherent in the soteriological union, the believer is incorporated into Christ. Participation in the Son, in all that he is, includes participation in his sonship with the Father. As Athanasius notes, believers become sons of God through the Son who indwells them.[130] Interpreting Athanasius, Thomas Torrance

---

128. See the argument of Moore, *Adopted for Life*, 67–68. While it is possible that Mary was also descended from David, there is no explicit textual evidence for it. The genealogies in both Matthew 1 and Luke 3 trace the Davidic line of descent from David to Jesus through Joseph, not Mary. See the discussion in Machen, *Virgin Birth*, 127–30.

129. Machen, *Virgin Birth*, 130. Though Jesus's virgin birth and lack of a biological father are unique, Machen's point is that there would be no challenge to the adoptive fatherhood of Joseph, cementing his status as his father by adoption.

130. Athanasius, *Against the Arians* 1.39 (NPNF2 4:329).

writes, "This does not mean that the relation between us and Christ is precisely the same as that between the Son and the Father, although it is grounded upon it, for there is no identity in nature or equality between us and Christ as there is between him and the Father. The union between us and Christ is not one of nature but one of adoption and grace effected through the gift of the Spirit who comes to dwell in us as he dwells in God."[131]

Cyril of Alexandria, in the same vein, sees the sonship of Christians derived directly from the Sonship of Christ. He writes,

> Christ is at once the only-begotten Son and the first-born Son. He is the only-begotten as God; he is the first-born through the saving union he has established between us and him by becoming man among many brethren. He became man that in him and through him we might be made sons of God both by nature and by grace: by nature, in him alone; by participation and grace, through him in the Spirit. Therefore, just as the attribute of the only-begotten has become proper to the humanity in Christ, since that humanity is united to the Word according to the economy of salvation, so also to be the first-born among many brethren has become proper to the Word, through his union with the flesh.[132]

Summarizing Cyril, Emile Mersch writes, "'In him and through him we are made sons of God both by nature and by grace.' To the mind of St. Cyril, the incarnation of the only-begotten Son extends that far."[133] Thus adoption is not merely a legal pronouncement—it is a real participation in the Son.

---

131. Torrance, *Trinitarian Faith*, 265.

132. Cyril of Alexandria, *De recta fide ad Theodosium* 30 (PG 46:1177), quoted in Mersch, *Theology of the Mystical Body*, 348–49. Here, Cyril's view of "nature" is different from that of Torrance. According to Torrance, Christ as son by "nature" equals he is the eternal son of God, and therefore unique. According to Cyril, other humans as sons by "nature" equals human re-creation and incorporation in the Son. Elsewhere (quoted in Mersch, *Theology of the Mystical Body*, 347), Cyril speaks of the believer being transformed "wholly into excellence," which may account for his use of nature. Either way, they are using "nature" in two different senses. Furthermore, Fairbairn (*Life in the Trinity*, 36–37n5), states that Cyril developed two technical words to describe the two different unities the persons of the Trinity share. The first is an ontological unity that created persons may not share. The second is a relational unity that is open to believers as well.

133. Mersch, *Theology of the Mystical Body*, 349.

To describe the depth of the filial relationship that is present in the incorporation and adoption, Donald Fairbairn notes that adoption allows humans access to the relationship the persons of the Trinity share. Although he is careful to maintain the ontological distinctions between Christ's sonship (by who he is) and that of other persons (derived, adopted, and created), he writes, "The fellowship we have with God is the same as that which the Son has with the Father. They [Father and Son] have that fellowship because they share the same nature; we have it because we have been linked to God through the incarnation."[134] The link is precisely the three types of *perichoresis* in action together: trinitarian, christological, and soteriological.

Christian believers are children of God because of their inclusion in the Son of God. The sonship of the Christian is fully derived from the sonship of Christ. Because a perichoretic relationship exists between the believer and Christ, the believer actively participates in Christ's sonship. All aspects of Christ's relationship with the Father, with the exception of the ontological differences noted above, are present in the adoptive relationship as well. It is due to the perichoretic active participation in the other that the two varieties of sonship are effectively one. Again, the *origin* of the sonship is different (Son by nature vs. children by grace), but the *relationship* is not, for the children by grace participate in the sonship of the Son by the Spirit.

The existence of a third type of *perichoresis* in the soteriological union makes the relationship between Father and Son the same as between Father and children in the Son. So Frank Porter states, "Paul seems to know no bounds when he sets out to show that the sonship of the Christian is the same as the sonship of Christ. He begins the parallelism with the eternal purpose of God (Rom 8:29; Eph 1:4–5) and does not end until the body itself becomes glorified, and Christians are co-heirs with Christ in his kingship (Gal 4:7; Rom 8:17)."[135] Because of the perichoretic relationship of mutual indwelling and active participation in the other between Christ and the believer, the two are inextricably bound together, both now and for eternity. Also because of the soterio-

---

134. Fairbairn, *Life in the Trinity*, 138. Here Fairbairn is summarizing the thoughts of Cyril of Alexandria as well.

135. Porter, *Mind of Christ*, 258–59. Again, the sonship of which Porter speaks is the relationship, not the ontological difference.

logical *perichoresis*, adopted children of God are as much members of the family as the eternal Son is.

The Father as "Abba"

In his words and teachings, Jesus repeatedly refers to God as the Father or his Father. The Aramaic word Jesus used to refer to his Father is "Abba" (Mark 14:36). Ralph Martin notes that this word probably results from childish babble added to the Aramaic word for father, *ab*.[136] Moreover, Martin provides evidence that "Abba" was probably the word Jesus used when addressing the Father in his numerous teachings and prayers, especially evidenced by its liturgical adaption in the letters of Paul to Galatia and Rome.[137] It is significant that the term Jesus used to convey his closeness to the Father is the same term adopted children use to note that same closeness.

The ability of the believer to cry "Abba" deserves closer attention. "Abba" shows the closeness and intimacy Father and Son enjoy.[138] By adoption, believers are now permitted to use that title to address the Father as well. When God the Son became flesh and incorporated believers into himself through the Spirit, they become adopted children with the right to address the Father in the same way Jesus did—as "Abba."[139] Moltmann, commenting on the significance of "Abba," writes, "In the Christ community we and they become children of God who also call God 'Abba, dear Father' (Rom 8:15; Gal 4:4–6). God the Spirit gives witness 'that we are children of God' (Rom 8:16). In community with Christ and in the power of the life-giving Spirit, we experience ourselves in God and God in us."[140]

Robert Peterson adds, "Our Spirit-given ability to cry 'Abba, Father' points to the intimacy of our relationship with God through adoption. We know the Father so closely that we are permitted to address him as his

---

136. Martin (*Reconciliation*, 217) notes that "*ab*" becomes "*abba*" in the same way that "dad" becomes "daddy" in English. For those who do not favor the "daddy" interpretation, see Burke, *Adopted into God's Family*, 94. In either case, interpreters agree it is a term of endearment from child to father, and is best translated with the meaning, "dear father."

137. Ibid., 217–18.

138. Peterson, *Adopted by God*, 115.

139. See Bouttier, *Christianity according to Paul*, 51–52; and Scott, *Adoption*, 182–83.

140. Moltmann, "God in the World," 376.

beloved and unique Son did."[141] Likewise, C. Baxter Kruger states that the Spirit takes the exclusive words of Jesus, "Abba, Father," and makes them our own.[142] The Son's address of "Abba" to the Father is based upon the relationship they already share. Because the relationship of the believer with the Father is derived from the existing soteriological perichoretic union, the believer in Christ likewise shares the same relationship to the Father. Therefore, the believer may use the same term of endearment for the Father that Jesus does. That may be why Paul saw fit to include the Aramaic expression for Father in his letters to Greek readers.[143]

In John 17:22, Jesus promises to give his followers glory so that they may be one even as he and the Father are one.[144] Paul writes in Romans 8:17 that the adoption of believers implies their joint-heirship with Christ. The promise of joint-heirship, in turn, depends on the believer's willingness to suffer with Christ. Philippians 3:10, as Cunningham notes, speaks of believers as participating in Christ's sufferings.[145] This suffering, part of the believer's experiential union with him, leads to the believer's glorification with Christ—the exact promise of John 17:22. Sonship, the type of familial relationship that allows believers to use the name "Abba," is closely tied to the glory that will result in the oneness that believers (and by extension each individual believer) will enjoy with the Godhead that the Father and Son presently experience. This adoption whereby the believer cries "Abba" is a gift to believers in their union with Christ.[146]

Adoption into the family of God brings the family relationship into reality for each believer. Here Moltmann speaks of the church as a whole, but his ideas may be extended to each individual believer. He writes, "The community of Christ's disciples shall not, however, only

---

141. Peterson, *Adopted by God*, 116.

142. Kruger, "Bearing Our Scorn," 18, http://www.perichoresis.org/x2/file/9fc3d7152ba9336a670e36d0ed79bc43.pdf. They *were* exclusive until Jesus opened them to believers through the Spirit.

143. See Martin, *Reconciliation*, 217–18.

144. The context of this text is that oneness operates on two levels. First is the believers' (and therefore each individual believer's) oneness with the Godhead, and then the believers' oneness with each other. This study is only concerned with the individual believer's relationship to Christ, and is thus obviously included in this text.

145. Cunningham, *These Three Are One*, 182.

146. Burke, *Adopted into God's Family*, 120–23. See also Murray, *Redemption Accomplished*, 170.

correspond to the divine Trinity by analogy. They shall also become a community included in the divine Trinity, 'so that they shall also be one in us.' This is the mystical dimension of the church: the human community in the divine community and vice versa, mutually indwelling one another."[147] Gruenler summarizes by stating, "Jesus's prayer [in John 17] reveals that the goal of the divine family is to bring the separated and fallen into a redeemed and unified family that reflects the relationship of the divine persons in their ultimate oneness."[148] Because each believer is adopted into the family of God, he is able to enjoy the Father-child relationship, which works itself out in *theosis*. As Thomas Weinandy writes, "The contention of the whole Pauline corpus is that we are taken into the intimate life of the Trinity, becoming genuine adopted sons and daughters of God. We enjoy the same rights and privileges as Jesus. We experience a heavenly life analogous to his own."[149] This is an eschatological reality with a foretaste for believers now. James Scott notes that the present aspect is the "Abba-cry" and participation in the "Son's Spirit-led sonship." The future aspect is the full adoption at the time of the resurrection of the body which precedes "the Abrahamic inheritance of universal sovereignty with the Son."[150]

The believer's prerogative to use "Abba," then, is due to the sonship (again, relationship, not ontology) of the believer being on the same level with the sonship of Christ. It is indicative of both shared sufferings now and a shared inheritance later.[151] As Mersch summarizes concerning believers, "As members of Christ they are members of the Son; we cannot escape this conclusion. We may and we must make distinctions; but we may admit no separation."[152] The Son is the Son by nature and eternity, while the believer is a son by grace in time.[153] But that is the only real difference between them. God the Father wants both kinds of sons to be in his "forever family."[154]

---

147. Ibid.

148. Gruenler, *Trinity and the Gospel of John*, 129.

149. Weinandy, *Father's Spirit of Sonship*, 35.

150. Scott, *Adoption as Sons of God*, 265–66.

151. See Porter, *Mind of Christ in Paul*, 259–60 for more of the benefits of adoption.

152. Mersch, *Theology of the Mystical Body*, 370.

153. Ibid., 372.

154. This term is part of contemporary adoption language. As an adoptive father,

Adoption and Soteriological Perichoresis

The relationship of the believer to the Father may now be seen as a chain with three links. The first link is the trinitarian *perichoresis* that unites the three persons of the Godhead. The second link is the incarnation with its christological *perichoresis* uniting the divine and human natures in Christ. The third link is the soteriological union, where the believer is united to Christ. It is the thesis of this study that this union is likewise a perichoretic relationship, albeit of a third type. This study has argued inductively that the biblical description of the soteriological union may rightly be called perichoretic. It has shown that descriptions of the union throughout Christian history have used terminology that strongly resembles the language of *perichoresis*. What light does the perichoretic soteriological union shed on adoption?

As argued in chapter 1, the trinitarian *perichoresis* is symmetric and mutual.[155] There is full and complete indwelling and participation among the persons of the Trinity, as they possess one (divine) nature. The christological *perichoresis* is neither symmetric nor complete, as Jesus's human nature is not infinite.[156] The soteriological *perichoresis* has asymmetry as well, since Christ is God by nature as well as human. Given this, there is still a perichoretic chain of three links, albeit resulting in an asymmetrical and incomplete *perichoresis* between the Father (and the Spirit) and the human believer. This perichoretic chain allows the relationship of human children to the Father to be the same as the relationship of Father and Son.

The previous subsection has shown that the believer's sonship is equal in all respects to that of Christ except for the ontological (that is, uncreated vs. created and nature vs. grace) difference between the two.[157] The relationship the Father has with his eternal Son is perichoretic. His relationship with the other children is perichoretic as well, since

---

this author has had the incredible privilege of bringing home two boys from South Korea and one daughter from China to become children by adoption. They are now a part of his "forever family," as they will always have a home. It is unthinkable that *the* Father would adopt believers *as sons* and place them beneath or love them any less than the Son. In words Jesus could have spoken, if an earthly father could love in this way, how much more will *the* Father love?

155. See also Thacker, *Postmodernism*, 53–54.

156. Jesus's humanity had a beginning, and therefore does not share in the eternality of the divine nature.

157. For a more complete explanation, see Hill, *Three-Personed God*, 292.

Christians are perichoretically included in the Son. As Emile Mersch interprets Augustine, "The unity we have in [Christ] and with him is so close that, to love the Son completely, God must love us along with him."[158] Even though the three links of the perichoretic chain result in an incomplete and asymmetrical *perichoresis*, it is still a perichoretic result. Believers become the true children of the Father in the Son, sharing a perichoretic relationship with the Father, although not the same type of *perichoresis* the Son enjoys with him. The Son's *perichoresis* with the Father is trinitarian, while the believer's is a three-link chain.

Summary of Adoption

This section has argued that God has willed to add to his family through the adoption of human persons. While there are biblical grounds for distinguishing Christ as eternal Son from believers as adopted children, this distinction has more to do with ontology than the resultant relationship. The term of endearment "Abba" shows that the Father is the real Father of both the Son and believers. Both the Son and the children suffer together, and are glorified together (Rom 8:17). Both have the same inheritance: to be revealed as children of God in the eschaton (Rom 8:19). Both have a perichoretic relationship with the Father, although the equality and symmetry of those relationships differ since the relationship between the Father and the believer is mediated through the "three divine onenesses."[159] Thus seeing the soteriological union as perichoretic enables the Christian to logically deduce that her relationship with the Father is perichoretic as well.

For a last piece of evidence for equal sonship as well as a comment on the role of the Spirit in adoption, Thomas Weinandy writes, "The same Spirit by which we become one with the oneness of the Father and the Son, is the same Spirit by which they themselves are one. As our oneness with God, our abiding, is founded upon the Spirit given to us by the Father, so the Son's oneness with the Father is established by the Spirit in which he is begotten and in which he eternally abides with the Father in love."[160] The adoption of believers as sons is of supreme impor-

---

158. Mersch, *Theology of the Mystical Body*, 351, citing Augustine, *In Ioan.* 111 (PL 35:1929).

159. See Fowler, "Three Divine Onenesses," http://www.christinyou.net/pages/3divineonenesses.html.

160. Weinandy, *Father's Spirit of Sonship*, 46. Here Weinandy is following Augustine's

tance. Michel Bouttier summarizes, "Thus Christ's presence takes us into the new dwelling-place, 'the household of God,' where we have a place as sons; such is the gospel proclaimed to the Galatians. Communion with the First-born fashions them into the image of the Father (Rom 8:29), teaches them a filial attitude, begins to replace pride by humility, prompts them to that obedience and gratitude that characterize legitimate children."[161] The next section will examine some possible theological benefits in seeing the soteriological union as a third type of perichoretic relationship.

FURTHER THEOLOGICAL BENEFITS OF SOTERIOLOGICAL PERICHORESIS

This section will highlight two further theological benefits in understanding the soteriological union as a third type of *perichoresis*. The first of these is that the word "perichoretic" has greater explanatory power than other adjectives to describe the depth and detail of the soteriological union. Second, like the trinitarian or christological *perichoresis*, the soteriological union must preserve the unity and diversity of the believer and Christ in the relationship. Overstressing unity or diversity leads to theological error. The two must be kept in balance, which is what *perichoresis* is uniquely able to do in the other theological contexts.

Why the Term "Perichoretic" Is Helpful

If describing the believer's union with Christ as a perichoretic relationship is not an unorthodox idea, what is gained by using the term? Why should theology consider a new term to describe the believer's union with Christ? Will it aid or deepen understanding? Below are some reasons to answer in the affirmative.

---

idea that the Spirit is the bond of love between Father and Son, as well as the Spirit's role in the conception of the human Jesus.

161. Bouttier, *Christianity according to Paul*, 52. Here, Bouttier evidently uses Rom 8:29 together with Heb 1:3, because Rom 8:29 speaks of the image of the Son. The Son is the image of the Father (Heb 1:3), so being changed into the image of the Son results in some way being changed to the image of the Father also. See also Rhoads, "Children of Abraham," 295. Rhoads states that "The relationship between brothers was the strongest bond in ancient familial relations." It was even stronger than father-son, because brothers were equals.

From chapter 1 above, it is currently more common to describe what the believer's union with Christ is not rather than what it is.[162] There is a lack of positive terminology for describing the union, and so theologians are utilizing the *via negativa*, which has its limits of description.

What positive terminology there is for describing the believer's union with Christ is mostly either inadequate or confusing. The most confusing term is "mystical union." Since there is no universally accepted definition of mysticism, "mystical union" can mean significantly different things to different people.[163] Such potential equivocation renders the term meaningless for discussion. Add to this the fear that "mystical" might equal "occult," and the term becomes a hindrance rather than a help.

Other positive terminology for the believer's union with Christ is not quite as descriptive as a perichoretic relationship. "Mutual indwelling," for example, does not tell the whole story, since mutual indwelling is not the entirety of the believer's union with Christ. Mutual active participation in the other is also present. "Vital union" does not explain the quality or source of the life, nor does it express the idea of indwelling. "Judicial union" does not adequately reflect the relationships among persons in the union. It seems a bit cold and impersonal as well. "Spiritual union" is good, but it does not adequately explain by what spirit the union is made, whether the human spirit or the Holy Spirit. Calvin's threefold terminology for union, which is a very comprehensive explanation, can be well summarized as what this study argues as perichoretic union.[164] There is no other adjective with the explanatory power to describe the believer's union with Christ as well as "perichoretic" does—at least not yet.

---

162. See chapter 1 above. See also Demarest, *Cross and Salvation*, 314–23, 330–33, and Erickson, *Christian Theology*, 965–66.

163. See the difference between John Calvin's description of mystical union and that of Wolfhart Pannenberg's. For Calvin (in Rankin, "Calvin's Correspondence," 232–50), mystical union is akin to what this study has called divine indwelling. On the other hand, Pannenberg (*Systematic Theology*, 2:452) believes mystical union entails absorption into the divine.

164. See Rankin, "Calvin's Correspondence," 250, for a full treatment. Calvin's threefold terminology, discussed in chapter 3 above, includes the incarnational union (God becoming flesh and uniting himself to humanity in that sense), the mystical union (the believer being joined to Christ by faith), and the spiritual union (the enjoyment of the blessings that flow from the mystical union).

One useful positive term to describe the believer's union with Christ is "adoptive union." This term possibly says more than the other descriptive terms in the preceding paragraph, but "adoption" itself, though it does imply a distinction between the Son and children in the Son, is often read as "less than real" or "less than biological" in Western eyes. The biblical portrayal of adoption in Christ means no such thing; it holds adoptive reality the same as eternal.[165] But the stigma associated with adoption in society limits the term's effectiveness. It also does not explain that the sonship the believer enjoys is due to direct incorporation in the Son, which exposes underlying perichoretic ideas, nor does it describe the mutual indwelling of Christ and the believer.

Returning to Helminiak's line of thought from chapter 1 above, a definition for union must explain, not just describe. In calling the soteriological union a third type of *perichoresis*, it assumes the existence of the first two types, especially the christological. Union with Christ is a union with the Son, who is already in a perichoretic union with the Father. It assumes both the shared humanity of the believer and Christ (for this is the believer both in and active in Christ) as well as the one-in-Spirit idea where Christ is both in and active in the believer through the Holy Spirit.[166] Where the above terminology is "kerygmatic," calling the believer's union with Christ a third type of *perichoresis* both reiterates the description of union to the faithful and explains what the union is and how it occurs.[167] Based on these factors, calling the soteriological union a third type of *perichoresis* is a superior explanation to the other terminology discussed above.

But why the novelty? Two millennia of theological reflection have passed. Why has the word not been more employed than it has in history? There are a few reasons for this. First, soteriology as a whole has not enjoyed many sustained periods of intense reflection in Christian history.[168] Tim Trumper notes three periods where soteriology has been at the

---

165. Otherwise, it is difficult to explain how the "only begotten" of John becomes the "firstborn of many" of Romans. The resurrection promise of "We will be like him" also rings true here (1 Cor 15).

166. See Helminiak, "One in Christ," 135–36.

167. Ibid., 114–15.

168. This is not to say, of course, that soteriology has been ignored throughout Christian history. It has always been very important. But there have been relatively few periods in Christian history where salvation was explicitly the main topic of discussion for a prolonged period of time. It was often the evidence, rather than the point

front of theological thinking—the days of Anselm, the Reformation, and the nineteenth and twentieth centuries.[169] He notes the energy expended on the trinitarian and christological controversies produced "fine tuning of the doctrines in question."[170] There has been no comparable energy to similarly define salvation in Christian history.

Second, chapter 3 above has shown the close relationship between the perichoretic relationship of Christ and the believer and *theosis*—the latter is based on the former. *Theosis* has a long history of describing Christian salvation, as has been shown above. Because the two descriptions for salvation—a third type of *perichoresis* and *theosis*—are so similar, it is quite possible that the third type of *perichoresis* has been explained well, except it has been couched in the language of *theosis*.

Third, the term *perichoresis* itself has been somewhat dormant since the days of the Reformation until recently, which has contributed to its neglect as a key to understanding Christian salvation, even during a period in which interest in salvation, according to Trumper, has been heightened. The term was not circulating in the Latin West in Anselm's day either.[171] So even during the periods of acute soteriological awareness, the idea of *perichoresis* was unavailable or avoided.

Fourth, a Western emphasis on legal categories to explain the union of the believer and Christ has caused some of the more relational concepts (such as *perichoresis*) to be relatively ignored. More will be said on this below, but for now, it is enough to state that the legal terminology has been dominant in Western theology since the days of Augustine. The perichoretic relationship between Christ and the believer for which this study argues, though very seldom stated in such language, has always been present, from the apostolic age until now.

---

of controversy. A quick examination of the main creeds of the Church reflects that soteriological language is not as doctrinally precise as, say, trinitarian or christological language.

169. Trumper, "Metaphorical Import II," 108.

170. Ibid., 109.

171. According to Fantino ("Circumincession," 1:315–16), the Greek word *perichoresis* did not make its way into Latin thinking (as *circumincessio*) until 1154 when Burgundio of Pisa translated John of Damascus's *On the Orthodox Faith* into Latin. This was forty-five years after the death of Anselm, so he would have not had access to the term.

The Tension of the Soteriological Perichoresis—Between the Ditches

There is one final theological consideration to explore in seeing the soteriological union as a third type of *perichoresis*. Why is the concept of *perichoresis* necessary at all, at any level? It is necessary because it is able to hold together two different persons or natures in union and distinction without either absorption or separation. Both of the historical varieties of *perichoresis*—the trinitarian and christological—require such a concept. Does soteriology require it as well? This study believes so.

As chapter 1 has noted, *perichoresis* in its trinitarian context holds together the unity of the Godhead while maintaining three distinct persons. It keeps orthodox Christian theology on the road between the two heretical ditches—modalism and tritheism.[172] Similarly, though Gregory of Nazianzus's christological use of *perichoresis* predated the heresies that argued the relationship of the divine and human natures in Christ, it is the most helpful way to see how the divine and human natures are joined in Christ without change, confusion, division, or separation.[173] Nestorianism so divided and separated the natures that it was as if there were two separate persons in Christ.[174] On the other hand, Eutychianism changed and confused the natures to the point that the divine nature in Christ overwhelmed the human.[175] Thus there are two heretical "ditches" in Christology as well—the Nestorian separation of the natures and the Eutychian merging of them.

Both the trinitarian and christological "ditches" result from either overstressing diversity (tritheism and Nestorianism) or overstressing unity (modalism and Eutychianism). Therefore, both doctrines have an orthodox understanding of *perichoresis* that preserves both unity and diversity without allowing one to be stressed over the other. This study has argued that the soteriological union between Christ and the believer is a third type of perichoretic relationship, along with the trinitarian and christological. Does soteriology have its "ditches" too?

The answer is yes. The third type of *perichoresis* guarantees the unity and diversity in the soteriological union. The overemphasis on unity in the soteriological union—the heretical "ditch" of divine absorption—has

---

172. Lytle, "Perichoretically-Embodied Ethics," 26.

173. Gregory wrote in the late fourth century, while the heresies of Nestorianism and Eutychianism did not become real problems until the early-to-mid fifth century.

174. See MacLeod, *Person of Christ*, 181–83.

175. Ibid., 183–85.

already been answered in chapter 1 above.[176] The other ditch, which is more subtle, is the overemphasis on diversity. Make no mistake, diversity does exist in the soteriological union—the creature-creator distinction must be affirmed. If the distinction is affirmed too strongly, however, it creates a theory of salvation detached from the person and work of Christ.[177] Thomas Torrance provides an answer that, if applied to the level of the individual believer rather than to the church as a whole, resembles the third type of *perichoresis* for which this study argues. Tee Gatewood writes, "Over and against the temptation to identify the church with Christ, and the temptation to separate the church from Christ, Torrance describes a relation of participation. The church is the body of Christ as it participates in Christ's mission in the power of the Spirit as a concrete embodiment of God's love."[178]

Donald Fairbairn and Baxter Kruger both argue that the heart of the Christian message is the eternal (perichoretic) relationship of the Father, Son, and Spirit.[179] The Godhead has freely decided to share that relationship with humans through the incarnation and the soteriological union. When the believer and Christ are separated too far in the soteriological union, a kind of "soteriological Nestorianism" results where the impartation of the divine life and nature to believers cannot occur, because the tie has been severed. What is "separated too far?" No one knows the line for sure, but there are clues that signal when separation is overstressed in the soteriological union.

One clue is making the believer's union with Christ part of the *ordo salutis* rather than the overarching framework in which the *ordo* sits. In his examination of the *ordo* in Paul, Richard Gaffin writes concerning the believer's union with Christ, "This is the central truth of salvation for Paul, the key soteriological reality comprising all others."[180]

---

176. Demarest (*Cross and Salvation*, 314–16) discusses some, including Eastern and medieval mystics, who see the soteriological union as absorption, or as he calls it, "ontological."

177. Speidell, "Trinitarian Ontology," 293–94. Speidell argues that one's conception of God as leaning toward either modalism or tritheism shapes how one views the community of the church and salvation in general.

178. Gatewood, "Alive to God in Christ," 15. He cites Torrance, *Royal Priesthood*, 30.

179. See Fairbairn, *Life in the Trinity*, 10–11, and any of Kruger's writings cited in chapter 3 above or in the bibliography.

180. Gaffin, *By Faith*, 36.

Elsewhere Gaffin sees the same thinking in Calvin, as the twofold grace of justification and sanctification both flow from the believer's union with Christ.[181] He writes concerning justification, "However crucial, it is not the stand-alone foundation of salvation."[182] Fairbairn argues that the Reformers placed great weight on topics like justification in order to separate themselves from the Roman Catholics. He writes, "The longer we assume something without explicitly stating it, the more likely we are to forget it. And this, I fear, is what has happened in evangelicalism more recently. We have faithfully majored on the truths the Reformers stressed, but we have underemphasized the context in which they spoke those truths, to the point that we have forgotten what they knew and assumed."[183] The Reformers, as chapter 3 has illustrated, knew and assumed the centrality of the believer's union with Christ in the context of the incarnation and explicitly taught the language of *theosis* as it relates to salvation.

If, as this study has argued, the soteriological union is a perichoretic relationship, albeit of a third type, then union with Christ must be the central idea in salvation. The historical grounds for this assertion have been demonstrated in chapter 3 above. The biblical grounds are partly noted in chapter 2, but there is more. William Mueller shows how Paul develops the following Christian doctrines with a basis in the soteriological union: election, calling, foreordination, justification, sanctification, unity with other believers, redemption, eternal life, the wisdom of Christ, Christian liberty, and all spiritual blessings.[184] This is almost the entire *ordo salutis*. Stanley Grenz adds glorification to the list as well: "In the dynamic of glorification we actually participate in the eternal relationship between the Father and the Son—who is the Spirit within us bringing us to glorify the Father through the Son. Therefore, the eternal community ultimately means the participation of creation through the Spirit in the glory of—even in the life of—the triune God (2 Peter 1:4)."[185] The entire *ordo salutis* is biblically based on the union of Christ

---

181. Gaffin, "Justification and Union," 253. See chapter 3 for some examples of those who disagree with Gaffin.

182. Ibid., 257.

183. Fairbairn, *Life in the Trinity*, 11.

184. Mueller, "Mystical Union," 209. He provides biblical citations for each instance.

185. Grenz, *Created for Community*, 275.

and the believer, and that view has held for the majority of Christian history. Any attempt to put the union on the same level with its benefits threatens to substitute the benefit for Christ himself, and thereby overemphasize the distinctions within the soteriological union.

A second clue is seeing the benefits of salvation in overly forensic and legal terms. While legal terminology helps clarify meaning, it is not a universally dominant metaphor in all branches of Christianity. Ross Aden traces the origin of the dominance of legal language to the Western Augustinian-Anselmian tradition, where "salvation is accomplished by the satisfaction of the demands of divine justice."[186] In such an interpretive framework, acquittal of guilt can precede (logically, not temporally) relationship, because justice and satisfaction need not be personal. It is a debt needing to be paid rather than a breach needing to be healed.[187] Thus the overuse or overemphasis of terminology that is subtly impersonal (penalty, justice, debt, price, payment, etc.) is a warning sign of potential over-separation of Christ and the believer in the soteriological union. Though justification may be forensic, it still biblically follows from a personal union with Christ (1 Cor 1:30).[188] Therefore justification must be rooted in personal rather than legal terminology.[189] Perhaps even the idea of "substitution," if contemplated apart from real participation in the other, may carry a separation that goes too far.[190]

Closely tied to the forensic metaphor is the doctrine of grace. Timothy Dearborn attempts to ground the doctrine of grace in the triune God, so that grace becomes identifiable as God's essential being.[191]

---

186. Aden, "Justification and Divinization," 104–5.

187. See Trumbull, *Blood Covenant*, 221.

188. See also Gaffin, "Justification," 264.

189. For some re-examinations of the salvific metaphors in relational language, see Mulcahy, *Cause of Our Salvation*, 429–38, as well as Shelton, *Cross and Covenant*, 117–44. Legal terminology may certainly be used, but the root should be personal, since justification occurs "in Christ," and never apart from Christ.

190. Heim ("Salvation as Communion," 325) says of substitution, "When Paul says, 'not I, but Christ in me,' he does not mean 'not me, but instead Christ who has now replaced me.'" Neither is it a unity (merging) of the two. The union between Christ and the believer is closer than just substitution. It is an indwelling and participation in the other that retains the distinctiveness of both parties.

191. Dearborn, "God, Grace, and Salvation," 271. He contrasts his view of grace with "monotheistic" views of grace that lead to grace becoming an attribute of God, such as his unmerited favor, eternal decree, healing power, salvific will, or cosmically present acceptance (all Dearborn's terminology).

Dearborn, building on the relational triunity of God, writes, "Biblically, grace is revealed as the triune God's being-in-communion. Because of this love in his innermost being, grace is God's actions to incorporate humanity into relation with himself. . . . Grace is the sum-total of all God's dealings with humanity."[192] He continues, "Grace is not simply the action of God in Christ, nor the power of God, nor the will of God manifested in Christ. It is neither merely God's attitude, attribute, nor presence. Those views depersonalize grace, making it something separable from Christ. Grace is a person, for grace is God's being in three persons, and God's life as the divine/man, Jesus Christ. Thus, as Paul says, life is Christ."[193] Grace as God's being has important ramifications, especially when one considers the soteriological union perichoretically.[194]

Thus grace, as embodied in Christ and as an onto-relational reality, cannot be "something automatic, or something divinely imposed."[195] Dearborn argues that salvation as onto-relational (perichoretic) is both ontological (humanity is "reconstituted in Christ's atoning life, death, and resurrection") and relational ("one must in faith be adopted by the Spirit into the incarnate Son's relationships within the Trinity").[196] Again,

---

192. Ibid., 272–73.

193. Ibid., 275–76. Dearborn subsequently surveys misrepresentations of grace as being misrepresentations of God. The idea of God as the supreme substance (which itself comes about, he argues, due to an inordinate stress on "one substance" as the foundation of divinity) degenerates into errors such as pan(en)theism, the sacramental "dispensing" of grace, and cosmically present grace that permeates universalism and liberation theology. It is probably no accident that the same Augustine who wanted to preserve the "one substance" of the Trinity also coined *ex opere operato* grace that led to western sacramentalism. The idea of God as the supreme subject makes grace "an act of the Father's will," rather than "the expression of the personal, free being of God in triune relationship" (281–82). This leads to the idea that God may be something other than what he has revealed in Christ, which itself plays out in the unconditional election to salvation and reprobation as well as more radical forms of inclusivism or universalism.

194. Ibid., 283. Dearborn's terminology for the relationship in the soteriological union is "onto-relational," a term first introduced by T. F. Torrance in chapter 3 above. Soteriological *perichoresis* seems to be a synonym for onto-relational, or at least very close to it.

195. Ibid., 289. This shows why T. F. Torrance's "twin heresies" are universalism and predestination. More exploration of this theme might prove fruitful in finding a way forward in the "divine sovereignty" and "free will" debates.

196. Ibid., 290.

if grace is not God himself, there is a separation in the soteriological union that may be too great.

A third clue is the separation of Christian doctrine and Christian life. Fairbairn notes that even though Jesus is the central figure of Christianity, Christians tend to make propositional statements the core of the faith. He writes that part of the reason Christian doctrine is "somewhat irrelevant to Christian life is that our theological discussions focus on the doctrines rather than on the God to whom those doctrines point. Theologians have unintentionally given the impression that the doctrines, the ideas about God, are the subject of our study. As a result, students and others unwittingly substitute truths about God for God."[197] Fairbairn proposes that one solution for this problem is to see the patristic doctrine of *theosis* as the link between doctrine and life.[198]

Richard Jensen, a Lutheran preaching professor, agrees. He quotes Luther as saying that "if you divide Christ's person from your own, you are in the Law."[199] He notes that this works itself out in preaching the necessity of the human agency to conform to God's righteous standard. Because of the division between Christ and the believer, the divine work is already accomplished. The human work remains. He states, "We preach the law and we think we are preaching the gospel. The gospel after all is a given. Our names have been written down in a heavenly book somewhere. It's all there. We are justified. So let's get on with it. Divine agency is a given. Human agency is the problem. We preach to the problem; we preach to inspire human agency."[200] He goes on to demonstrate how utilizing the language of *theosis* and union with Christ can repair the separation between Christ and the believer in salvation. This study has stated that *theosis* flows from the perichoretic soteriological union, because it is the experiential outworking of the union already present. Thus seeing salvation perichoretically would keep believers out of the ditch.

Thus one may be approaching the "ditch" of "soteriological Nestorianism" (separating Christ and the believer) whenever something besides the soteriological union becomes the "central" idea in salvation,

---

197. Fairbairn, *Life in the Trinity*, 4–5.

198. Ibid., 6.

199. Jensen, "*Theosis* and Preaching," 433. The quotation is provided without citation in Jensen's article.

200. Ibid., 434.

when inordinate stress is placed upon the legal and forensic aspects of salvation rather than the participatory ones, or Christian doctrine is severed from Christian life. There may be several other warning signs of the ditch that separates the Creator (Christ) and the creature (believer) to such an extent that there is no longer any union. Therefore, as in the case of the trinitarian or christological *perichoresis*, the soteriological (third type) of *perichoresis* helps to hold the unity and distinction in the believer's union with Christ together without either unity or distinction being overemphasized.

CHAPTER SUMMARY

This chapter has attempted to show that the biblical pictures of the soteriological union—covenant, marriage, and adoption—both enlighten and are enlightened by understanding the union as a perichoretic relationship, albeit of a third type. Also, it has attempted to explain why seeing the union as a perichoretic one best fits the evidence, and that *perichoresis* in the union holds together the unity and diversity between the believer and Christ. There is a considerable overlap in the biblical pictures, as they are describing the same reality from different vantage points. This chapter closes with a couple of quotes that show how easily one can move from one picture to another in deepening one's understanding of the soteriological union.

Michael Horton has made some progress by coining the phrase "covenantal union" to describe the soteriological union.[201] He writes,

> It is no wonder that the marital analogy figures so prominently in the biblical drama. The two become "one flesh" not in any kind of ontological synthesis, reducing the other to oneself (or vice versa), but in covenant. The sort of union that a covenantal approach entails corresponds to the analogies of marriage and adoption, in which the two becoming "one flesh" or the child being made an heir is constituted by both legal and organic solidarity, while retaining their otherness.[202]

"Covenantal union" is definitely a better way to describe the believer's union with Christ than most of the existing terminology. *Perichoresis*, albeit of a third type, probably still wields more explanatory power than

---

201. Horton, *Lord and Servant*, 13.
202. Ibid., 15.

covenantal union, though, because of its incorporation of the themes of *theosis* and adoption. It is good to see others working toward better explanations of the soteriological union as well. Similarly, Scott Walker Hahn writes, "The covenant serves as the transcendent principle that reveals the moral and theological frame of reference for the family."[203] Since Hahn claims the basis for a covenant is a father-son type of relationship, Christ as the eternal Son is the perfect representation for the initiator of the new and final covenant, in both a relational and a moral sense.[204] Here it may be seen that covenant, marriage, and adoption all display the same idea—the soteriological union—while further deepening the understanding of just how truly it is a *perichoresis* of a third type. The next chapter will discuss some possible implications of this thesis and show where some opportunities for further thinking exist.

203. Hahn, *Kinship by Covenant*, 656.
204. Ibid., 659–67.

5

Possible Implications and Conclusion

In the previous three chapters, this study has argued that the soteriological union between Christ and the believer constitutes a third type of perichoretic relationship. This argument has progressed through biblical, historical, and theological evidence. The last section of chapter 4 has addressed why this argument is a potentially fruitful way of looking at the soteriological union. This chapter will now explore some of the possible implications of a perichoretic relationship between Christ and the believer. These implications will be presented in two groups. First are the implications for doctrine and systematic theology. Second are the implications for some further issues, such as the justification debates, Christian ethics, and personal Christian living. Much of the work in these areas has already been explored. The value of the perichoretic union in most instances is that it provides a direct link to these already-existing implications. The chapter will conclude with a brief discussion of areas for possible further research and a summary of major findings.

DOCTRINAL IMPLICATIONS

If the soteriological union is rightly to be seen as a perichoretic relationship, several doctrinal implications follow, as well as personal ones. The thesis of this investigation provides an important link in the chain of many recent theological conclusions. First, in the field of Christian epistemology, Justin Thacker asserts that a perichoretic relationship between Christ and the believer is a prerequisite for human knowledge of God.[1] This study provides the biblical, historical, and theological considerations Thacker largely assumes. Following closely behind epistemology, there

---

1. Thacker, *Postmodernism*.

are serious ramifications for the major doctrines of the Christian faith. These will be briefly mentioned, showing why viewing the soteriological union as a third type of *perichoresis* is a fruitful theological enterprise.

Soteriological Perichoresis and Christian Epistemology

Justin Thacker builds a theological epistemology based on the perichoretic relationship in the soteriological union. He argues that knowledge of God in a Cartesian sense is not possible because humanity is not constituted as disembodied minds.[2] Rather, he argues that one cannot know God "objectively and theoretically. Rather, knowledge of God necessarily involves a transformation of our whole being in worship and obedience."[3] He argues that to know God is to relate to God and to relate in a perichoretic fashion.[4]

Thacker builds on the work of two of the twentieth century's most influential thinkers—Karl Barth and Michael Polanyi.[5] Barth subscribed to a fully relational knowledge of God. He writes, "Knowledge in the biblical sense directly includes, indeed, it is itself at root, *metanoia*, conversion, the transformation of the νους, and therefore of the whole man, in accordance with the one known by him. . . . To know him . . . is to receive and have the νους of Jesus Christ himself, and thus to know in fellowship with the one who is known."[6] Similarly, Polanyi described using tools (which Thacker extends to words, skills, and percepts) as a process in which both the user and the tool indwell one another.[7] The theological ramification, in Thacker's words, is that "we know God just to the extent that we allow our participation in Christ's rationality to function tacitly in this manner. That is, we do not know God by considering explicitly, as it were, our participation in him, but rather we know God just as that participation governs our interactions with both his revelation and the

---

2. Ibid., 45.
3. Ibid., 49.
4. Ibid., 49–51.
5. See also Martin, *Incarnate Ground of Christian Faith*. Martin argues, following T. F. Torrance, that the incarnation is a proper epistemological ground for Christian education. That ground is replicated by the Spirit in the lives of believers. Though not exactly the idea for which this study argues, it does resemble it in the two traditional ideas of *perichoresis*, and hints at the soteriological union as well.
6. Barth, *CD* IV/3.1, 185, quoted in Thacker, *Postmodernism*, 50.
7. Thacker, *Postmodernism*, 89. Thacker quotes Polanyi, *Knowing and Being*, 59.

world."[8] He continues to state that such knowledge is one of mutual indwelling, and therefore it serves to "highlight the perichoretic nature of our participation in Christ."[9] In other words, "When we know God it is not so much that we are given something. Rather we become something, that is, partakers in Christ's redeemed humanity."[10] Thacker emphasizes knowledge as participation, because one must be in Christ in order to see Christ or know Christ as God.[11]

If Thacker is correct in his assertion that knowledge of God is relational and knowing consists also in "being known," then a perichoretic relationship between the knower (the believer) and the known (God) is essential for knowledge to occur.[12] If such a perichoretic relationship does not exist, then God cannot be known fully in a relational way. There will forever be a gulf between humans and God so that knowledge is limited to the cognitive aspect only, which is far short of the biblical idea of salvation (1 Cor 13). Therefore, in Thacker's view, a perichoretic relationship between a believer and Christ must precede any knowledge of God on the part of the believer—that is, the perichoretic relationship in the soteriological union is the foundation for theological epistemology.[13] This study has argued (along with Thacker) that the soteriological union provides such a perichoretic relationship, albeit of a third type. The ramifications of his ethical ideas will be examined later in this chapter. For now, the direct influence of the soteriological *perichoresis* on the other doctrines of the Christian faith will become the focus.

Other Theological Areas to Explore

The previous chapter highlighted some soteriological benefits of seeing the union of the believer and Christ as a third type of *perichoresis*. Other theological avenues to explore include doctrines within almost every branch of systematic theology. Some that seem directly connected to this study include issues in anthropology and hamartiology. Paul employs "in Christ" language to describe the depths of the believer's re-

8. Ibid., 90.
9. Ibid.
10. Ibid., 64.
11. Ibid., 92.
12. Ibid., 48.
13. Of course, one could know about God without the presence of such a relationship, but real, saving knowledge of God is not possible without the relationship.

lationship with Christ—so deep that this study argues that it may rightly be called perichoretic. He also utilizes "in Adam" language to describe unredeemed humanity. Perhaps it would be fruitful to explore possible perichoretic vestiges present within the human race.[14] In addition, a study of the relational aspects of sin would be helpful. If salvation as a personal enterprise remedies sin, then perhaps sin is more personal than theology has realized.

Chapter 4 only scratched the surface of other important issues. Exploring any or all of the salvation terminology (justification, regeneration, redemption, expiation, propitiation, atonement, etc.) relationally in depth would be quite rewarding. A deeper study into baptism and the Lord's Supper from the standpoint of soteriological *perichoresis* should shed light on their meaning for the church as well.

OTHER IMPLICATIONS

This section explores some additional benefits of seeing the soteriological union as a third type of *perichoresis*. Ideas to be explored here include a possible third way in the recent debates over justification, the impact on Christian ethics, and influences in the everyday lives and relationships of Christians. These may be avenues for further research or areas where this study provides additional light to work already being done.

A "Third Way" in the Justification Debates?

One of the benefits of seeing the soteriological union as a third type of *perichoresis* is it provides a third alternative in the recent justification debates between the traditional Reformed position of the imputation of Christ's righteousness and the so-called "New Perspective on Paul" view of covenantal nomism.[15] This chapter will not summarize the debates

---

14. See Harrison, "Greek Patristic Foundations," 399–412. Her idea of *theosis* (399) comes very close to what this study has called a third type of *perichoresis*: "What is most central to [*theosis*] is a sharing in the joyous interchange of mutual self-giving love and devotion to other persons that has its source and heart in the communal life of the three divine persons themselves, who invite other persons, the angels and humans they have together created, to join in their eternal community."

15. Here, the traditional Reformed position on justification—the doctrine McCormack ("Crisis of Protestantism," 81) calls *the* doctrine of the Reformation—is summarized by Packer ("Justification," 643) as God's declaration of righteousness based upon a person's faith in what Christ has done. On the other side, theologians who hold to the New Perspective on Paul are often called covenantal nomists, because they be-

but only offer a potential way to help resolve them.[16] In these recent debates, each of the two sides seem to stress the case for either imputation or covenantal nomism to the exclusion of the other. If one is to see the soteriological union as perichoretic, perhaps both sides of the issue hold explanatory power simultaneously.

This study has argued that one of the reasons the soteriological union may be properly called a perichoretic relationship is because of its mutual indwelling and participatory nature. While Romans 4:21–24 shows that imputation is a biblical doctrine, several biblical texts underscore the participatory nature of justification as well, especially 1 Corinthians 1:30.[17] Based on the early church's view of the soteriological union, Daniel Powers argues they saw the work of Christ from a participatory rather than a substitutionary point of view. Since believers are included in every aspect of the work of Christ, Jesus's "justification and exaltation could be interpreted as their own. Consequently, believers are able to participate in the grace and justification that God granted to Jesus by raising him from the dead. Every notion of an exchange, whereby Jesus is perceived as being imputed with the believers' sin and the believers imputed with Jesus's righteousness, is absent."[18]

---

lieve the law God requires believers to keep is the covenant itself. Packer (644) states that those who follow the New Perspective believe that justification is a result of being in covenant with God. In addition, there are Reformed thinkers who believe that the only imputation occurring in justification is the imputation of human sin to Christ. For example, see Gundry, "Nonimputation of Christ's Righteousness," 18–45.

16. One of the leading voices on the side of imputed righteousness is Piper, whose notable works on the subject include *Counted Righteous* and "John Piper Responds," *Desiring God*, http://www.desiringgod.org/ResourceLibrary/Articles/ByDate/2003/1522_John_Piper_Responds_to_Don_Garlington_on_the_Imputation_of_Righteousness/. Notable covenantal nomists include Wright, *What St. Paul Really Said*, and Dunn, *New Perspective on Paul*. For a scholarly treatment of the issue, see the two-volume series edited by Carson, Seifrid, and O'Brien, *Justification and Variegated Nomism*, as well as Waters, *Justification and the New Perspectives*, and Kruse, *Paul, the Law, and Justification*, 289–90.

17. 1 Corinthians 1:30 reads, "But by His doing you are in Christ Jesus, who became to us wisdom from God, and righteousness and sanctification, and redemption." See also the comments by Barrett, *First Epistle to the Corinthians*, 59–61.

18. Powers, *Salvation through Participation*, 234. This study does not believe that justification must be either via imputation or via participation. They are both correct, especially when the soteriological union is viewed as perichoretic. As will be explained below, imputation cannot stand without participation, and participation is not complete without imputation. Thus Powers is not completely correct, because imputation is *implied* in participation.

Two recent authors, Brian Vickers and Don Garlington, believe that union with Christ is the key to resolving the tension.[19] Garlington writes, "Stress on union with Christ rather than imputation places Christology, rather than soteriology, at the forefront of Paul's theology (and that of the New Testament generally). The showcase of the apostle's thought is *not* justification, as time-honored as that notion is in Reformation theology. It is, rather, the union with Christ, or the 'in Christ' experience."[20] He adds, "Hand in hand with the preeminence of the person of Christ is that union with him bespeaks a personal (covenant) relationship that is obscured when legal and transactional matters are given as much prominence as they are in traditional Reformed thought. 'Imputation' is a transferal of a commodity from one person to another; but union means that we take up residence, as it were, within the sphere of the other's existence."[21] Garlington's language is similar to that of others in this study used to demonstrate the soteriological union as a perichoretic relationship of a third type.

Finally, how does describing the believer's union with Christ as a perichoretic relationship help provide a third way in the debates? The Reformed position, while biblical, does not say all that the Bible does. There are two noticeable weaknesses to many current Reformed explanations of justification. First, though it may be implied, there is little mention of the doctrine of union as its biblical basis—that is, there is no "*sola unio*" to go along with "*sola fide*."[22] The danger of the doctrine of

19. Vickers, from the Reformed camp, has argued as much in his *Jesus' Blood and Righteousness*. Garlington is from the New Perspective camp.

20. Garlington, "Imputation or Union with Christ?"

21. Ibid. In Piper's "Response," he acknowledges Garlington's emphasis on union with Christ.

22. In addition to the discussion above concerning the *ordo salutis*, see the writings and interpretations of both Martin Luther and John Calvin in chapter 3 above as examples of those who grounded justification in union. See also Mueller, "Mystical Union," 208, and Murray, *Redemption Accomplished*, 164. For a shift in the thinking of Reformers after Luther and Calvin, see Oden, *Justification Reader*, 39, and his discussion of several Reformed confessions. A further reading of these confessions reveals that none of them mention union with Christ as part of their respective articles or clauses on justification. The French Reformed Confession alludes to the idea of union in a chapter prior to the one on justification. The Belgic Confession stresses imputation without mentioning union. The Westminster Standards likewise stresses imputation, does not mention union, and excludes the possibility of infusing righteousness into the believer. In roughly a century after Calvin, his doctrine of union as the basis of justification was not mentioned in the Westminster Confession. This confession still

imputation standing alone without stressing its basis in union is that it can easily obscure the point that justification is not an arbitrary, groundless act. Rather justification occurs in accordance with the existing soteriological union of the believer and Christ.[23] That union, the one in which the believer and Christ indwell and participate in one another, allows what belongs to Christ to become the believer's and vice versa. Thus imputation occurs but only because the soteriological union that logically (not temporally) precedes it is so intimate that it may rightly be called perichoretic.

Second, the word used to describe imputation is often "substitution" or "exchange" rather than "participate."[24] Although "substitution" and "exchange" are helpful to a point, they do not go far enough to explain what occurs in the soteriological union. The Bible does indicate that Christ is the substitute for the sinner (2 Cor 5:21 and Gal 3:13), but even in these texts there is a mutual participation already in view. Shelton writes concerning such texts, "They do not focus exclusively on Christ's objectively absorbing the judicial penalty which humanity has called down on itself because of its sin. On the contrary Paul sees the atoning death of Jesus . . . as 'inclusive substitution,' in which the whole self of the sinful person is given to Christ as an offering of one's life, in response to Christ giving his whole self as an offering of covenant restoration for humanity."[25] If the argumentation of this study is correct, then justification, as important as it is, is the means to an end—the end being including humans in the incarnate Son so that they might be adopted as children of the Father and partake of the divine nature.[26] The will of God is to utilize the life, death, and resurrection of Christ to reproduce his life in human persons. If the soteriological union may rightly be called a

---

guides much Reformed thinking today. Moreover, Bird ("Incorporated Righteousness, 253–56) says that the successors to the Reformers developed justification into the central doctrine in Reformed theology.

23. Gaffin, *Resurrection and Redemption*, 152. He utilizes the term "existential union" to describe the believer's union with Christ. Shelton (*Cross and Covenant*, 112–14) argues that, contrary to the Greek and Roman idea of "just" as an ethical norm, the Hebrew idea of "just," developed from the Old Testament, is a right relationship through covenant. Covenant, as has been shown in chapter 4 above, conveys the type of relationship this study calls a third type of *perichoresis*.

24. Powers, *Salvation through Participation*, 234.

25. Shelton, *Cross and Covenant*, 121.

26. See also the argument of Kruger, *Great Dance*, 31–33.

third type of *perichoresis*, then God wants the whole person in a participatory way, which includes the more traditional atonement themes of substitution and exchange within the perichoretic relationship.[27]

Despite the contributions of the New Perspective on justification, its glaring weakness remains the denial of the biblical doctrine of imputation in favor of the affirmation of the covenant.[28] Imputation need not be eliminated, for it is still a biblical doctrine. What the New Perspective seems to miss here is filled in by seeing the soteriological union as a perichoretic relationship. If two persons mutually indwell and participate in one another, as this study has repeatedly stressed as the two components of perichoretic relationships, then what one has is imputed to the other. In this way, the perichoretic relationship allows for both the imputation the Reformed want to preserve as well as the covenant reality of the New Perspective. While more research needs to be done here, it does seem to be a fruitful starting point.

Soteriological Perichoresis and Christian Ethics

Already noted in this chapter for his contributions in Christian epistemology, Justin Thacker connects Christian ethics with the soteriological *perichoresis*. He argues that "knowing is never neutral with respect to ethics, but rather embodies, whether implicitly or explicitly, some ethical stance."[29] Knowledge of God, which Thacker has shown above to be a perichoretic enterprise, cannot stand apart from the ethical import to love others. He argues his case from several fronts, most clearly in that knowledge of anything consists of a real experience of it.[30] In the Bible, knowledge of evil is the experience, or ethics, of evil. To know is to participate.

---

27. The "whole person" evokes the holocaust, or whole burnt offering, discussed in chapter 4 above. This sacrifice was primarily participation, but could evoke ideas of substitution and exchange within it. See Shelton, *Cross and Covenant*, 55–57.

28. Vickers, *Jesus' Blood and Righteousness*, 60.

29. Thacker, *Postmodernism*, 100.

30. Ibid., 101. Thacker argues (48–51) that the biblical idea of knowledge includes emotional and experiential interaction rather than merely mental cognition. He argues that this goes all the way back to Genesis 2 in that eating the fruit of the "tree of the knowledge of good and evil" involves an experience of evil as well as a cognitive ability to understand factually what evil is. Thacker's point is that knowledge is both propositional and personal/experiential, much like the revelation of God.

Another approach Thacker's integration of theological epistemology and ethics takes is that the knowledge of God already implies that God knows the knower. Since God's knowledge of the believer "impacts every sphere of our existence," and has been historically expressed in God's call and election of his people, the believer's knowledge of God has amounted to the appropriate response to the call of God.[31] This response requires the act of the whole person, which includes ethical implications.[32] Therefore knowledge of God and by God integrates the whole of human existence, involving the ethical as well as the cognitive. By this line of reasoning, because knowledge of God is based on a perichoretic relationship, Christian ethics must flow from a perichoretic soteriological union as well.

Finally, because the epitome of Christ-likeness is to be radically self-giving and other-centered, a perichoretic soteriological union should guarantee that the believer replicates the ethics that are present in Christ.[33] That is, it is impossible to say or believe that "Jesus is Lord" with "any kind of theological content in the absence of a personal experience of Christ's lordship over one's life."[34] Therefore, Christian ethics as practiced by believers is impossible without knowledge of God. The knowledge of God itself is based on the pre-existing perichoretic relationship between Christ and the believer. As Thacker summarizes, "Under a theological paradigm, no separation can be made between our knowledge of God [which is perichoretic] and our obedience to God in our love for the other."[35] Thus the soteriological *perichoresis* is vital to a clear understanding of Christian ethics. Again, Thacker has worked out the implications. This study provides the biblical, historical, and theological foundation to declare that the soteriological union is indeed perichoretic.

---

31. Ibid., 106–7.

32. Ibid., 109.

33. Ibid., 111–12. Thacker argues from Phil 2 that Jesus's equality with God is proven in his self-emptying, so that a believer who shares the mind of Christ is compelled to act in the same manner.

34. Ibid., 114. Thacker goes on to explore this concept in the context of Paul's explanation that one cannot say that "Jesus is Lord" except by the Spirit (1 Cor 12:3). One could of course say the words without the Spirit (see the discussion in Thacker of Lindbeck, *Nature of Doctrine*, 64), but not the words as the Spirit intends them.

35. Ibid., 46.

Miroslav Volf argues much the same in his essay "The Trinity is Our Social Programme."[36] Volf argues for a "self-donation" which builds on the idea of *perichoresis* as "making room for others." He argues that Christians should make room for others as the divine persons do.[37] Volf cites Rowan Williams, who writes, "Generosity, mercy, and welcome are imperatives for the Christian because they are a participation in the divine activity."[38] While not as explicit as Thacker, Volf acknowledges that Christian ethics flows from Christian epistemology, with some caveats.[39]

Alan Torrance follows suit in his essay "On Deriving 'Ought' from 'Is.'" He insists that participation in Christ is the determining factor for theological ethics.[40] Departing from the communion meal, Torrance writes that Christ "took bread (meaning, he took our humanity), gave thanks (offered that life of gratitude which is the true response in our place), broke it (died in and through taking the alienation of humanity to himself), and gave (giving us back our humanity, renewed and sanctified in him). Christian ethics denotes nothing less, therefore, than the gift of participating by the Spirit in that exchange."[41]

Torrance rejects natural revelation as a source for Christian ethics.[42] Instead, he appeals to the direct revelation of God as the only pos-

---

36. Volf, "Trinity Is Our Social Programme," 105–24.

37. Ibid., 116–17.

38. Ibid., 118. The citation is from Williams, "Interiority and Epiphany," 42.

39. Ibid., 106–7. Volf's two caveats include the human inability to fully comprehend and know God because the human is a creature and human ideas about God do not necessarily correspond to reality, as well as the effects of sin that are so entrenched in humanity distort direct comprehension.

40. Torrance, "On Deriving 'Ought' from 'Is,'" 170.

41. Ibid., 175.

42. Ibid., 178. Torrance claims that natural law, which he identifies as the underpinning of both Scholastic Calvinism and Puritanism, is not sufficient to ground Christian ethics, because it produced both ethical (United States) and unethical (Apartheid) systems. Torrance argues that the Calvinist *duplex cognitio* or two-fold knowledge of God (natural and special revelation) and its attendant nature-grace model (where grace perfects nature and "'nature' includes *our prior and diverse readings of nature* by the light of 'natural' reason and our own, innate, (natural) moral sense," italics in original) allow a division between natural and special revelation which led Barth to reject the former, because both sides of an issue can appeal to nature. Rather, if the way God has revealed himself in Christ is the appeal, there are fewer gray areas, though some still exist.

sible source for ethical behavior for the people of God.[43] The ultimate revelation is in Jesus Christ. To summarize, Torrance writes, "Christian doctrine is 'ethics-laden' and Christian ethics is 'doctrine-laden.' Both articulate the triune grammar of our covenantal participation in Christ. As every theologian worth her salt should recognize, the imperatives of ethical law derive from, repose upon, and witness to, the indicatives of grace. The Christian ethicist must derive 'ought' from 'is.'"[44]

Practical Concerns for Christians

There are many ways in which the reality of the soteriological union can aid in living out the faith both individually and communally. As Graham Buxton writes, "Since human beings do not possess the capacity to indwell, it is more appropriate to posit an asymmetrical relationship between God and humanity—but a relationship, nonetheless, which is intensely alive, creatively dynamic, and as mutually reciprocal as the divine-human distinction is able to offer."[45] This subsection will examine the practical results of this relationship in the soteriological union this study has called a third type of *perichoresis*.

One of the individual benefits of seeing the perichoretic nature of the believer's union with Christ is that a Christian has a firm basis, and an expectation, to reflect the glory and holiness of God.[46] The command "Be holy, for God is holy" takes on new meaning. The believer first of all possesses holiness due to the mutual indwelling and participation between Christ and the Christian.[47] The possession of holiness needs to extend to the life of the Christian, especially when operating on the

---

43. Ibid., 181. Torrance appeals to the Ten Commandments as destroying any independent appeal to nature for what is right. It is in the context of covenant (Mosaic) that ethical commands are made. Therefore (as 1 John 4:9–10 states), as God has loved us (meaning the work of God through the incarnation and salvation) so ought we to love each other. The work of God in salvation is the basis for the ethical imperative (ibid., 182).

44. Ibid., 185.

45. Buxton, *Trinity, Creation, and Pastoral Ministry*, 151. Here, Buxton understands indwelling as a spatial phenomenon. A human cannot physically indwell another.

46. Ng, "Reconsideration of the Use of the Term 'Deification,'" 39.

47. See also Willis, *Notes on the Holiness of God*. His study probes the holiness of God in depth as well as how this translates into the lives of his redeemed creatures. See especially page 141, as he relates the holiness of God interwoven with the *koinonia*, "the saints' partnership in the gospel."

assumption that God seeks to reproduce his life in his people. At a more basic level, the existence of this relationship provides the means for Christian revelation. Justin Thacker writes, "Our participation in him, then, becomes the 'ground and grammar' of our meaningful reception of his revelation. Hence, participation and revelation are merely two aspects of the same single event. It is participation in Christ that enables us faithfully to receive the revelation, and we can only receive the revelation to the extent that we are participating in Christ."[48]

Simon Chan argues that Christian salvation and the resulting life are based directly in the triune life of God. He states that the trinitarian *perichoresis* guarantees the ability for Christian spiritual life to be "essentially relational without ceasing to be particular."[49] Following Colin Gunton, he continues, "The *perichoresis* of the Trinity characterized by the distinct persons-in-relation offers a pattern for human relationship. It also provides a basis for Christians' participation in the trinitarian life. Far from being just a model, *perichoresis* is the effective means by which the life of particularity-in-relationality can be realized."[50] A further insight into the connection of the perichoretic relationships and Christian living is that life and work are inseparable.[51] Therefore, the church (made up of closely-linked individuals) continues the mission of God because it possesses the life of God, which is perichoretic.

This line of thinking conforms to the thought of Paul in both Galatians 2:20 and Colossians 3:4, where he calls the life of Christ the life of the believer. The soteriological union is so intimate that the lives are intertwined, and become one yet distinct. The holiness of the believer is the holiness of Christ due to the perichoretic union they share. Because the relationship is more than forensic in nature, it allows for both a "positional" holiness and "progressive" transformation.

Likewise, there are tremendous benefits of seeing the believer's union with Christ as a third type of *perichoresis* for living out the Christian faith in community. The first benefit is the sharing of material goods, just as the persons of the Trinity share their lives. Jürgen Moltmann believes one may see the perfect expression of this sharing in the first Christian

---

48. Thacker, *Postmodernism*, 92.
49. Chan, *Spiritual Theology*.
50. Ibid. Chan goes on to cite Gunton, *One, the Three, and the Many*.
51. Ibid., 54.

congregation, with its "primitive Christian communism."⁵² In describing this way of living, he states that the way of life was not new. "Rather, it was the social expression of the new trinitarian experience of God in us and our community in God. It was in particular the social expression of the experienced Spirit, the Spirit of the resurrection, since those who have found eternal life no longer need to cling to the goods of this world and accumulate property. Once the fear of death has disappeared from life, the greed for life disappears as well."⁵³

This way of living, if it can be resuscitated, can perhaps be a needed corrective for the individualism of the Enlightenment and modern society. As David Cunningham argues, the Enlightenment focus on the autonomous self, from which many present social ills arise, is fully antitrinitarian.⁵⁴ This idea has some implications for Christians both in the way they share their wealth and the role of the church in social relief.⁵⁵ Cunningham notes that such sharing of all goods in the early church shows a "community in which real participation is possible."⁵⁶

Second, Graham Buxton argues that the perichoretic life God shares with believers can be beneficial in allowing Christians to form healing relationships with one another. He writes that God "gives us bodies and a history through which we might participate in his own divine *perichoresis*. Human beings participate in the triune life of compassion as they enter into mutually enriching compassionate relationships, characterized by openness, vulnerability, and availability."⁵⁷ James Torrance adds, "Christ takes up our relationships, sanctifies them and makes us one in his Body, in union with him. Our mutual loving of one another, as in our love for God, is participatory loving. As the Son indwells the Father, and we dwell in him, so we indwell one another in 'perichoretic unity,' setting forth the *perichoresis* which is in the triune God."⁵⁸ It is the perichoretic

52. Moltmann, "God in the World," 377.

53. Ibid.

54. Cunningham, *These Three Are One*, 170–71. For a discussion of Enlightenment dualism, see Martin, *Incarnate Ground*, 7–13.

55. One is reminded here of the christological hymn in Phil 2:5–11, where Paul says "Have this attitude in yourselves which was also in Christ Jesus." He then goes on to describe how Christ did not grasp onto his equality with God, but emptied himself and took on the form of a servant.

56. Cunningham, *These Three Are One*, 186.

57. Buxton, *Trinity, Creation, and Pastoral Ministry*, 191.

58. Torrance, "Contemplating the Trinitarian Mystery," 147. Although it is not the

power in the soteriological union that allows the compassion of the Son to be reproduced in the believer through the Spirit.

Another benefit of the perichoretic soteriological union is that it should be the goal of every Christian to promote unity in the faith with one another. The great (and not so great) divisions that exist in the Christian world often do not promote the message of the gospel, especially when those divisions are hostile. While the richness of the various Christian traditions is to be commended, the traditions should not become more important than the unity of the Spirit. Simply put, if two groups are both genuine believers, then they should be able to put aside their differences to recognize one another, even if they choose to remain in their own traditions. When traditions supersede the unity of the Holy Spirit and the perichoretic nature implied therein, something is terribly wrong. This calls for healing wounds anywhere from brand new to several hundred years old.

Another benefit for the community lies in intercessory prayer. In the soteriological union, Christ is the intercessor for the believer for the Father. Because the perichoretic union exists for both the individual and the community, the act of interceding on behalf of another becomes a perichoretic act. As Paul Fiddes writes, "Intercessory prayer is an experience of connectedness and mutuality, because it is praying 'in God' who lives in relationships. In intercession we meet others in the *perichoresis*, the divine dance of Father, Son, and Spirit."[59] Commenting on the Son's act of intercession, he continues, "This Son communicates eternally with the Father, not in order to plead a case for us as a kind of lawyer in heaven, but so that we can lean upon the prayers he makes and make this movement of prayer our own. We enter into the life of prayer already going on within the communion of God's being; we pray to the Father, through the Son, and in the Spirit. This is why the everlasting God 'has time for us.'"[60] In the same vein, Stephen Seamands adds empathic listening as a ministry that flows from mutual indwelling.[61]

---

point of this study to show that the relationships among believers are perichoretic, it is the next logical step and is an area for further research. More to the point of this work, it allows those already in the perichoretic soteriological union with Christ to be able to form deep unions with other Christians as well.

59. Fiddes, *Participating in God*, 123. See also Seamands, *Ministry in the Image of God*, 152–54, and Jenson, *Systematic Theology*, 1:228.

60. Ibid.

61. Seamands, *Ministry in the Image of God*, 150–52.

Much the same can be said for Christian worship. James Torrance states that worship is "the gift of participating through the Spirit in the (incarnate) Son's communication with the Father—the gift of participating, in union with Christ, in what *he* has done for us once and for all by his self-offering to the Father in his life and death on the cross, and what *he* is continuing to do for us in the presence of the Father, and in *his* mission from the Father to the world."[62] He writes in *Worship, Community, and the Triune God of Grace*, "Christian worship is, therefore, our participation through the Spirit in the Son's communion with the Father, in his vicarious life of worship and intercession."[63] True Christian worship, then, is not necessarily something the believer must do on her own. Rather, it is a participation in the perfect worship of Christ in his *perichoresis* with the Father, which can only be accomplished due to a perichoretic (though of a third type) relationship between the believer and Christ. Much the same applies to preaching and pastoral theology.[64]

AREAS FOR FURTHER RESEARCH

There are several areas for further research which can build off the argument presented in this study. First, one possible area of fruitfulness is to examine the relationship between the believer and the Holy Spirit. As noted in chapter 2 above, Paul's language of "in Christ" and other phrases have parallels with the ministry of the Holy Spirit and his indwelling in believer's lives. There was not space to fully explore that connection here, but it could prove to be a worthwhile companion study to this one.

An area that seems to be of growing interest, especially in the intersection of theology and science, is the possibility that *perichoresis* is inherent in all creation. While it may not be the case that the created world enjoys a *perichoresis* as intimate or close as the soteriological union, and certainly not as the christological or trinitarian unions, there may be room to explore it more deeply. The challenge will be to resist the temptation to slip into panentheism.

Certainly the next logical step beyond this particular study is to examine the possibility that the relationships in the church are perichoretic. These would be human-to-human perichoretic relationships based

---

62. Torrance, "Contemplating the Trinitarian Mystery," 142.

63. Torrance, *Worship, Community, and the Triune God*, 15.

64. See Jensen, "*Theosis* and Preaching," and Purves, *Reconstructing Pastoral Theology*.

on each human being in soteriological union with Christ. One may even be able to argue that perichoretic relationships are transitive. Nothing in this investigation has proven otherwise. This would complement many good works on the body of Christ chapter 2 surveyed. As this study has attempted to link theology proper to Christology to soteriology, perichoretic relationships within the church would extend the link to ecclesiology. That would be an important step in the unification of a solidly trinitarian systematic theology.

CONCLUSION

This study has attempted to show that the soteriological union between the believer and Christ may rightly be called a perichoretic relationship, albeit of a third type. Building on the introductory material from chapter 1, chapter 2 has shown that the Bible describes the soteriological union as one that is so close and intimate that it possesses many of the same characteristics that the trinitarian and christological varieties of *perichoresis* possess, so that calling it a third type of *perichoresis* is warranted. Chapter 3 has demonstrated that what this study calls a third type of perichoretic union has been very similarly expressed, though not often in the exact words, by many of the leading theologians of the church. Chapter 4 has affirmed that three biblical-theological metaphors of the believer's union with Christ—covenant, marriage, and adoption—highlight aspects of the perichoretic relationship present in the union. The last section of chapter 4 has provided two benefits of calling the soteriological union perichoretic—explanatory power and the preservation of both unity and diversity. Finally, this chapter has named a few potential ramifications for the doctrine of perichoretic union and some areas for possible further study.

To summarize, there are four conclusions that may be drawn about the perichoretic union of the believer and Christ. First, there is sufficient evidence—from the Bible, history, and theological reflection—to affirm that the soteriological union is indeed perichoretic. There is a both a mutual indwelling and an active participation in the other—defining characteristics of both trinitarian and christological *perichoresis*—taking place now that will be fully realized in the eschaton. The mutual indwelling and active participation in the other between Christ and the believer facilitates the Christian becoming a partaker of the divine nature, and is described in such metaphors as covenant, marriage, and adoption into God's family.

Second, at the present time, the perichoretic relationship in the union is but a reflection of the trinitarian *perichoresis*. Humans are creatures bound by space and time. It is not possible for humans to completely indwell another in the same fashion the persons of the Trinity do with each other. At this time, one may only speak analogously of the relationship between the believer and Christ as perichoretic. The believer remains in a world where re-creation is not yet complete. Moreover, the believer lacks the infinity of God that makes the trinitarian *perichoresis* so complete. A human person is just not able to completely indwell God in the fullest. In these manners there is a strong analogy, as this study has demonstrated.

Third, the reflection of the perichoretic relationship between Christ and the believer may become much more like the trinitarian *perichoresis* at the *parousia*, when believers are changed to be like Christ and the "manifestation of the sons of God" takes place. At this point in time, the union may well become asymptotically close to the inter-trinitarian relationships. The biblical promise is that "we will be like [Christ]." Does that include a fuller enjoyment of the perichoretic reality with both him and each other? It probably does, as 1 Corinthians 13:10–12 intimates; but that knowledge remains hidden now.

Fourth, there are some real benefits theologically in understanding the union of the believer and Christ as a perichoretic relationship. It can provide an alternative voice in the justification debates. It adds some vitality to the traditional *ordo salutis*, giving it a framework within which to both operate and be accountable. It is a helpful way to look at theological ethics. It can be extended to ecclesiological relationships as well as the rest of creation. It perhaps adds some meaning to the sacraments of baptism and the Lord's Supper.

Perhaps greater than all these, though, it allows a full appreciation for the language of Jesus in John 17—that we may be one, even as Father and Son are one. The revival of trinitarian discourse in the last fifty years has compelled Christian theology to attempt to ground much of its reflection in the life of the Godhead. Theology proper, Christology, and pneumatology have always been grounded in the triune God. This study has been a humble effort to explore salvation as a relational participation with Christ through the Spirit to the Father, thereby allowing soteriology to flow directly through the three great, mysterious, and even perichoretic unions from the Godhead. Further research may show that ecclesiology, anthropology, and hamartiology can be similarly understood within the triune, relational paradigm. In the end, this study has shown that it should not be improper to say that the Christian, in her union with Christ, relates perichoretically to the one who eternally exists in *perichoresis*.

Bibliography

PRIMARY SOURCES

Ambrose. *On the Christian Faith*. Pages 201–314 in vol. 10 of *The Nicene and Post-Nicene Fathers*, Series 2. Edited by Philip Schaff and Henry Wace. 13 vols. Repr., Peabody, MA: Hendrickson, 1994.

Aquinas, Thomas. "Summa Theologica 112:1." In *Nature and Grace: Selections from the Summa Theologica of Thomas Aquinas*. Edited and translated by A. M. Fairweather. Library of Christian Classics 11. Philadelphia: Westminster, 1954.

Athanasius. *Against the Arians*. Pages 306–447 in vol. 4 of *The Nicene and Post-Nicene Fathers*, Series 2. Edited by Philip Schaff and Henry Wace. 13 vols. Repr., Peabody, MA: Hendrickson, 1994.

———. *On the Incarnation*. Pages 55–110 in *Christology of the Later Fathers*. Library of Christian Classics 3. Edited by Edward A. Hardy. Philadelphia: Westminster, 1954.

Augustine. *On Nature and Grace*. Page 332 in Norman Russell, *The Doctrine of Deification in the Greek Patristic Tradition*. Translated by Henry Chadwick. Oxford: Oxford University Press, 2004.

———. "Sermon on Psalm 49." Page 331 in Norman Russell, *The Doctrine of Deification in the Greek Patristic Tradition*. Translated by Henry Chadwick. Oxford: Oxford University Press, 2004.

———. "Sermon 166.4.4." Pages 208–10 in *Sermons III/5 (148–183) on the New Testament*. Vol. III/5 of *The Works of Saint Augustine: A Translation for the 21st Century*. Edited by John E. Rotelle. Translated by Edmund Hill. New Rochelle, NY: New City, 1993.

———. "Sermon 192.1.1." Pages 46–49 in *Sermons III/6 (184–229z) on the Liturgical Seasons*. Vol. III/6 of *The Works of Saint Augustine: A Translation for the 21st Century*. Edited by John E. Rotelle. Translated by Edmund Hill. New Rochelle, NY: New City, 1993.

Basil of Caesarea. *Letter 93*. Page 179 in vol. 8 of *The Nicene and Post-Nicene Fathers*, Series 2. Edited by W. Sanday. 13 vols. Repr., Peabody, MA: Hendrickson, 1994.

Calvin, John. *Commentary on the Epistles of Paul the Apostle to the Corinthians, Vol. I*. Calvin's Commentaries 20. Translated by John Pringle. Grand Rapids: Baker, 1999.

———. *Commentary on John*. Vol. 75 of *Corpus Reformatorum*. Edited by Guilielmus Baum, Eduardus Cunitz, and Eduardus Reuss. 101 Vols. Brunsvigae: Schwetschke, 1834–1907.

———. *The Epistles of Paul the Apostle to the Romans and to the Thessalonians*. Translated by Ross Mackenzie. Grand Rapids: Eerdmans, 1960.

———. *Institutes of the Christian Religion*. 2 vols. Library of Christian Classics 20–21. Edited by John T. McNeill. Translated by Ford Lewis Battles. Philadelphia: Westminster, 1960.

———. *The Gospel according to St. John 11–21 and the First Epistle of John.* Translated by T. H. L. Parker. Grand Rapids: Eerdmans, 1961.

Cyril of Alexandria. *Commentary on the Gospel of John.* Page 257 in *Ancient Christian Commentary on Scripture.* Edited by Joel C. Elowsky. Downers Grove, IL: InterVarsity, 2007.

Cyril of Jerusalem. *Catechetical Lecture 20.* Pages 147–48 in vol. 7 of *The Nicene and Post-Nicene Fathers,* Series 2. Edited by W. Sanday. 13 vols. Repr., Peabody, MA: Hendrickson, 1994.

Gregory of Nazianzus. *Oration 101.* Pages 439–43 in vol. 7 of *The Nicene and Post-Nicene Fathers,* Series 2. Edited by W. Sanday. 13 vols. Repr., Peabody, MA: Hendrickson, 1994.

———. *Oration on Holy Baptism.* Pages 360–77 in vol. 7 of The *Nicene and Post-Nicene Fathers,* Series 2. Edited by W. Sanday. 13 vols. Repr., Peabody, MA: Hendrickson, 1994.

———. *Third Theological Oration.* Pages 160–76 in *Christology of the Later Fathers.* Library of Christian Classics 3. Edited by Edward A. Hardy. Philadelphia: Westminster, 1954.

Hilary of Poitiers. *On the Trinity.* Pages 40–233 in vol. 9 of *The Nicene and Post-Nicene Fathers,* Series 2. Edited by W. Sanday. 13 vols. Repr., Peabody, MA: Hendrickson, 1994.

Ignatius. *Epistle to the Ephesians.* Pages 49–58 in vol. 1 of *The Ante-Nicene Fathers.* Edited by A. Cleveland Coxe. 12 vols. Repr., Peabody, MA: Hendrickson, 1994.

———. *Epistle to the Smyrnaeans.* Pages 86–92 in vol. 1 of *The Ante-Nicene Fathers.* Edited by A. Cleveland Coxe. 12 vols. Repr., Peabody, MA: Hendrickson, 1994.

Irenaeus. *Against Heresies.* Pages 315–567 in vol. 1 of *The Ante-Nicene Fathers.* Edited by A. Cleveland Coxe. 12 vols. Repr., Peabody, MA: Hendrickson, 1994.

Jerome. *Against Jovinianus.* Pages 346–416 in vol. 6 of *The Nicene and Post-Nicene Fathers,* Series 2. Edited by Philip Schaff and Henry Wace. 13 vols. Repr., Peabody, MA: Hendrickson, 1994.

John Chrysostom. *Homily 5 on the Epistles of Paul to the Corinthians.* Pages 22–28 in vol. 12 of *The Nicene and Post-Nicene Fathers,* Series 1. Edited by Talbot W. Chambers. 13 vols. Repr., Peabody, MA: Hendrickson, 1994.

John of Damascus. *On the Orthodox Faith.* Pages 1–104 in vol. 9 of *The Nicene and Post-Nicene Fathers,* Series 2. Edited by Philip Schaff and Henry Wace. 13 vols. Repr., Peabody, MA: Hendrickson, 1994.

Justin Martyr. *Dialogue with Trypho.* Pages 194–270 in vol. 1 of *The Ante-Nicene Fathers.* Edited by A. Cleveland Coxe. 12 vols. Repr., Peabody, MA: Hendrickson, 1994.

———. *First Apology.* Pages 163–93 in vol. 1 of *The Ante-Nicene Fathers.* Edited by A. Cleveland Coxe. 12 vols. Repr., Peabody, MA: Hendrickson, 1994.

Luther, Martin. *Sämmtlichte Schriften.* 11 Vols. St. Louis: Concordia, 1892.

———. *Lectures on Galatians (1535).* Vol. 26 of *Luther's Works.* Edited and translated by Jaroslav Pelikan. St. Louis: Concordia, 1967.

———. *Commentary on Galatians.* Translated by Erasmus Middleton. Grand Rapids: Kregel, 1979.

———. "The Freedom of the Christian." Pages 585–629 in *Martin Luther's Basic Theological Writings.* Edited by Timothy Lull. Minneapolis: Fortress, 1989.

Maximus the Confessor. *Mystigogia.* Pages 181–225 in *Maximus the Confessor: Selected Writings.* Translated by George Berthold. Mahwah, NJ: Paulist, 1985.

Origen. *Against Celsus.* Pages 395–669 in vol. 4 of *The Ante-Nicene Fathers.* Edited by A. Cleveland Coxe. 12 vols. Repr., Peabody, MA: Hendrickson, 1994.
———. *Commentary on the Gospel according to John, Books 1–10.* The Fathers of the Church 80. Translated by Ronald E. Heine. Washington, DC: Catholic University of America Press, 1989.
———. *On First Principles.* Pages 239–382 in vol. 4 of *The Ante-Nicene Fathers.* Edited by A. Cleveland Coxe. 12 vols. Repr., Peabody, MA: Hendrickson, 1994.
Tertullian. *On Baptism.* Pages 669–79 in vol. 3 of *The Ante-Nicene Fathers.* Edited by A. Cleveland Coxe. 12 vols. Repr., Peabody, MA: Hendrickson, 1994.

COMMENTARIES

Barrett, C. K. *The First Epistle to the Corinthians.* Harper New Testament Commentaries. New York: Harper & Row, 1968.
———. *The Gospel according to St. John.* Philadelphia: Westminster, 1978.
Bauckham, Richard. *Jude and 2 Peter.* Word Biblical Commentary 50. Waco: Word, 1983.
Beasley-Murray, George R. *John.* 2nd ed. Word Biblical Commentary 36. Dallas: Word, 1999.
Bernard, J. H. *A Critical and Exegetical Commentary on the Gospel According to St. John.* 2 vols. International Critical Commentary. Edinburgh: T&T Clark, 1963.
Borchert, Gerald. *John 12–21.* New American Commentary 25B. Nashville: Broadman & Holman, 2002.
Brodie, Thomas L. *The Gospel according to John: A Literary and Theological Commentary.* New York and Oxford: Oxford University Press, 1993.
Brown, Raymond E. *The Gospel According to John.* 2 vols. Anchor Bible 29–29A. Garden City, NY: Doubleday, 1966–70.
Bruce, F. F. *The Epistle to the Hebrews.* New International Commentary of the New Testament. Grand Rapids: Eerdmans, 1964.
Carson, D. A. *The Gospel according to John.* Pillar New Testament Commentary. Grand Rapids: Eerdmans, 1991.
Cranfield, C. E. B. *A Critical and Exegetical Commentary on the Epistle to the Romans.* International Critical Commentary. 2 vols. Edinburgh: T&T Clark, 1975.
———. *Romans: A Shorter Commentary.* Grand Rapids: Eerdmans, 1985.
Davids, Peter H. *The Letters of 2 Peter and Jude.* Pillar New Testament Commentary. Grand Rapids: Eerdmans, 2006.
Fee, Gordon D. *The First Epistle to the Corinthians.* New International Commentary on the New Testament. Grand Rapids: Eerdmans, 1987.
France, R. T. *The Gospel of Matthew.* New International Commentary on the New Testament. Grand Rapids: Eerdmans, 2007.
George, Timothy. *Galatians.* New American Commentary 30. Nashville: Broadman & Holman, 1994.
Green, Gene L. *Jude and 2 Peter.* Baker Exegetical Commentary on the New Testament. Grand Rapids: Baker, 2008.
Hartley, John E. *Leviticus.* Word Biblical Commentary 4. Dallas: Word, 1982.
Hoehner, Harold W. *Ephesians: An Exegetical Commentary.* Grand Rapids: Baker Academic, 2002.

Keener, Craig S. *The Gospel of John: A Commentary*. 2 vols. Peabody, MA: Hendrickson, 2003.
Keil, C. F., and F. Delitzsch. *Keil and Delitzsch on the Pentateuch, Vol. II*. Edinburgh: T&T Clark, 1887.
Köstenberger, Andreas J. *John*. Baker Exegetical Commentary on the New Testament. Grand Rapids: Baker Academic, 2004.
Lane, William L. *The Gospel according to Mark*. New International Commentary on the New Testament. Grand Rapids: Eerdmans, 1974.
Lenski, R. C. H. *The Interpretation of John's Gospel*. Minneapolis: Augsburg, 1943.
Longenecker, Richard N. *Galatians*. Word Biblical Commentary 41. Dallas: Word, 1990.
Lincoln, Andrew T. *The Gospel according to St. John*. Black's New Testament Commentaries. London: Continuum, 2005.
Moo, Douglas. *Romans 1–8*. The Wycliffe Exegetical Commentary. Chicago: Moody, 1991.
———. *The Epistle to the Romans*. New International Commentary on the New Testament. Grand Rapids: Eerdmans, 1996.
Morris, Leon. *The Gospel according to Matthew*. Pillar New Testament Commentary. Grand Rapids: Eerdmans, 1992.
———. *The Gospel according to John*. New International Commentary on the New Testament. Grand Rapids: Eerdmans, 1995.
Mounce, Robert H. *Romans*. New American Commentary 27. Nashville: Broadman & Holman, 1995.
Rooker, Mark F. *Leviticus*. New American Commentary 3A. Nashville: Broadman & Holman, 2000.
Schnackenburg, Rudolf. *The Gospel according to St. John*. Translated by Cecily Hastings et al. 3 vols. New York: Seabury, 1980–90.
Schreiner, Thomas R. *Romans*. Baker Exegetical Commentary on the New Testament 6. Grand Rapids: Baker Academic, 1998.
———. *1, 2 Peter, Jude*. New American Commentary 37. Nashville: Broadman & Holman, 2003.
Walvoord, John F., and Roy B. Zuck, ed. *The Bible Knowledge Commentary: Old Testament*. Wheaton, IL: Victor, 1985.
Wenham, Gordon J. *The Book of Leviticus*. New International Commentary on the Old Testament. Grand Rapids: Eerdmans, 1979.
Witherington, Ben III. *John's Wisdom: A Commentary on the Fourth Gospel*. Louisville: Westminster John Knox, 1995.

MONOGRAPHS

Akin, Daniel L., ed. *A Theology for the Church*. Nashville: Broadman & Holman, 2007.
Anderson, Gary A. *Sacrifices and Offerings in Ancient Israel: Studies in their Social and Political Importance*. Harvard Semitic Monograph Series 41. Atlanta: Scholars Press, 1987.
Appold, Mark L. *The Oneness Motif in the Fourth Gospel: Motif Analysis and Exegetical Probe into the Theology of John*. Tübingen: Mohr Siebeck, 1976.

Ball, David Mark. *"I Am" in John's Gospel: Literary Function, Background, and Theological Implications*. Journal for the Study of the New Testament Supplement Series 124. Sheffield: Sheffield Academic Press, 1996.
Balswick, Jack O., and Judith K. Balswick. *A Model for Marriage: Covenant, Grace, Empowerment, and Intimacy*. Downers Grove, IL: IVP Academic, 2006.
Balthasar, Hans Urs von. *Cosmic Liturgy: The Universe according to Maximus the Confessor*. Translated by Brian E. Daley. San Francisco: Ignatius, 2003.
Baltzer, Klaus. *The Covenant Formulary in Old Testament, Jewish, and Early Christian Writings*. Translated by David E. Green. Philadelphia: Fortress, 1971.
Barcley, William B. *Christ in You: A Study of Paul's Theology and Ethics*. Lanham, MD: University Press of America, 1999.
Barth, Karl. *Church Dogmatics*. 14 volumes. Edited by G.W. Bromiley et al. Translated by J. C. Campbell et al. Edinburgh: T&T Clark, 1956–2004.
Bartos, Emil. *Deification in Eastern Orthodox Theology: An Evaluation and Critique of the Theology of Dumitru Staniloae*. Paternoster Theological Monographs. Milton Keynes, UK, and Waynesboro, GA: Paternoster, 1999.
Bauckham, Richard. *The Theology of Jürgen Moltmann*. Edinburgh: T&T Clark, 1995.
Bauckham, Richard, and Carl Mosser, eds. *The Gospel of John and Christian Theology*. Grand Rapids: Eerdmans, 2008.
Beale, G. K. *The Temple and the Church's Mission: A Biblical Theology of the Dwelling Place of God*. New Studies in Biblical Theology 17. Downers Grove, IL: InterVarsity, 2004.
Beckwith, Roger T., and Martin J. Selman, eds. *Sacrifice in the Bible*. Grand Rapids: Baker, 1995.
Behr, John. *The Way to Nicaea*. Crestwood, NY: St. Vladimir's Seminary Press, 2001.
Best, Ernest. *One Body in Christ: A Study in the Relationship of the Church of Christ in the Epistles of the Apostle Paul*. London: SPCK, 1955.
Billings, J. Todd. *Calvin, Participation, and the Gift: The Activity of Believers in Union with Christ*. Changing Paradigms in Historical and Systematic Theology. Oxford: Oxford University Press, 2007.
Bindley, T. H. *The Ecumenical Documents of the Faith*. 4th ed. Westport, CT: Greenwood, 1950.
Blaising, Craig A., and Darrell L. Bock, eds. *Dispensationalism, Israel, and the Church: The Search for Definition*. Grand Rapids: Zondervan, 1992.
Boff, Leonardo. *Trinity and Society*. Translated by Paul Burns. Maryknoll, NY: Orbis, 1998.
Bouttier, Michel. *Christianity according to Paul*. Translated by Frank Clarke. Studies in Biblical Theology 49. Naperville, IL: Alec R. Allenson, 1966.
Braaten, Carl, and Robert W. Jenson, eds. *Union with Christ: The New Finnish Interpretation of Luther*. Grand Rapids: Eerdmans, 1998.
Brunn, Emilie Zum, and Georgette Epiney Burgard. *Women Mystics in Medieval Europe*. Translated by Sheila Hughes. New York: Paragon House, 1989.
Bullett, Gerald. *The English Mystics*. London: Michael Joseph, 1950.
Burke, Trevor J. *Adopted into God's Family: Exploring a Pauline Metaphor*. New Studies in Biblical Theology 22. Downers Grove, IL: InterVarsity, 2006.
Butin, Philip W. *Revelation, Redemption, and Response: Calvin's Trinitarian Understanding of the Divine-Human Relationship*. Oxford: Oxford University Press, 1995.

Buxton, Graham. *The Trinity, Creation, and Pastoral Ministry: Imaging the Perichoretic God*. Waynesboro, GA: Paternoster, 2005.
Caird, G. B. *New Testament Theology*. Edited by L. D. Hurst. Oxford: Clarendon, 1995.
Callaway, Joseph A. *Faces of the Old Testament*. Macon, GA: Smyth and Helwys, 1995.
Calov, Abraham. *Theologia Postiva*. Wittenberg, 1652.
Carson, D. A. *The Farewell Discourse and Final Prayer of Jesus: An Exposition of John 14–17*. Grand Rapids: Baker, 1980.
Carson, D. A., Peter T. O'Brien, and Mark A. Siefrid, eds. *Justification and Variegated Nomism*. 2 vols. Grand Rapids: Baker Academic, 2001–2004.
Cerfaux, Lucien. *The Christian in the Theology of St. Paul*. Translated by Lilian Soiron. New York: Herder and Herder, 1967.
Chan, Simon. *Spiritual Theology: A Systematic Study of the Christian Life*. Downers Grove, IL: InterVarsity, 1998.
Chavasse, Claude. *The Bride of Christ: An Enquiry into the Nuptial Element in Early Christianity*. London: Religious Book Club, 1939.
Chemnitz, Martin. *The Two Natures in Christ*. St. Louis: Concordia, 1971.
Chennattu, Rekha M. *Johannine Discipleship as a Covenant Relationship*. Peabody, MA: Hendrickson, 2006.
Collins, Paul M. *Trinitarian Theology West and East: Karl Barth, the Cappadocian Fathers, and John Zizioulas*. Oxford: Oxford University Press, 2001.
Colyer, Elmer, ed. *The Promise of Trinitarian Theology: Theologians in Dialogue with T. F. Torrance*. Lanham, MD: Rowman & Littlefield, 2001.
———. *How to Read T. F. Torrance: Understanding his Trinitarian and Scientific Theology*. Downers Grove, IL: InterVarsity, 2001.
Cook, James I., ed. *Saved by Hope: Essays in Honor of Richard C. Oudersluys*. Grand Rapids: Eerdmans, 1978.
Cooper, John W. *Panentheism: The Other God of the Philosophers*. Grand Rapids: Baker Academic, 2006.
Corduan, Winfried. *Mysticism: An Evangelical Option?* Grand Rapids: Zondervan, 1991.
Crisp, Oliver D. *Divinity and Humanity: The Incarnation Reconsidered*. Cambridge: Cambridge University Press, 2007.
Cunningham, David S. *These Three Are One: The Practice of Trinitarian Theology*. Malden, MA: Blackwell, 1998.
Daly, Robert J. *The Origins of the Christian Doctrine of Sacrifice*. Philadelphia: Fortress, 1978.
Daniélou, Jean. *God and the Ways of Knowing*. Translated by Walter Roberts. New York: Meridian, 1957.
Dawes, Gregory W. *The Body in Question: Metaphor and Meaning in the Interpretation of Ephesians 5:21–33*. Biblical Interpretation Series 30. Leiden: Brill, 1998.
Dawson, Gerrit Scott, ed. *An Introduction to Torrance Theology: Discovering the Incarnate Savior*. London: T&T Clark, 2007.
de Vaux, Roland. *Ancient Israel: Its Life and Institutions*. Translated by John McHugh. New York: McGraw-Hill, 1961.
Deissmann, Adolf. *Die neutestamentliche Formel 'in Christo Jesu.'* Marburg: N. G. Elwert'sche Verlagsbuchhandlung, 1892.
———. *St. Paul: A Study in Social and Religious History*. Translated by Lionel R. M. Strachan. London: Hodder and Stoughton, 1912.

Demarest, Bruce. *The Cross and Salvation*. Wheaton, IL: Crossway, 1997.
Demarest, Bruce, and Gordon A. Lewis. *Integrative Theology*. 3 Vols. Grand Rapids: Academie Books, 1987.
Dunn, James D. G. *The Theology of Paul's Letter to the Galatians*. Cambridge: Cambridge University Press, 1993.
———. *The Theology of Paul the Apostle*. Grand Rapids: Eerdmans, 1998.
———. *The New Perspective on Paul*. Tübingen: Mohr Siebeck, 2005.
Dyrness, William A. *Themes in Old Testament Theology*. Downers Grove, IL: InterVaristy, 1979.
Edersheim, Alfred. *The Temple: Its Ministry and Services*. Peabody, MA: Hendrickson, 1994.
Eichrodt, Walther A. *Theology of the Old Testament*. Translated by J. A. Baker. 3 Vols. Philadelphia: Westminster, 1961.
Elwell, Walter A., ed. *Evangelical Dictionary of Theology*. 2nd ed. Grand Rapids: Baker, 2004.
Engelsma, David J. *Marriage: The Mystery of Christ and the Church: The Covenant-Bond in Scripture and History*. Rev. ed. Grandville, MI: Reformed Free Publishing Association, 1998.
Erickson, Millard J. *The Word Became Flesh: A Contemporary Incarnational Christology*. Grand Rapids: Baker, 1991.
———. *God in Three Persons: A Contemporary Interpretation of the Trinity*. Grand Rapids: Baker, 1995.
———. *Christian Theology*. 2nd ed. Grand Rapids: Baker, 1998.
Evans, William B. *Imputation and Impartation: Union with Christ in American Reformed Theology*. Milton Keynes, UK, and Colorado Springs: Paternoster, 2008.
Fairbairn, Donald. *Life in the Trinity: An Introduction to Christian Theology with the Help of the Church Fathers*. Downers Grove, IL: IVP Academic, 2009.
Fee, Gordon D. *God's Empowering Presence: The Holy Spirit in the Letters of Paul*. Peabody, MA: Hendrickson, 1994.
———. *Paul, the Spirit, and the People of God*. Peabody, MA: Hendrickson, 1996.
———. *Pauline Christology: An Exegetical-Theological Study*. Peabody, MA: Hendrickson, 2007.
Ferguson, Everett, ed. *Studies in Early Christianity: Doctrines of Human Nature, Sin, and Salvation in the Early Church*. New York and London: Garland, 1993.
Fiddes, Paul S. *Participating in God: A Pastoral Doctrine of the Trinity*. Louisville: Westminster John Knox, 2000.
Furnish, Victor P. *The Love Command in the New Testament*. Nashville: Abingdon, 1972.
Gaffin, Richard B. Jr. *Resurrection and Redemption: A Study in Paul's Soteriology*. Phillipsburg, NJ: Presbyterian and Reformed, 1987.
———. *By Faith, Not by Sight: Paul and the Order of Salvation*. London and Colorado Springs: Paternoster, 2006.
Garcia, Mark A. *Life in Christ: Union with Christ and Twofold Grace in Calvin's Theology*. Studies in Christian History and Thought. Colorado Springs: Paternoster, 2008.
Garrett, James Leo Jr.. *Systematic Theology*. 3 vols. Grand Rapids: Eerdmans, 1995.
George, Timothy, ed. *God the Holy Trinity: Reflections on Christian Faith and Practice*. Grand Rapids: Baker Academic, 2006.

Gilson, Etienne. *The Mystical Theology of St. Bernard*. Translated by A. H. C. Downes. Kalamazoo, MI: Cistercian, 1990.

Gorman, Michael J. *Inhabiting the Cruciform God: Kenosis, Justification, and* Theosis *in Paul's Narrative Soteriology*. Grand Rapids: Eerdmans, 2009.

Gordon, A. J. *In Christ*. New York: Fleming H. Revell, 1880.

Green, Joel B. and Max Turner, eds. *Jesus of Nazareth, Lord and Christ: Essays on the Historical Jesus and New Testament Christology*. Grand Rapids: Eerdmans, 1994.

Grenz, Stanley J. *Created for Community: Connecting Christian Belief with Christian Living*. 2nd ed. Grand Rapids: Baker, 1998.

———. *Rediscovering the Triune God: The Trinity in Contemporary Theology*. Minneapolis: Fortress, 2004.

Gross, Jules. *The Divinization of the Christian according to the Greek Fathers*. Translated by Paul A. Onica. Anaheim: A & C, 2004.

Grudem, Wayne C. *Systematic Theology*. Grand Rapids: Zondervan, 1994.

Gruenler, Royce Gordon. *The Trinity in the Gospel of John: A Thematic Commentary on the Fourth Gospel*. Grand Rapids: Baker, 1986.

Gundry, Robert H. Soma *in Biblical Theology with an Emphasis on Pauline Anthropology*. Cambridge: Cambridge University Press, 1976.

Gunton, Colin E. *The Actuality of Atonement: A Study of Metaphor, Rationality, and Christian Tradition*. Grand Rapids: Eerdmans, 1989.

———. *The One, the Three, and the Many: God, Creation, and the Culture of Modernity*. Cambridge: Cambridge University Press, 1993.

———. *Father, Son, and Holy Spirit: Toward a Fully Trinitarian Theology*. London and New York: T&T Clark, 2003.

Gunton, Colin E., and Daniel W. Hardy, eds. *On Being the Church: Essays on the Christian Community*. Edinburgh: T&T Clark, 1989.

Guthrie, Donald L. *New Testament Theology*. Downers Grove, IL: InterVarsity, 1981.

Habets, Myk. *Theosis in the Theology of Thomas Torrance*. Burlington, VT: Ashgate, 2009.

Hagner, Donald A., and Murray J. Harris. *Pauline Studies: Essays Presented to Professor F. F. Bruce on his 70th Birthday*. Exeter: Paternoster, 1980.

Hahn, Scott Walker. *Kinship by Covenant: A Biblical, Theological Study of Covenant Types and Texts in the Old and New Testaments*. Ann Arbor: UMI, 1995.

Hale, Clarence B. *The Meaning of 'In Christ' in the Greek New Testament*. Dallas: Summer Institute of Linguistics, 1991.

Hall, David W., and Peter A. Lillback, eds. *A Theological Guide to Calvin's Institutes: Essays and Analyses*. Phillipsburg, NJ: Presbyterian and Reformed, 2008.

Hamilton, James M. Jr. *God's Indwelling Presence: The Holy Spirit in the Old and New Testaments*. Nashville: B&H Academic, 2006.

Hanson, Anthony Tyrrell. *The Prophetic Gospel: A Study of John and the Old Testament*. New York: T&T Clark, 1991.

Harkey, Simeon. *Justification by Faith as Held and Taught by Lutherans*. Philadelphia: Lutheran Board of Publication, 1875.

Hart, Trevor, and Daniel Thimell, eds. *Christ in Our Place: The Humanity of God in Christ for the Reconciliation of the World*. Princeton Theological Monograph Series. Exeter: Paternoster, 1989.

Hawthorne, Gerald F., and Ralph P. Martin, eds. *Dictionary of Paul and His Letters*. Downers Grove, IL: InterVarsity: 1993.

Henry, Carl F. H., ed. *Basic Christian Doctrines*. New York: Holt, Rinehart, and Winston, 1962.
Hill, William J. *The Three-Personed God: The Trinity as a Mystery of Salvation*. Washington: Catholic University of America Press, 1982.
Hillers, Delbert R. *Covenant: The History of a Biblical Idea*. Baltimore: The Johns Hopkins University Press, 1969.
Hoenecke, Adolf. *Dogmatik*. 4 Vols. Milwaukee: NPH, 1912.
Hooker, Morna D. *From Adam to Christ: Essays on Paul*. Cambridge: Cambridge University Press, 1990.
Horton, Michael. *Covenant and Salvation: Union with Christ*. Louisville: Westminster John Knox, 2007.
———. *Lord and Servant: A Covenant Christology*. Louisville: Westminster John Knox, 2005.
Hoskins, Paul M. *Jesus as the Fulfillment of the Temple in the Gospel of John*. Colorado Springs: Paternoster, 2006.
Hudson, Nancy J. *Becoming God: The Doctrine of Theosis in Nicholas of Cusa*. Washington, DC: Catholic University of America Press, 2007.
Hugenberger, Gordon Paul. *Marriage as a Covenant: A Study of Biblical Law and Ethics Governing Marriage Developed from the Perspective of Malachi*. Supplements to Vetum Testamentum 52. Leiden: Brill, 1994.
Husbands, Mark, and Daniel J. Treier, eds. *Justification: What's at Stake in the Current Debates*. Downers Grove, IL: InterVarsity: 2004.
Huttar, Charles A., ed. *Imagination and the Spirit: Essays in Literature and the Christian Faith Presented to Clyde S. Kilby*. Grand Rapids: Eerdmans, 1971.
Jenson, Robert W. *Systematic Theology, Vol. 1—The Triune God*. New York: Oxford University Press, 1997.
Kalluveettil, Paul. *Declaration and Covenant: A Comprehensive Review of Covenant Formulae from the Old Testament and the Ancient Near East*. Rome: Pontifical Biblical Institute, 1982.
Kanagaraj, Jey J. *'Mysticism' in the Gospel of John: An Inquiry into its Background*. Journal for the Study of the New Testament Supplement Series 158. Sheffield: Sheffield Academic Press, 1998.
Keathley, Kenneth. *Salvation and Sovereignty: A Molinist Approach*. Nashville: B&H Academic, 2010.
Kelly, J. N. D. *Early Christian Doctrines*. Rev. ed. Peabody, MA: Prince, 2007.
Kennedy, Kevin Dixon. *Union with Christ and the Extent of the Atonement in Calvin*. Studies in Biblical Literature 48. New York: Peter Lang, 2002.
Kerr, Alan R. *The Temple of Jesus' Body: The Temple Theme and the Gospel of John*. Journal of the Study of the New Testament Supplement Series 220. London: Sheffield, 2002.
Kittel, Gerhard, ed. *Theological Dictionary of the New Testament*. 10 vols. Translated by Geoffrey W. Bromiley. Grand Rapids: Eerdmans, 1962–71.
Koester, Craig R. *Symbolism in the Fourth Gospel: Meaning, Mystery, Community*. Minneapolis: Fortress, 1995.
Köstenberger, Andreas, and Scott R. Swain. *Father, Son, and Spirit: The Trinity and John's Gospel*. New Studies in Biblical Theology 24. Downers Grove, IL: InterVarsity, 2008.

Kress, Robert. *The Church: Communion, Sacrament, Communication.* New York: Paulist, 1985.
Kruger, C. Baxter. *Jesus and the Undoing of Adam.* Jackson, MS: Perichoresis, 2003.
———. *The Great Dance: The Christian Vision Revisited.* Vancouver: Regent College Publishing, 2005.
Kruse, Colin G. *Paul, the Law, and Justification.* Peabody, MA: Hendrickson, 1996.
Lacoste, Jean-Yves, ed. *The Encyclopedia of Christian Theology.* 3 vols. New York: Routledge, 2005.
LaCugna, Catherine Mowry. *God for Us: The Trinity and Christian Life.* San Francisco: Harper Collins, 1992.
Ladd, George Eldon. *A Theology of the New Testament.* Rev. ed. Edited by Donald A. Hagner. Grand Rapids: Eerdmans, 1993.
Landman, Isaac, ed. *The Universal Jewish Encyclopedia.* 10 vols. New York: Universal Jewish Encyclopedia, 1948.
Lee, Kye Won. *Living in Union with Christ: The Practical Theology of Thomas F. Torrance.* Issues in Systematic Theology 11. New York: Peter Lang, 2003.
Letham, Robert. *The Work of Christ.* Contours of Christian Theology. Downers Grove, IL: InterVarsity, 1993.
———. *The Holy Trinity: In Scripture, History, Theology, and Worship.* Phillipsburg, NJ: Presbyterian and Reformed, 2004.
Leupp, Roderick T. *The Renewal of Trinitarian Theology: Themes, Patterns, and Explorations.* Downers Grove, IL: InterVarsity, 2008.
Lindbeck, George. *The Nature of Doctrine: Religion and Theology in a Postliberal Age.* London: SPCK, 1984.
Lull, Timothy, ed. *Martin Luther's Basic Theological Writings.* Minneapolis: Fortress, 1989.
Machen, J. Gresham. *The Virgin Birth of Christ.* New York and London: Harper and Brothers, 1932.
MacLeod, Donald. *The Person of Christ.* Contours of Christian Theology. Downers Grove, IL: InterVarsity, 1998.
Maloney, George A. *Entering into the Heart of Jesus: Meditations on the Indwelling Trinity in St. John's Gospel.* New York: Alba House, 1987.
———. *The Undreamed Has Happened: God Lives within Us.* Scranton, PA: University of Scranton Press, 2003.
Mantzaridis, Georgios I. *The Deification of Man: St. Gregory Palamas and the Orthodox Tradition.* Translated by Liadain Sherrard. Crestwood, NY: St. Vladimir's Seminary Press, 1984.
Martin, Ralph P. *Reconciliation: A Study of Paul's Theology.* New Foundations Theological Library. Atlanta: John Knox, 1981.
Martin, Robert K. *The Incarnate Ground of Christian Faith: Toward a Christian Theological Epistemology for the Educational Ministry of the Church.* Lanham, MD: University Press of America, 1998.
Mascall, E. L. *Christ, the Christian, and the Church: A Study of the Incarnation and its Consequences.* London: Longmans Green & Co., 1946.
———. *The Importance of Being Human: Some Aspects of the Christian Doctrine of Man.* New York: Columbia University Press, 1958.
McCaffrey, James. *The House with Many Rooms: The Temple Theme of John 14:2–3.* Analecta biblica 114. Rome: Pontifical Biblical Institute, 1988.

McCarthy, Dennis J. *Old Testament Covenants: A Survey of Current Opinions*. Atlanta: John Knox, 1972.

———. *Treaty and Covenant*. Analecta biblica 21. Rome: Pontifical Biblical Institute, 1963.

McCready, Douglas. *He Came Down from Heaven: The Preexistence of Christ and the Christian Faith*. Downers Grove, IL: InterVarsity, 2005.

McGowan, A. T. B., ed. *Always Reforming: Explorations in Systematic Theology*. Downers Grove, IL: InterVarsity, 2006.

McKenzie, Steven L. *Covenant*. St. Louis: Chalice, 2000.

McKnight, Scot. *Jesus and His Death: Historiography, the Historical Jesus, and Atonement Theory*. Waco: Baylor, 2005.

McWhirter, Jocelyn. *The Bridegroom Messiah and the People of God: Marriage in the Fourth Gospel*. Cambridge: Cambridge University Press, 2006.

Mendenhall, George E. *Law and Covenant in Israel and the Ancient Near East*. Pittsburgh: Biblical Colloquium, 1955.

Mersch, Emile. *The Whole Christ: The Historical Development of the Doctrine of the Mystical Body in Scripture and Tradition*. Translated by John R. Kelly. Milwaukee: Bruce, 1938.

———. *The Theology of the Mystical Body*. Translated by Cyril Vollert. London: B. Herder, 1951.

Mielziner, Moses. *Jewish Law of Marriage and Divorce*. Cincinnati: Bloch, 1884.

Miletic, Stephen Francis. *"One Flesh": Eph. 5:22–24, 31—Marriage and The New Creation*. Analecta biblica 115. Rome: Editrice Pontificio Instituto Biblico, 1998.

Moltmann, Jürgen. *The Trinity and the Kingdom: The Doctrine of God*. Translated by Margaret Kohl. San Francisco: Harper and Row, 1981.

———. *History and the Triune God: Contributions to Trinitarian Theology*. Translated by John Bowden. New York: Crossroad, 1992.

———. *Experiences in Theology: Ways and Forms of Christian Theology*. Translated by Margaret Kohl. Minneapolis: Fortress, 2000.

Moltmann, Jürgen, and Elisabeth Moltmann-Wendel. *Humanity in God*. London: SCM, 1984.

Moltmann, Jürgen, and Carmen Riwuzumwami, eds. *Wo ist Gott? Gottesräume—Lebensräume*. Neukirchen: Neukirchener Verlag, 2002.

Moore, Russell. *Adopted for Life: The Priority of Adoption for Christian Families and Churches*. Wheaton, IL: Crossway, 2009.

Morris, Leon. *The Apostolic Preaching of the Cross*. Grand Rapids: Eerdmans, 1965.

———. *The Atonement: Its Meaning and Significance*. Downers Grove, IL: InterVarsity, 1983.

Morris, Thomas V. *The Logic of God Incarnate*. Eugene: Wipf and Stock, 2001.

Morrison, John Douglas. *Knowledge of the Self-Revealing God in the Thought of Thomas Forsyth Torrance*. Issues in Systematic Theology 2. New York: Peter Lang, 1997.

Moule, C. F. D. *The Origin of Christology*. Cambridge: Cambridge University Press, 1977.

Mulcahy, Eamonn. *The Cause of our Salvation: Soteriological Causality according to some Modern British Theologians 1988–1998*. Tesi Gregoriana Serie Teologia 140. Rome: Editrice Pontifica Universita Gregoriana, 2007.

Murray, John. *Redemption Accomplished and Applied*. Edinburgh: Banner of Truth, 1961.

Oden, Thomas C. *The Justification Reader*. Grand Rapids: Eerdmans, 2002.
Ortlund, Raymond C. Jr. *God's Unfaithful Wife: A Biblical Theology of Spiritual Adultery*. New Studies in Biblical Theology 2. Downers Grove, IL: InterVarsity, 1996.
Packer, J. I., and Loren Wilkinson, eds. *Alive to God: Studies in Spirituality Presented to James Houston*. Vancouver: Regent College Publishing, 1992.
Pannenberg, Wolfhart. *Systematic Theology*. 3 vols. Translated by Geoffrey W. Bromiley. Grand Rapids: Eerdmans, 1994.
Penny, Robert L., ed. *The Hope Fulfilled: Essays in Honor of O. Palmer Robertson*. Phillipsburg, NJ: Presbyterian and Reformed, 2008.
Peters, Ted. *God as Trinity: Relationality and Temporality in Divine Life*. Louisville: Westminster John Knox, 1993.
Peterson, Robert A. *Adopted by God: From Wayward Sinners to Cherished Children*. Phillipsburg, NJ: Presbyterian and Reformed, 2001.
Pink. A. W. *Exposition of the Gospel of John (John 8–15:6)*. Grand Rapids: Zondervan, 1945.
———. *The Divine Covenants*. Grand Rapids: Baker, 1973.
Piper, John. *Counted Righteous in Christ*. Wheaton, IL: Crossway, 2002.
Polanyi, Michael. *Knowing and Being: Essays by Michael Polanyi*. Chicago: University of Chicago Press, 1969.
Porter, Frank Chamberlain. *The Mind of Christ in Paul: Light from Paul on Present Problems of Christian Thinking*. New York: Charles Scribner's Sons, 1930.
Posset, Franz. *Pater Bernhardus: Martin Luther and Bernard of Clairvaux*. Kalamazoo, MI: Cistercian, 1999.
Powers, Daniel G. *Salvation through Participation: An Examination of the Notion of the Believers' Corporate Unity with Christ in Early Christian Soteriology*. Contributions to Biblical Exegesis and Theology 29. Leuven: Peeters, 2001.
Prestige, G. L. *God in Patristic Thought*. London, SPCK, 1956.
Pryor, John W. *John: Evangelist of the Covenant People*. Downers Grove, IL: InterVarsity, 1992.
Purves, Andrew. *Reconstructing Pastoral Theology: A Christological Foundation*. Louisville: Westminster John Knox, 2004.
Purves, Jim. *The Triune God and the Charismatic Movement*. Carlisle: Paternoster, 2004.
Quaegebuer, J., ed. *Ritual and Sacrifice in the Ancient Near East*. Orientalia lovaniensia analecta 55. Leuven: Peeters, 1993.
Rahner, Karl. *The Trinity*. Translated by Joseph Donceel. London: Burns and Oates, 1970.
Reid, J. K. S. *Our Life in Christ*. Philadelphia: Westminster, 1963.
Richardson, Alan, and John Bowden, eds. *The Westminster Dictionary of Christian Theology*. Philadelphia: Westminster, 1983.
Ridderbos, Herman. *Paul: An Outline of His Theology*. Translated by John Richard DeWitt. Grand Rapids: Eerdmans, 1975.
———. *The Gospel of John: A Theological Commentary*. Translated by John Vriend. Grand Rapids: Eerdmans, 1997.
Robertson, O. Palmer. *Christ of the Covenants*. Phillipsburg, NJ: Presbyterian and Reformed, 1980.
Russell, Norman. *Cyril of Alexandria*. New York: Routledge, 2000.
———. *The Doctrine of Deification in the Greek Patristic Tradition*. Oxford: Oxford University Press, 2004.

Sampley, J. Paul. *And the Two Shall Become One Flesh: A Study of Traditions in Ephesians 5:21–33.* Society for New Testament Studies Monograph Series 16. Cambridge: Cambridge University Press, 1971.
Sanders, E. P. *Paul and Palestinian Judaism: A Comparison of Patterns of Religion.* Philadelphia: Fortress, 1977.
———. *Paul.* Oxford: Oxford University Press, 1991.
Schreiner, Thomas R. *Paul—Apostle of God's Glory in Christ: A Pauline Theology.* Downers Grove, IL: InterVarsity, 2001.
Schweitzer, Albert. *The Mysticism of Paul the Apostle.* Translated by William Montgomery. London: A&C Black, 1931.
Schwöbel, Chrisoph, and Colin E. Gunton, eds. *Persons, Divine and Human: King's College Essays in Theological Anthropology.* Edinburgh: T&T Clark, 1991.
Scott, James M. *Adoption as Sons of God: An Exegetical Investigation into the Background of ΥΙΟΘΕΣΙΑ in the Pauline Corpus.* Wissenschaftliche Untersuchungen zum Neuen Testament 2. Reihe 48. Tübingen: J. C. B. Mohr, 1992.
Seamands, Stephen. *Ministry in the Image of God: The Trinitarian Shape of Christian Service.* Downers Grove, IL: InterVarsity, 2005.
Segovia, Fernando F. *Love Relationships in the Johannine Tradition.* SBL Dissertation Series 58. Chico, CA: Scholars Press, 1982.
———. *The Farewell of the Word: The Johannine Call to Abide.* Minneapolis: Fortress, 1991.
Shelton, R. Larry. *Cross and Covenant: Interpreting the Atonement for 21st Century Mission.* Tyrone, GA: Paternoster, 2006.
Sherman, Robert. *King, Priest, and Prophet: A Trinitarian Theology of the Atonement.* New York: T&T Clark, 2004.
Showers, Renald. *Maranatha Our Lord, Come! A Definitive Study of the Rapture of the Church.* Bellmawr, NJ: Friends of Israel Gospel Ministry, 1995.
Smail, Thomas A. *The Forgotten Father: Rediscovering the Heart of the Christian Gospel.* London: Hodder and Stoughton, 1980.
Smedes, Lewis B. *Union with Christ: A Biblical View of the New Life in Jesus Christ.* Rev. ed. Grand Rapids: Eerdmans, 1983.
Smith, D. Moody. *The Theology of the Gospel of John.* Cambridge: Cambridge University Press, 1995.
Smith, Gordon T. *A Holy Meal: The Lord's Supper in the Life of the Church.* Grand Rapids: Baker Academic, 2005.
Smith, William Robertson. *Lectures on the Religion of the Semites.* New York: Macmillan, 1927.
Son, Sang-Won Aaron. *Corporate Elements in Pauline Anthropology: A Study of Terms, Idioms, and Concepts in the Light of Paul's Usage and Background.* Analecta biblica 114. Rome: Editrice Pontificio Istituto Biblico, 2001.
Staniloae, Dumitru. *The Experience of God.* Translated and edited by Ioan Ionita and Robert Barringer. Brookline, MA: Holy Cross Orthodox Press, 1994.
Stepp, Perry Leon. *The Believer's Participation in the Death of Christ: "Corporate Identification" and a Study of Romans 6:1–14.* Mellen Biblical Press Series 49. Lewiston, NY: Mellen Biblical Press, 1996.
Stewart, James. *A Man in Christ: The Vital Elements of St. Paul's Religion.* New York: Harper and Brothers, 1935.

Stoffer, Dale R., ed. *The Lord's Supper: Believer's Church Perspectives*. Scottdale, PA: Herald, 1994.

Szarmach, Paul E., ed. *An Introduction to the Medieval Mystics of Europe*. Albany: SUNY Press, 1984.

Tamburello, Dennis E. *Union with Christ: John Calvin and the Mysticism of St. Bernard*. Louisville: Westminster John Knox, 1994.

Tannehill, Robert C. *Dying and Rising with Christ: A Study in Pauline Theology*. Eugene: Wipf and Stock, 2006.

Tarwater, John K. *Marriage as Covenant: Considering God's Design at Creation and the Contemporary Moral Consequences*. Lanham, MD: University Press of America, 2006.

Thacker, Justin. *Postmodernism and the Ethics of Theological Knowledge*. Hampshire: Ashgate, 2007.

Thatcher, Adrian. *Marriage after Modernity: Christian Marriage in Postmodern Times*. New York: NYU Press, 1999.

Thettayil, Benny. *In Spirit and Truth: An Exegetical Study of John 4:19–26 and a Theological Investigation of the Replacement Theme in the Fourth Gospel*. Contributions to Biblical Exegesis and Theology 46. Leuven: Peeters, 2007.

Thomas, John Christopher. *Footwashing in John 13 and the Johannine Community*. Journal for the Study of the New Testament Supplement Series 61. Sheffield: Sheffield Academic Press, 1991.

Thompson, Marianne Meye. *The God of the Gospel of John*. Grand Rapids: Eerdmans, 2001.

Thompson, John. *Modern Trinitarian Perspectives*. Oxford: Oxford University Press, 1994.

Torrance, Alan J. *Persons in Communion: An Essay on Trinitarian Description and Human Participation with Special Reference to Volume One of Karl Barth's* Church Dogmatics. Edinburgh: T&T Clark, 1996.

Torrance, Alan J., and Michael Banner, eds. *The Doctrine of God and Theological Ethics*. London, T&T Clark, 2006.

Torrance, James B. *Worship, Community, and the Triune God of Grace*. Downers Grove, IL: InterVarsity, 1995.

Torrance, Thomas F. *Conflict and Agreement in the Church, Volume Two: The Ministry and the Sacraments of the Gospel*. London: Lutterworth, 1960.

———. *Theology in Reconstruction*. Grand Rapids: Eerdmans, 1965.

———. *Space, Time, and Incarnation*. London: Oxford University Press, 1969.

———. *Theology in Reconciliation*. Grand Rapids: Eerdmans, 1975.

———. *The Ground and Grammar of Theology*. Charlottesville, VA: University of Virginia Press, 1980.

———. *Reality and Scientific Theology*. Edinburgh: Scottish Academic Press, 1981.

———. *The Mediation of Christ*. Grand Rapids: Eerdmans, 1983.

———. *The Trinitarian Faith: The Evangelical Theology of the Ancient Catholic Church*. Edinburgh: T&T Clark, 1988.

———. *Royal Priesthood*. Edinburgh: T&T Clark, 1993.

———. *Trinitarian Perspectives: Toward Doctrinal Agreement*. Edinburgh: T&T Clark, 1994.

———. *The Christian Doctrine of God: One Being, Three Persons*. Edinburgh: T&T Clark, 1996.

———. *Incarnation: The Person and Life of Christ*. Edited by Robert T. Walker. Downers Grove, IL: IVP Academic, 2008.
———, ed. *The Incarnation: Ecumenical Studies in the Nicene-Constantinopolitan Creed*. Eugene: Wipf and Stock, 1998.
Trumbull, H. Clay. *The Blood Covenant*. Philadelphia: John D. Wattles, 1898.
Turner, H. E. W. *The Patristic Doctrine of Redemption*. London: A. R. Mowbray, 1952.
Van Belle, G., J. G. van der Watt, and P. Maritz, eds. *Theology and Christology in the Fourth Gospel*. Leuven: Leuven University Press, 2005.
Van Buren, Paul. *Christ in Our Place: The Substitutionary Character of Calvin's Doctrine of Reconciliation*. Edinburgh and London: Oliver and Boyd, 1957.
Van der Watt, Jan G. *Family of the King: Dynamics of Metaphor in the Gospel according to John*. Leiden: Brill, 2000.
Van Gemeren, Willem A., ed. *New International Dictionary of Old Testament Theology and Exegesis*. 5 vols. Grand Rapids: Zondervan, 1997.
Vellanickal, M. *The Divine Sonship of Christians in the Johannine Writings*. Analecta biblia 72. Rome: Pontifical Biblical Institute, 1977.
Verity, G. B. *Life in Christ: A Study of Coinherence*. London: Longmans, Green, and Co., 1954.
Vickers, Brian. *Jesus' Blood and Righteousness*. Wheaton, IL: Crossway, 2006.
Volf, Miroslav. *After Our Likeness: The Church as the Image of the Trinity*. Grand Rapids: Eerdmans, 1998.
Wahlstrom, Eric H. *The New Life in Christ*. Philadelphia: Muhlenberg, 1950.
Waters, Guy Prentiss. *Justification and the New Perspectives on Paul: A Review and Response*. Phillipsburg, NJ: Presbyterian and Reformed, 2004.
Weinandy, Thomas G. *The Father's Spirit of Sonship: Reconceiving the Trinity*. Edinburgh: T&T Clark, 1995.
Weinandy, Thomas G., Daniel A. Keating, and John P. Yocum, eds. *Aquinas on Doctrine: A Critical Introduction*. London and New York: T&T Clark, 2004.
Whiteley, D. E. H. *The Theology of St. Paul*. Philadelphia: Fortress, 1964.
Wickenhauser, Alfred. *Pauline Mysticism: Christ in the Mystical Teaching of St. Paul*. Translated by Joseph Cunningham. Freiburg: Herder and Nelson, 1960.
Wickham, L. R. *Cyril of Alexandria: Select Letters*. Oxford: Clarendon, 1983.
Williams, Charles. *The Descent of the Dove: A Short History of the Holy Spirit in the Church*. London: Religious Book Club, 1939.
———, *The Image of the City and Other Essays*. London: Oxford University Press, 1958.
———. *He Came Down from Heaven*. Repr., Grand Rapids: Eerdmans, 1984.
Williamson, Paul R. *Sealed with an Oath: Covenant in God's Unfolding Purpose*. New Studies in Biblical Theology 23. Downers Grove, IL: InterVarsity, 2007.
Willis, David. *Notes on the Holiness of God*. Grand Rapids: Eerdmans, 2002.
Windeatt, Barry, ed. *English Mystics of the Middle Ages*. Cambridge: Cambridge University Press, 1994.
Witherington, Ben III. *The Jesus Quest: The Third Search for the Jew of Nazareth*. 2nd ed. Downers Grove, IL: InterVarsity, 1997.
Wright, N. T. *The New Testament and the People of God*. Minneapolis: Fortress, 1992.
———. *What Saint Paul Really Said*. Grand Rapids: Eerdmans, 1997.
Zizioulas, John D. *Being as Communion: Studies in Personhood and the Church*. Crestwood, NY: St. Vladimir's Seminary Press, 1985.

ARTICLES

Aden, Ross. "Justification and Divinization." *Dialog* 32 (Spr 1993): 102–7.

Alfeyev, Hilarion. "The Deification of Man in Eastern Patristic Tradition (With Special Reference to Gregory Nazianzen, Symeon the New Theologian and Gregory Palamas)." *Colloquium* 36 (2004): 109–22.

Allan, John A. "The 'In Christ' Formula in Ephesians." *New Testament Studies* 5 (1958): 54–62.

Anderson, Megory, and Philip Culbertson. "The Inadequacy of the Christian Doctrine of Atonement in Light of the Levitical Sin Offering." *Anglican Theological Review* 68 (1996): 303–28.

Archer, Gleason L. Jr. "Covenant." Pages 299–301 in *Evangelical Dictionary of Theology.* 2nd ed. Edited by Walter A. Elwell. Grand Rapids: Baker, 2001.

Attfield, D. G. "'I in You and You in Me': *Perichoresis* and Salvation." *Theology* 109 (2006): 421–29.

Ayres, Lewis. "Deification and the Dynamics of Nicene Theology: The Contribution of Gregory of Nyssa." *St. Vladimir's Theological Quarterly* 49 (2005): 375–94.

Barrett, Jordan. "Biography of Colin E. Gunton." *Theopedia.* http://www.theopedia.com/Colin_E._Gunton.

Beckwith, Roger T. "The Death of Christ as a Sacrifice in the Teaching of Paul and Hebrews." Pages 130–35 in *Sacrifice in the Bible.* Edited by Roger T. Beckwith and Martin J. Selman. Grand Rapids: Baker, 1995.

Bercot, David W., ed. "Deification of Man." Pages 199–200 in *A Dictionary of Early Christian Beliefs.* Peabody, MA: Hendrickson, 1998.

Bird, Michael. "Incorporated Righteousness: A Response to Recent Evangelical Discussion Concerning the Imputation of Christ's Righteousness in Justification." *Journal of the Evangelical Theological Society* 47 (Jun 2004): 253–75.

Bonner, Gerald. "Augustine's Conception of Deification." *Journal of Theological Studies* 37 (1986): 369–86.

Brand, Paul, and Philip Yancey. "Blood, Part 2: The Miracle of Life." *Christianity Today.* http://www.christianitytoday.com/ct/2003/julyweb-only/7-7-45.0.html?start=6.

Burns, J. Patout. "The Economy of Salvation: Two Patristic Traditions." Pages 224–46 in *Studies in Early Christianity: Doctrines of Human Nature, Sin, and Salvation in the Early Church.* Edited by Everett Ferguson. New York and London: Garland, 1993.

Canlis, Julie. "Calvin, Osiander and Participation in God." *International Journal of Systematic Theology* 6 (Apr 2004): 169–84.

Carlson, Richard P. "The Role of Baptism in Paul's Thought." *Interpretation* 47 (July 1993): 255–66.

Carpenter, Craig B. "A Question of Union with Christ? Calvin and Trent on Justification." *Westminster Theological Journal* 64 (Fall 2002): 363–86.

Chia, Roland. "Trinity and Ontology: Colin Gunton's Ecclesiology." *International Journal of Systematic Theology* 9 (Oct 2007): 452–68.

Christensen, Michael J. "John Wesley: Christian Perfection as Faith Filled with the Energy of Love." Pages 219–29 in *Partakers of the Divine Nature: The History and Development of Deification in the Christian Tradition.* Edited by Michael J. Christensen and Jeffrey A. Wittung. Grand Rapids: Baker, 2007.

Cohn, Marcus. "Marriage in Rabbinical Law." Pages 370–76 in vol. 7 of *The Universal Jewish Encyclopedia.* Edited by Isaac Landman. New York: Universal Jewish Encyclopedia, 1948.

Colijn, Brenda B. "Paul's Use of the 'In Christ' Formula." *Ashland Theological Journal* 23 (1991): 9–26.

Coloe, Mary F. "Welcome into the Household of God: The Foot Washing in John 13." *Catholic Biblical Quarterly* 66 (July 2004): 400–15.

Cook, James I. "The Concept of Adoption in the Theology of Paul." Pages 133–44 in *Saved by Hope: Essays in Honor of Richard C. Oudersluys*. Edited by James I. Cook. Grand Rapids: Eerdmans, 1978.

Cooke, Bernard. "Synoptic Presentation of the Eucharist as Covenant Sacrifice." *Theological Studies* 21 (1960): 1–44.

Crisp, Oliver D. "Problems with *Perichoresis*." *Tyndale Bulletin* 56 (2005): 119–40.

Crump, David. "Re-examining the Johannine Trinity: *Perichoresis* or Deification." *Scottish Journal of Theology* 59 (2006): 395–412.

Culpepper, R. Alan. "Johannine Hypodeigma: A Reading of John 13." *Semeia* 53 (1991): 133–52.

Dearborn, Timothy A. "God, Grace, and Salvation." Pages 265–93 in *Christ in Our Place: The Humanity of God in Christ for the Reconciliation of the World*. Princeton Theological Monograph Series. Edited by Trevor Hart and Daniel Thimell. Exeter: Paternoster, 1989.

DeBoer, Martinus C. "Jesus' Departure to the Father in John: Death or Resurrection?" Pages 1–20 in *Theology and Christology in the Fourth Gospel*. Edited by G. Van Belle, J. G. van der Watt, and P. Maritz. Leuven: Leuven University Press, 2005.

Deddo, Gary W. "The Holy Spirit in T. F. Torrance's Theology." Pages 81–114 in *The Promise of Trinitarian Theology: Theologians in Dialogue with T. F. Torrance*. Edited by Elmer M. Colyer. Lanham, MD: Rowman and Littlefield, 2001.

———. "Our Participation in Christ's Continuing Ministry." Pages 135–56 in *An Introduction to Torrance Theology: Discovering the Incarnate Savior*. Edited by Gerrit Scott Dawson. London: T&T Clark, 2007.

Del Colle, Ralph. "'Person' and 'Being' in John Zizioulas' Trinitarian Ontology: Conversations with Thomas Torrance and Thomas Aquinas." *Scottish Journal of Theology* 54 (2001): 70–86.

Derickson, Gary W. "Viticulture and John 15:1–6." *Journal of the Grace Evangelical Society* 18 (Spring 2005): 40–41.

Dragas, George Dionysius. "Exchange or Communication of Properties and Deification: *Antidosis* or *Communicatio Idiomatum* and *Theosis*." *Greek Orthodox Theological Review* 43 (1998): 377–99.

Dulles, Avery. "The Trinity and Christian Unity." Pages 69–82 in *God the Holy Trinity: Reflections on Christian Faith and Practice*. Edited by Timothy George. Grand Rapids: Baker Academic, 2006.

Duncan, J. Ligon, III. "What is Covenant Theology?" http://www.fpcjackson.org/resources/apologetics/Covenant%20Theology%20&%20Justification/ligoncovt.htm.

Edgington, Allen. "Footwashing as an Ordinance." *Grace Theological Journal* 6 (1985): 425–34.

Edwards, Ruth B. "The Christological Basis of the Johannine Footwashing." Pages 367–83 in *Jesus of Nazareth, Lord and Christ: Essays on the Historical Jesus and New Testament Christology*. Edited by Joel B. Green and Max Turner. Grand Rapids: Eerdmans, 1994.

Fairbairn, Donald. "Patristic Soteriology: Three Trajectories." *Journal of the Evangelical Theological Society* 50 (June 2007): 289–310.

Fantino, Jacques. "Circumincession." Pages 315–16 in vol. 1 of *The Encyclopedia of Christian Theology*. Edited by Jean-Yves Lacoste. 3 vols. New York: Routledge, 2005.

Finlan, Stephen. "Can We Speak of *Theosis* in Paul?" Pages 68–80 in *Partakers of the Divine Nature: The History and Development of Deification in the Christian Tradition*. Edited by Michael J. Christensen and Jeffrey A. Wittung. Grand Rapids: Baker, 2007.

Florovsky, Georges. "Father Florovsky on Palamas: Essence/Energy." http://www.nicenetruth.com/home/2009/05/fr-florovsky-on-palamas.html#more.

Fowler, James A. "Three Divine Onenesses." *Christ in You Ministries*. http://www.christinyou.net/pages/3divineonenesses.html.

Gaffin, Richard B. Jr. "'Life-Giving Spirit': Probing the Center of Paul's Pneumatology." *Journal of the Evangelical Theological Society* 41 (1998): 573–89.

———. "Union with Christ: Some Biblical and Theological Reflections." Pages 271–88 in *Always Reforming: Explorations in Systematic Theology*. Edited by A. T. B. McGowan. Downers Grove, IL: InterVarsity, 2006.

———. "Justification and Union with Christ." Pages 248–69 in *A Theological Guide to Calvin's* Institutes: *Essays and Analyses*. Edited by David W. Hall and Peter A. Lillback. Phillipsburg, NJ: Presbyterian and Reformed, 2008.

Garlington, Don. "Imputation or Union with Christ? A Response to John Piper." *The Paul Page*. http://www.thepaulpage.com/Imputation.pdf.

Gatewood, Tee. "Alive to God in Christ: The Spirit and the Church in the Torrance Tradition." *Crux* 44 (2008): 9–19.

Gifford Lecture Series, "Biography—Jürgen Moltmann." http://www.giffordlectures.org/Author.asp?AuthorID=217.

Grundmann, Walter. "Σύν/μέτα." Pages 766–97 in vol. 7 of *Theological Dictionary of the New Testament*. Edited by Gerhard Kittel. Translated by Geoffrey W. Bromiley. Grand Rapids: Eerdmans, 1970.

Gundry, Robert H. "The Nonimputation of Christ's Righteousness." Pages 17–45 in *Justification: What's at Stake in the Current Debates*. Edited by Mark Husbands and Daniel J. Treier. Downers Grove, IL: InterVarsity: 2004.

Gunton, Colin E. "Trinity, Ontology, and Anthropology: Towards a Renewal of the Doctrine of the *Imago Dei*." Pages 47–61 in *Persons, Divine and Human: King's College Essays in Theological Anthropology*. Edited by Christoph Schwöbel and Colin E. Gunton. Edinburgh: T&T Clark, 1991.

———. "The Church on Earth: The Roots of Community." Pages 48–80 in *On Being the Church: Essays on the Christian Community*. Edited by Colin E. Gunton and Daniel W. Hardy. Edinburgh: T&T Clark, 1989.

Habets, Myk. "'Reformed *Theosis*?' A Response to Gannon Murphy." *Theology Today* 65 (2009): 489–98.

Hadfield, Alice Mary. "Coinherence, Substitution and Exchange in Charles Williams' Poetry and Poetry-Making." Pages 229–58 in *Imagination and the Spirit: Essays in Literature and the Christian Faith Presented to Clyde S. Kilby*. Edited by Charles A. Huttar. Grand Rapids: Eerdmans, 1971.

Hallonsten, Gösta, "*Theosis* in Recent Research: A Renewal of Interest and a Need for Clarity." Pages 281–93 in *Partakers of the Divine Nature: The History and Development of Deification in the Christian Tradition*. Edited by Michael J. Christensen and Jeffrey A. Wittung. Grand Rapids: Baker, 2007.

Hanson, K. C. "Blood and Purity in Leviticus and Revelation." http://www.kchanson.com/ARTICLES/blood.html.
Harris, Murray J. "Appendix: Prepositions and Theology in the Greek New Testament." Pages 1171–1215 in vol. 3 of the *New International Dictionary of New Testament Theology.* Edited by Colin Brown. 3 vols. Grand Rapids: Zondervan, 1986.
Harrison, Verna. "*Perichoresis* in the Greek Fathers." *St. Vladimir's Theological Quarterly* 35 (1991): 53–65.
———. "*Theosis* as Salvation: An Orthodox Perspective." *Pro Ecclesia* 6 (Fall 1997): 429–43.
———. "Greek Patristic Foundations of Trinitarian Anthropology." *Pro Ecclesia* 14 (Fall 2005): 399–412.
Hauck, Friedrich. "οφειλω." Pages 559–66 in vol. 5 of *Theological Dictionary of the New Testament.* Edited by Gerhard Friedrich. Edited and translated by Geoffrey L. Bromiley. Grand Rapids: Eerdmans, 1967.
Heim, Mark. "Salvation as Communion: Partakers of the Divine Nature." *Theology Today* 61 (2004): 322–33.
Helminiak, Daniel A. "Human Solidarity and Collective Union in Christ." *Anglican Theological Review* 70 (1998): 34–59.
Heron, Alasdair. "*Communicatio Idiomatum* and *Deificatio* of Human Nature: A Reformed Perspective." *Greek Orthodox Theological Review* 43 (1998): 367–76.
Hooker, Morna D. "Interchange in Christ." *Journal of Theological Studies* 22 (1971): 349–61.
Houston, James M. "Spirituality and the Doctrine of the Trinity." Pages 48–69 in *Christ in our Place: The Humanity of God in Christ for the Reconciliation of the World.* Princeton Theological Monograph Series. Edited by Trevor Hart and Daniel Thimell. Exeter: Paternoster, 1989.
Hultgren, Arlan J. "The Johannine Footwashing as a Symbol of Eschatological Hospitality." *New Testament Studies* 28 (1982): 539–46.
Hilkert, Mary Catherine. "Catherine Mowry LaCugna's Trinitarian Theology." *Horizons* 27 (2000): 338–42.
Hunsinger, George. "The Dimension of Depth: Thomas F. Torrance on the Sacraments of Baptism and the Lord's Supper." *Scottish Journal of Theology* 54 (2001): 155–76.
Jensen, Richard A. "Theosis and Preaching: Implications for Preaching in the Finnish Luther Research." *Currents in Theology and Mission* 31 (2004): 432–37.
Jenson, Philip P. "The Levitical Sacrificial System." Pages 23–40 in *Sacrifice in the Bible.* Edited by Roger T. Beckwith and Martin J. Selman. Grand Rapids: Baker, 1995.
Jenson, Robert W. "Response to Mark Seifrid, Paul Metzger, and Carl Trueman on Finnish Luther Research." *Westminster Theological Journal* 65 (Fall 2003): 245–50.
Johnson, Marcus. "Luther and Calvin on Union with Christ." *Fides et Homina* 39 (2007): 59–77.
———. "New or Nuanced Perspective on Calvin? A Reply to Thomas Wenger." *Journal of the Evangelical Theological Society* 51 (2008): 559–72.
Jones, R. Tudor. "Union with Christ: The Existential Nerve of Puritan Piety." *Tyndale Bulletin* 41 (1990): 186–208.
Kaiser, Walter C. Jr. "The Old Promise and the New Covenant." *Journal of the Evangelical Theological Society* 15 (1972): 11–23.
Kangas, Ron. "In My Father's House: The Unleavened Truth of John 14." *Affirmation and Critique* 5 (Apr 2000): 22–36.

Keating, Daniel A. "Justification, Sanctification, and Divinization." Pages 139–59 in *Aquinas on Doctrine: A Critical Introduction*. Edited by Thomas G. Weinandy, Daniel A. Keating, and John P. Yocum. London and New York: T&T Clark, 2004.

Keathley, Kenneth. "The Work of God: Salvation." Pages 686–764 in *A Theology for the Church*. Edited by Daniel L. Akin. Nashville: Broadman & Holman, 2007.

Kent, Homer A. Jr. "The New Covenant and the Church." *Grace Theological Journal* 6 (1985): 289–98.

Kerr, Nathan A. "*Theoria* and the Doctrinal Language of Perfection." Pages 175–88 in *Partakers of the Divine Nature: The History and Development of Deification in the Christian Tradition*. Edited by Michael J. Christensen and Jeffrey A. Wittung. Grand Rapids: Baker, 2007.

Kharlamov, Vladimir. "*Theosis* in Patristic Thought." *Theology Today* 65 (2008): 158–68.

Kress, Robert. "The Church *Communio*: Trinity and Incarnation as the Foundations of Ecclesiology." *The Jurist* 36 (1976): 127–58.

———. "Unity in Diversity and Diversity in Unity: Toward an Ecumenical Perichoretic Kenotic Trinitarian Ontology." *Dialog and Alliance* 4 (Fall 1990): 66–70.

Kruger, C. Baxter. "Bearing our Scorn: Jesus and the Way of Trinitarian Love." http://www.perichoresis.org/x2/file/9fc3d7152ba9336a670e36d0ed79bc43.pdf.

———. "The Doctrine of the Knowledge of God in the Theology of T. F. Torrance: Sharing in the Son's communion with the Father in the Spirit." *Scottish Journal of Theology* 43 (2008): 366–89.

———. "Irenaeus' Vision of the Incarnation." http://baxterkruger.blogspot.com.

———. "Interview with Dr. Baxter Kruger." http://www.perichoresis.org/content/1/3/22.html.

LaCugna, Catherine Mowry. "Reconceiving the Trinity as the Mystery of Salvation." *Scottish Journal of Theology* 38 (1985): 1–23.

Laney, J. Carl. "Abiding Is Believing: The Analogy of the Vine in John 15:1–6." *Bibliotheca Sacra* 146 (1989): 55–66.

Lawler, Michael G. "*Perichoresis*: New Theological Wine in an Old Theological Wineskin." *Horizons* 22 (1995): 49–66.

Leithart, Peter J. "Making Room." http://rdtwot.wordpress.com/2008/03/03/making-room-by-peter-j-leithart/.

Macchia, Frank D. "Is Footwashing the Neglected Sacrament? A Theological Response to John Christopher Thomas." *Pneuma* 19 (1997): 239–49.

Mannermaa, Tuomo. "Justification and *Theosis* in Lutheran-Orthodox Perspective." Pages 25–41 in *Union with Christ: The New Finnish Interpretation of Luther*. Edited by Carl E. Braaten and Robert W. Jenson. Grand Rapids: Eerdmans, 1998.

———. "Why is Luther So Fascinating? Modern Finnish Luther Research." Pages 1–24 in *Union with Christ: The New Finnish Interpretation of Luther*. Edited by Carl E. Braaten and Robert W. Jenson. Grand Rapids: Eerdmans, 1998.

Marshall, Bruce D. "Justification as Declaration and Deification." *International Journal of Systematic Theology* 4 (2002): 3–28.

Marshall, Molly T. "Participating in the Life of God: A Trinitarian Pneumatology." *Perspectives on Religious Studies* 30 (2003): 139–50.

Martin, D. D. "Mysticism." Page 806 in *Evangelical Dictionary of Theology*. 2nd. ed. Edited by Walter A. Elwell. Grand Rapids: Baker, 2001.

McCarthy, Dennis J. "The Symbolism of Blood and Sacrifice." *Journal of Biblical Literature* 88 (1969): 166–76.

———. "Further Notes on the Symbolism of Blood and Sacrifice." *Journal of Biblical Literature* 92 (1973): 205–10.

McConville, Gordon J. "*Berit.*" Pages 1:747–55 in *New International Dictionary of Old Testament Theology and Exegesis*. Edited by Willem A. VanGemeren. 5 vols. Grand Rapids: Zondervan, 1997.

McCormack, Bruce. "The Crisis of Protestantism in the West." Pages 81–117 in *Justification: What's at Stake in the Current Debates*. Edited by Mark Husbands and Daniel J. Treier. Downers Grove, IL: InterVarsity: 2004.

McDougall, Joy Ann. "Room of One's Own? Trinitarian *Perichoresis* as Analogy for the God-Human Relationship." Pages 133–41 in *Wo ist Gott? Gottesräume-Lebensräume*. Edited by Jürgen Moltmann and Carmen Riwuzumwami. Neukirchen: Neukirchener Verlag, 2002.

McGuckin, J. A. "The Strategic Adaptation of Deification in the Cappadocians." Pages 95–114 in *Partakers of the Divine Nature: The History and Development of Deification in the Christian Traditions*. Edited by Michael J. Christensen and Jeffrey A. Wittung. Grand Rapids: Baker Academic, 2008.

Mealand, David L. "The Language of Mystical Union in the Johannine Writings." *Downside Review* 95 (1977): 19–34.

Metzger, Paul Louis. "Mystical Union with Christ: An Alternative to Blood Transfusions and Legal Fictions." *Westminster Theological Journal* 65 (2003): 201–13.

Miles, Jack. "Israel as Foundling: Abandonment, Adoption, and the Fatherhood of God." *Hebrew Studies* 46 (2005): 7–24.

Mitchell, Curtis. "Praying 'In My Name.'" *Chafer Theological Seminary Journal* 4 (1998): 27.

Moltmann, Jürgen. "God in the World—The World in God: *Perichoresis* in Trinity and Eschatology." Pages 369–80 in *The Gospel of John and Christian Theology*. Edited by Richard Bauckham and Carl Mosser. Grand Rapids: Eerdmans, 2008.

Mosser, Carl. "The Greatest Possible Blessing: Calvin and Deification." *Scottish Journal of Theology* 55 (2002): 36–56.

———. "The Earliest Patristic Interpretations of Psalm 82, Jewish Antecedents, and the Origin of Christian Deification." *Journal of Theological Studies* 56 (2005): 30–74.

Mueller, William A. "The Mystical Union." Pages 206–12 in *Basic Christian Doctrines*. Edited by Carl F. H. Henry. New York: Holt, Rinehart, and Winston, 1962.

Ng, Nathan K. K. "A Reconsideration of the Use of the Term 'Deification' in Athanasius." *Coptic Church Review* 22 (2001): 34–42.

Nispel, Mark D. "Christian Deification and the Early *Testimonia*." *Vigiliae Christianae* 53 (1999): 289–304.

Oepke, Albrecht. "Ἐν." Pages 537–43 in vol. 2 of *Theological Dictionary of the New Testament*. Edited by Gerhard Kittel. Translated by Geoffrey W. Bromiley. Grand Rapids: Eerdmans, 1962.

Olson, Roger E. "Deification in Contemporary Theology." *Theology Today* 64 (2007): 186–200.

Otto, Randall E. "The Use and Abuse of *Perichoresis* in Recent Theology." *Scottish Journal of Theology* 54 (2001): 366–84.

Packer, J. I. "Justification." Pages 643–47 in *Evangelical Dictionary of Theology*. 2nd ed. Edited by Walter A. Elwell. Grand Rapids: Baker, 2001.

Pelser, Gert M. M. "Could the 'Formulas' *Dying* and *Rising with Christ* Be Expressions of Pauline Mysticism?" *Neotestamentica* 32 (1998): 115–34.

Piper, John. "John Piper Responds to Don Garlington on the Imputation of Righteousness." *Desiring God.* http://www.desiringgod.org/ResourceLibrary/Articles/ByDate/2003/1522_John_Piper_Responds_to_Don_Garlington_on_the_Imputation_of_Righteousness/.

Purves, Andrew. "The Christology of Thomas F. Torrance." Pages 51–80 in *The Promise of Trinitarian Theology: Theologians in Dialogue with T. F. Torrance.* Edited by Elmer M. Colyer. Lanham, MD: Rowman and Littlefield, 2001.

Rankin, W. Duncan. "Calvin's Correspondence on our Threefold Union with Christ." Pages 232–50 in *The Hope Fulfilled: Essays in Honor of O. Palmer Robertson.* Edited by Robert L. Penny. Phillipsburg, NJ: Presbyterian and Reformed, 2008.

Redmond, Robert R. Jr. "*Participatio Christi*: H. R. Mackintosh's Theology of the *Unio Mystica*." *Scottish Journal of Theology* 49 (1996): 201–22.

Ricker, George. "Covenant in the Old Testament." *International Standard Bible Encyclopedia Online.* http://www.searchgodsword.org/enc/isb/view.cgi?number=T2377.

Rhoads, David. "Children of Abraham, Children of God: Metaphorical Kinship in Paul's Letter to the Galatians." *Currents in Theology and Mission* 31 (2004): 282–97.

Ritschl, Dietrich. "Hippolytus' Conception of Deification: Remarks on the Interpretation of *Refutation* X, 34." *Scottish Journal of Theology* 12 (1959): 388–99.

Saarinen, Risto. "The Presence of God in Luther's Theology." *Lutheran Quarterly* (1994): 3–14.

Schwöbel, Chrisoph. "Introduction." Pages 1–29 in *Persons, Divine and Human: King's College Essays in Theological Anthropology.* Edited by Christoph Schwöbel and Colin E. Gunton. Edinburgh: T&T Clark, 1991.

Scoutieris, Constantine. "The People of God—Its Unity and Glory: A Discussion of John 17:17–24 in the Light of Patristic Thought." *Greek Orthodox Theological Review* 30 (1985): 399–420.

Segovia, Fernando F. "John 13:1–20: The Footwashing in the Johannine Tradition." *Zeitschrift fur die Neutestamentliche Wissenschaft* 73 (1982): 31–51.

Seifrid, Mark A. "In Christ." Pages 433–6 in *Dictionary of Paul and His Letters.* Edited by Gerald F. Hawthorne and Ralph P. Martin. Downers Grove, IL: InterVarsity: 1993.

———. "Paul, Luther, and Justification in Gal 2:15–21." *Westminster Theological Journal* 65 (2003): 215–30.

Sheeley, Steven M. "Nothing (a)B(o)ut the Blood: Images of Jesus' Death in the New Testament." *Perspectives in Religious Studies* 35 (2008): 109–19.

Simmons, Ernest L. "Quantum *Perichoresis*: Quantum Field Theory and the Trinity." *Theology and Science* 4 (2006): 37–50.

Smalley, Stephen S. "The Christ-Christian Relationship in Paul and John." Pages 95–105 in *Pauline Studies: Essays Presented to Professor F. F. Bruce on his 70th Birthday.* Edited by Donald A. Hagner and Murray J. Harris. Exeter: Paternoster, 1980.

Smith, Ralph A. "The Trinitarian Covenant in John 17." http://www.berith.org/essays/j17/10.html.

Smith, S. M. "*Perichoresis*." Page 906 in *Evangelical Dictionary of Theology.* 2nd ed. Edited by Walter A. Elwell. Grand Rapids: Baker, 2004.

Son, Sang-Won Aaron. "Implications of Paul's 'One Flesh' Concept for His Understanding of the Nature of Man." *Bulletin for Biblical Research* 11 (2001): 108–22.

Sorc, Ciril. "*Die perichoretischen Beziehungen im Leben der Trinität und in der Gemeinschaft der Menschen.*" *Evangelische Theologie* 58 (1998): 100–19.

Speidell, Todd H. "A Trinitarian Ontology of Persons in Society." *Scottish Journal of Theology* 47 (1994): 283–300.

Stamoolis, J. J. "*Theosis*." Page 1181 in *Evangelical Dictionary of Theology*. 2nd ed. Edited by Walter A. Elwell. Grand Rapids: Baker, 2001.

Starr, James. "Does 2 Peter 1:4 Speak of Deification?" Pages 81–92 in *Partakers of the Divine Nature: The History and Development of Deification in the Christian Tradition*. Edited by Michael J. Christensen and Jeffrey A. Wittung. Grand Rapids: Baker Academic, 2007.

Staton, John E. "A Vision of Unity—Christian Unity in the Fourth Gospel." *Evangelical Quarterly* 69 (1997): 291–305.

Stibbs, A. M. "The Meaning of the Word 'Blood' in Scripture." http://www.theologicalstudies.org.uk/pdf/blood_stibbs.pdf.

Stortz, Martha Ellen. "Indwelling Christ, Indwelling Christians: Living as Marked." *Currents in Theology and Mission* 34 (2007): 165–78.

Thomas, John Christopher. "Footwashing within the Context of the Lord's Supper." Pages 169–84 in *The Lord's Supper: Believer's Church Perspectives*. Edited by Dale R. Stoffer. Scottdale, PA: Herald, 1994.

Torrance, Alan J. "The Ecumenical Implications of Catherine Mowry LaCugna's Trinitarian Theology." *Horizons* 27 (2000): 347–53.

———. "On Deriving 'Ought' from 'Is': Christology, Covenant, and *Koinonia*." Pages 167–90 in *The Doctrine of God and Theological Ethics*. Edited by Alan J. Torrance and Michael Banner. London: T&T Clark, 2006.

Torrance, David F. "Thomas Forsyth Torrance: Minister of the Gospel, Pastor, and Evangelical Theologian." Pages 1–30 in *The Promise of Trinitarian Theology: Theologians in Dialogue with T. F. Torrance*. Edited by Elmer M. Colyer. Lanham, MD: Rowman and Littlefield, 2001.

Torrance, James B. "Contemplating the Trinitarian Mystery of Christ." Pages 140–51 in *Alive to God: Studies in Spirituality Presented to James Houston*. Edited by J. I. Packer and Loren Wilkinson. Vancouver: Regent College Publishing, 1992.

———. "The Vicarious Humanity of Christ." Pages 127–47 in *The Incarnation: Ecumenical Studies in the Nicene-Constantinopolitan Creed*. Edited by Thomas F. Torrance. Eugene, OR: Wipf and Stock, 1998.

Torrance, Thomas F. "The Goodness and Dignity of Man in the Christian Tradition." *Modern Theology* 44 (1989): 309–22.

———. "The Doctrine of the Virgin Birth." *Scottish Bulletin of Evangelical Theology* 12 (1994): 8–25.

Trueman, Carl R. "Is the Finnish Line a New Beginning? A Critical Assessment of the Reading of Luther Offered by the Helsinki Circle." *Westminster Theological Journal* 65 (2003) 231–44.

Trumper, Tim. "The Metaphorical Import of Adoption: A Plea for Realisation I: The Adoption Metaphor in Biblical Language." *Scottish Bulletin of Evangelical Theology* 14 (1996): 129–45.

———. "The Metaphorical Import of Adoption: A Plea for Realisation II: The Adoption Metaphor in Theological Usage." *Scottish Bulletin of Evangelical Theology* 15 (1997): 98–115.

Turner, H. E. W. "Coinherence." Page 112 in *The Westminster Dictionary of Christian Theology*. Edited by Alan Richardson and John Bowden. Philadelphia: Westminster, 1983.

Vervenne, Marc. "'The Blood Is the Life and the Life Is the Blood': Blood as the Symbol of Life in Biblical Tradition (Gen 9:4)." Pages 451–70 in *Ritual and Sacrifice in the Ancient Near East*. Edited by J. Quaegebeur. Orientalia lovaniensia analecta 55. Leuven: Peeters, 1993.

Vishnevskaya, Elena. "Divinization as Perichoretic Embrace in Maximus the Confessor." Pages 132–45 in *Partakers of the Divine Nature: The History and Development of Deification in the Christian Tradition*. Edited by Michael J. Christensen and Jeffrey A. Wittung. Grand Rapids: Baker Academic, 2007.

Vlach, Michael A. "New Covenant Theology Compared with Covenantalism." *The Masters Seminary Journal* 18 (2007): 201–19.

Volf, Miroslav. "'The Trinity Is Our Social Programme': The Doctrine of the Trinity and the Shape of Social Engagement." Pages 105–24 in *The Doctrine of God and Theological Ethics*. Edited by Alan J. Torrance and Michael Banner. London: T&T Clark, 2006.

Ware, Bruce A. "The New Covenant and the People(s) of God." Pages 68–97 in *Dispensationalism, Israel, and the Church: The Search for Definition*. Edited by Craig A. Blaising and Darrell L. Bock. Grand Rapids: Zondervan, 1992.

Wedderburn, A. J. M. "Some Observations on Paul's Use of the Phrases 'In Christ' and 'With Christ.'" *Journal for the Study of the New Testament* 25 (1985): 83–97.

Weiss, Herold. "Footwashing in the Johannine Community." *Novum Testamentum* 21 (1979): 298–325.

Wenger, Thomas L. "The New Perspective on Calvin: Responding to Recent Interpretations." *Journal of the Evangelical Theological Society* 50 (2007): 311–28.

———. "Theological Spectacles and a Paradigm of Centrality: A Reply to Marcus Johnson." *Journal of the Evangelical Theological Society* 51 (2008): 573–90.

Wenham, Gordon J. "The Theology of Old Testament Sacrifice." Pages 75–87 in *Sacrifice in the Bible*. Edited by Roger T. Beckwith and Martin J. Selman. Grand Rapids: Baker, 1995.

Whitcomb, John. "Christ's Atonement and Animal Sacrifices in Israel." *Grace Theological Journal* 6 (1985): 201–17.

Williams, Rowan. "Interiority and Epiphany: A Reading in New Testament Ethics." *Modern Theology* 13 (1997): 29–51.

Wolters, Al. "'Partners of the Deity': A Covenantal Reading of 2 Peter 1:4." *Calvin Theological Journal* 25 (1990): 28–44.

Zizioulas, John. "On Being a Person: Towards an Ontology of Personhood." Pages 33–46 in *Persons, Divine and Human: King's College Essays in Theological Anthropology*. Edited by Christoph Schwöbel and Colin E. Gunton. Edinburgh: T&T Clark, 1991.

UNPUBLISHED WORKS

Akin, Daniel L. "Bernard of Clairvaux: Evangelical of the Twelfth Century." PhD diss., University of Texas at Arlington, 1989.

Boehmer, David John. "Kierkegaard and the 'Finnish' Luther on the Presence of Christ in Faith, or, Jesus Embraces *Perichoresis*?" MA thesis, Toronto School of Theology, 2008.

Fischer, John. "Identification with Christ: A Study of Paul's Use of 'Syn' Compounds." MA thesis, Trinity Evangelical Divinity School, 1972.

Forsee, Bruce Alan. "The Role of Union with Christ in Sanctification." PhD diss., Bob Jones University, 1985.
Greear, James D. "*Theosis* and Muslim Evangelism: How the Recovery of a Patristic Understanding of Salvation Can Aid Evangelical Missionaries in the Evangelization of Islamic Peoples." PhD diss., Southeastern Baptist Theological Seminary, 2003.
Helminiak, Daniel A. "One in Christ: An Exercise in Systematic Theology." PhD diss., Boston College, 1979.
Heltzel, Peter Goodwin. "*Perichoresis* in the Trinitarian Theology of Thomas F. Torrance." MDiv thesis, Gordon-Conwell Theological Seminary, 1997.
Hill, William J. "Proper Relations to the Indwelling Divine Persons." STL thesis, Pontificia Studiorum Universitas a Sancto Thoma Aquinate in Urbe, 1955.
Lytle, R. Matthew: "Perichoretically-Embodied Ethics: A Biblical-Theological and Historical-Theological Analysis of the Importance of Perichoretic Relationships for Christian Ethics." PhD diss., Southeastern Baptist Theological Seminary, 2008.
Rakestraw, Robert W. "Becoming Like God: An Evangelical Doctrine of *Theosis*." Paper presented at the annual meeting of the Evangelical Theological Society, Lisle, IL, November 17–19, 1995.
Richardson, Kurt Anders. "Trinitarian Reality: The Interrelation of Uncreated and Created Being in the Thought of Thomas Forsyth Torrance." PhD diss., Univeristy of Basel, 1993.
Sanders, Matthew Lee. "*Perichoresis*: Historical Overview, Scriptural Basis, and Use in Contemporary Trinitarian Theology." MA thesis, Southwestern Baptist Theological Seminary, 2000.
Schmelling, Timothy R. "Life in Christ: A Study of the '*unio mystica*' and its Relation to *Theosis*." MDiv thesis, Bethany Lutheran Theological Seminary, 2002.
Spivey, Walt. "The Scope of the Phrase 'In Christ.'" PhD diss., Grace Theological Seminary, 1982.
Terveen, J. L. "Union with Christ: Pauline Christological Touchstone in Colossians 2:8–15." Paper presented at the annual meeting of the Evangelical Theological Society, Toronto, November 20–22, 2003.
Thieme, Robert B. III. "Union with Christ." Paper presented at the regional meeting of the Evangelical Theological Society, April 4, 1987.
Twombly, Charles Craig. "*Perichoresis* and Personhood in the Thought of John of Damascus." PhD diss. Emory University, 1992.
Vishnevskaya, Elena. "*Perichoresis* in the Context of Divinization: Maximus the Confessor's Vision of a Blessed and Most Holy Embrace." PhD diss., Emory University, 2004.
Wethington, Mark Wesley. "Paul and John: A Comparative Study of their Language of Internalization." PhD diss., Duke University, 1984.
Womack, James A. "A Comparison of *Perichoresis* in the Writings of Gregory of Nazianzus and John of Damascus." ThM thesis, Dallas Theological Seminary, 2005.

Subject Index

Abba 158–60, 162
Adoption 5, 106, 141 n 65, 152–63, 165
Anhypostasis 81
Christ, language concerning
    "Christ in you" 5, 68–72
    "In Christ" 5, 30, 53–62, 72, 105,
        113 n 186, 125, 177, 180
    "With Christ" 5, 62–7, 147
Christological heresies 167
Circumincessio 19, 132
Circuminsessio 19
Coinherence 20, 51, 104, 107–8, 111
    n 177,
Communicatio idiomatum 18, 61
Council of Florence 20
Covenant 29, 127–143, 151
Covenant, new 5, 135, 138 n 53, 139
Deification, see *theosis*
Divinization, see *theosis*
Election 30, 169
Enhypostasis 81, 113, 187
Enlightenment 1, 104
Epistemology 175–7
Ethics 6, 182–5
Footwashing 38–42
Grace 170–1
Hypostatic union 22, 27, 29 n. 122, 37,
    45, 61, 79, 101, 106, 113 n 186,
    121, 123
Interpenetration 72
John, writings of 5, 32, 33–53, 123, 153
Joy 60
Justification 6–7, 30, 96, 169–70,
    178–182
Koinonia 35
Love 60
Marriage 5–6, 29, 95, 112, 142–152
Medieval period 5, 94–5

Mysticism 51
New Perspective on Paul 6, 178–182
Onto-relational 115, 171
Ordo salutis 169–70
Panentheism 21, 109, 111, 171 n 193
Participation 39, 41–42, 62–7, 73, 80,
    85–94, 95, 98, 101, 103, 106,
    116–8, 120, 121 n 226, 124–5,
    131, 133, 137–8, 140–1, 143 n
    73, 147, 148 n 98, 151, 154–7,
    160–1, 169–70, 176–7, 179,
    181–2, 185–7, 189
Patristic era 5, 19. 83–94
Paul, writings of 5, 53–74, 145–6,
    153–4
Peace 60
Perichoresis, christological 18, 24–5,
    27–9, 34, 44, 48, 57, 73, 79, 81,
    92, 102, 110, 137 n 48, 141, 146
    n 88, 152, 157, 161, 163, 167,
    173, 190
Perichoresis, trinitarian 15–20, 24–25,
    28–29, 34–35, 37, 42, 44, 48, 51,
    57, 60, 65, 69, 73, 77, 99 n 112,
    106, 108, 110–1, 112 n 182, 114,
    120–1, 124–5, 131, 141, 146 n
    88, 148–52, 157, 161, 163, 167,
    173, 186–92
Peter, writings of 74–76
Reformation 5, 166
Righteousness 60
Sacrifice 130–6
Sanctification 30, 60, 169
Soteriological Nestorianism 168, 172
Substitution 170, 181
Theosis 2, 11–4, 74–5, 77, 78–82, 83–
    94, 95, 98–100, 102, 104, 116 n

Theosis - continued
    206, 118–9, 122, 125, 135, 138, 160, 166, 172
Trinity 1–2, 25, 30, 34, 61, 72, 81, 103–10, 114, 117, 119, 122–3, 126, 170, 187
    Trinity *ad intra* 25, 30, 123 n 237, 132, 148, 171
    Trinity *ad extra* 25, 123 n 237
Union with Christ 7–11, 12, 14, 40, 49, 64, 80, 83–94, 95–104, 106, 114–119, 120 n 220, 121, 124, 127, 137–41, 143, 145, 148 , 154, 156–7, 163–6, 168–70, 172–3, 180, 185–6, 191
Universalism 31–32
Virgin birth 154–5

www.ingramcontent.com/pod-product-compliance
Lightning Source LLC
Chambersburg PA
CBHW070304230426
43664CB00014B/2636